Gender Divisions
and
Social Change

NICKIE CHARLES

Lecturer in Sociology
University College of Swansea

Harvester Wheatsheaf
Barnes & Noble Books

First published in Great Britain 1993 by
Harvester Wheatsheaf
Campus 400, Maylands Avenue
Hemel Hempstead
Hertfordshire, HP2 7EZ
A division of
Simon & Schuster International Group

First published in the United States of America 1993 by
Barnes & Noble Books
4720 Boston Way
Lanham, MD 20706

Typeset in 10/12pt Sabon
by Photoprint, Torquay, Devon

Printed and bound in Great Britain by
Biddles Ltd, Guildford and King's Lynn

British Library Cataloguing in Publication Data

A catalogue record for this book is available from
the British Library

ISBN 0–7450–0806–2 (hbk)
ISBN 0–7450–0807–0 (pbk)

Library of Congress Cataloging-in-Publication Data

Available from the publisher

ISBN 0–389–21007–2 (hbk)

1 2 3 4 5   97 96 95 94 93

For my parents

CONTENTS

ACKNOWLEDGEMENTS

I am glad to be able to thank publicly those who have contributed in various ways to the writing of this book. Firstly, I am grateful to Professor Bill Williams who provided me with the opportunity to write what follows by inviting me to contribute a volume on gender to the series he edits. I also wish to thank Jane Cowan, Felicia Hughes-Freeland, Ursula Sharma and Luis Valenzuela for reading and commenting on various drafts of various chapters, and Chris Harris for supplying me with the limericks. My father, Freddie Charles, has ploughed through substantial parts of the manuscript and his critical comments have played their part in making this book what it is. Indeed, his critical (and supportive) comments have helped to shape my intellectual development more than he probably realises. My mother, Mary Charles, has also been inveigled into reading parts of the manuscript even though she thought that a holiday would do me much more good than getting this book to the publishers!

Unfortunately I cannot blame anyone mentioned here for the shortcomings of what follows and, in the normal way, I accept responsibility for the final outcome.

Swansea,
September 1992

INTRODUCTION

This book explores the relationship between processes of social and economic change and gender divisions. It is about women's subordination and the sorts of social arrangements that are associated with it. It is also about women and men and the social relations within which individuals have to make sense of their lives and reproduce themselves and their societies. Central to it is an attempt to understand the relationship between gender divisions and the organisation of production and reproduction. That such a book can be written and published owes everything to the women's liberation movement and the impact of feminism upon sociology and upon society. The impact of the women's movement upon society is discussed in the final chapter of the book; here I wish to discuss the impact of feminism upon sociology. It is appropriate to begin at the beginning, when the women's movement was in its infancy, in order to appreciate the distance that has been travelled in the past twenty years.

Twenty years ago gender was not a topic that concerned sociologists. Social divisions of class and status were considered central to the sociological enterprise but there was no inkling that gender might be an important aspect of stratification in modern, industrial societies. Indeed, sociological studies concentrated largely on men, men as workers in factories, men as members of communities, young men as members of youth cultures and so on (Goldthorpe et al., 1970; Dennis, Henriques & Slaughter, 1969; McRobbie & Garber, 1976). The language of even the more radical and challenging textbooks appeared to talk only of men:

1

Perhaps the most fruitful distinction with which the sociological imagination works is between 'the personal troubles of milieu' and 'the public issues of social structure' . . . In these terms, consider unemployment. When, in a city of 100,000, only one man is unemployed, that is his personal trouble, and for its relief we properly look to the character of the man, his skills, and his immediate opportunities. But when in a nation of 50 million employees, 15 million men are unemployed, that is an issue, and we may not hope to find its solution within the range of opportunities open to any one individual. (Mills, 1970: 14–15)

Women were mentioned as wives and mothers but never as workers or actors on the political scene. Studies of women were few and far between, unless they dealt with women within the family, and even these did not regard gender divisions within households as worthy of comment. Such divisions were, after all, natural and not the proper concern of sociologists.

The situation is very different today. So what has happened? Has sociology really been transformed by feminism? Or is the tremendous growth of women's studies and gender studies a passing phase that will be forgotten in the post-feminist era? I do not have the answers to these questions. But one of the most important achievements of feminism is its insistence that gender be problematised as a proper object of study, rather than being accepted as natural and, therefore, outside the remit of the social sciences. This has not been achieved without struggle and, as we shall see in the pages that follow, the battle still rages. Here I consider the impact that feminism has had on sociology and the issues and debates that have emerged and with which I engage in this book.

FEMINISM AND SOCIOLOGY

It has been suggested that the relationship between feminism and the social sciences can be divided into four phases. The first is the pre-feminist era when women were almost totally neglected as objects of study; the second is marked by the emergence of a critique of this neglect; in the third stage research is undertaken on women in order to 'add them on' to existing studies; and the fourth consists of the full theoretical integration of gender into the discipline (Walby, 1988; Oakley, 1989). This schema may not be totally accurate, but it gives an indication of the process that has been taking place since the early 1970s. It is, of course, not altogether true that women were neglected prior to the emergence of second wave feminism. There were a few studies, notable by their scarcity, that dealt with women as paid workers as well as wives and mothers (Myrdal & Klein, 1968; Hunt, 1968; Jephcott, Seear & Smith, 1962). And even Talcott Parsons suggests that the nuclear family typical of industrial society may produce intolerable strains for women (Parsons, 1954). However, most studies, when women were mentioned, included them as mothers and wives, as part of the family rather than as actors in the world of paid employment and politics. This is as true of social anthropology as it is of sociology despite its apparent greater concern with relations of kinship. Women, because they became visible only in the context of the family, were not central to sociology which was mainly concerned with the 'public' world of paid employment, class divisions and the state, a focus which was a legacy bequeathed to it by the founding 'fathers' (Stacey, 1981; Sydie, 1987).

The founding 'fathers' had accepted that the gender division of labour which they observed in families in a burgeoning industrial society was in some way natural and therefore unworthy of study. Women gave birth to children and lactated and because of this were bound to look after them. They always had done and they always would do (Sydie, 1987; Kandal, 1988). The facts of biological reproduction and the corresponding structure of the family were assumed to limit women's participation in significant social activity. Even Engels, who incorporated Morgan's ethnographic evidence in his discussion of the emergence of women's subordination, assumed a natural basis for the division of labour between women and men (see Chapter 1 for a full discussion of this). There are two levels of criticism that can be brought to bear on this conceptualisation of gender divisions and their relation to biological reproduction, both of which have been mobilised by feminists in an attempt to counter the assumptions underlying sociological theory. The first involves the accumulation of evidence demonstrating that gender roles and gender identities vary cross-culturally and are learnt (Oakley, 1972); the second involves a critique of the conceptual categories which underlie the theories which have dominated sociology (Sydie, 1987; Wallace, 1989).

In the 1970s feminists concentrated upon accumulating empirical evidence that pointed to the enormous variation in gender roles and identities that exist within human society, and even to the existence of a third gender in many societies. This not only questioned the assumption that the social roles of women and men are given by the facts of biological reproduction, but also questioned the dichotomous division of individuals at birth into male and female which characterises Western societies (Albers, 1989). Evidence was also amassed to show that gender roles were learned through a process of socialisation rather than being innate and biologically determined. Latterly, more attention has been paid to the conceptual categories which provide the framework for classical sociological theory (Stacey, 1981; Sydie, 1987; Wallace, 1989 and see Chapter 1). It has been argued that Western philosophical thought is constructed in terms of mutually exclusive dichotomous categories. Women are defined as different from men and, because men are rational, active, competitive and aggressive women must by definition be irrational or emotional, passive, cooperative and peaceful. Another dichotomy, which has been particularly significant within sociology and social anthropology is the nature-culture dichotomy and the association of women with nature and men with culture. This is looked at in detail in Chapter 1. However, even though the underlying categories of the Western philosophical tradition on which classical sociological theory is based have been subject to a critique, it is a much more difficult task for feminism to escape these categories and much feminist thought remains trapped in this conceptual straitjacket (Bacchi, 1990). The social and political effects of this are discussed in Chapter 8. Here, suffice it to say that within feminist sociology there are two dichotomous pairs which have assumed particular significance: the private and the public and production and reproduction. Feminists' attempts to explain gender divisions of labour by resorting to these dichotomies fall into the very framework that they are attempting to discard. It is tautological to explain women's subordination by their association with reproduction or with the private sphere if, by definition, these spheres are feminine within the categories of Western thought and women are defined as reproductive and domestic (private). The circularity of these categories haunts the analysis presented here.

The arguments about nature and nurture, biology and culture, and their respective roles in the formation of gender identities and gender divisions continue. Within sociology, biology and nature are championed by the sociobiologists while feminists argue either that biology of itself has no effect on women's social role or that, if it does have an effect, that effect is socially and culturally determined and varies with the economic organisation of society (Sayers, 1982; Oakley, 1972; Barrett, 1980). These debates are taken up in Chapter 1.

As well as challenging the assumptions that have been made about the naturalness of gender divisions of labour and the resulting invisibility of women within sociology, feminist sociologists have carried out studies which have attempted to bring women into the sociological picture. This has been an attempt to rectify the imbalance that existed within the discipline by adding women on. Thus a plethora of studies has been carried out demonstrating that women are involved in paid work, they go on strike, they are involved in spectacular youth cultures, they vote independently and, perhaps most importantly, they work even when they are not in paid employment. This startling discovery emerged from studies of women and housework and women in the Third World and has given rise to important conceptual shifts within sociology and to a continuing debate about the relation between unpaid (domestic) labour and paid employment (Dex, 1985; Oakley, 1974). Indeed, work that is unpaid, unvalued and unrecognised in Western capitalist industrial societies was also ignored in sociological theory until feminists pointed out its significance. Feminists argued that the 'public' world of production, paid work, the economy and the state was premised upon women's unpaid work within the 'private', domestic sphere (Stacey, 1981). Indeed, work had hitherto been defined as that which is carried out within the public sphere and is paid. Witness the oft-repeated refrain, 'Oh, I don't work, I'm just a housewife.' The importance of women's work, paid or unpaid, is encapsulated by the information which became widely known during the UN decade for women, that women do two-thirds of the world's work, receive 10% of the world's income and own 1% of the world's resources (Spender, 1985; Scott, 1985). This reappraisal of work, particularly work that is performed outside the wage–capital relation, has ramifications for development policies and the problems of poverty and hunger that they appear to be exacerbating (Blumberg, 1989). These issues are explored in Chapters 6 and 7. It also has implications for the way in which the social division of labour is conceptualised. Stacey has argued that classical sociological theory, because of its focus on the public world of paid work, has a limited understanding of the social division of labour (Stacey, 1981). It is limited because it fails to conceptualise the unpaid work which is carried out by women and, thereby, renders invisible the divisions of labour based on gender which form an integral part of the social division of labour.

Adding women on has therefore led to a questioning of some of the basic concepts of sociology and feminists are now pointing out that conceptualising gender is crucial to even its most mainstream concerns. This is perhaps best illustrated by the debates about class. Within sociology class has been conceptualised in a number of ways, ranging from definitions of class in terms of occupation and status to defining it in terms of an individual's relation to the means of production. However, it has usually been men's occupations or status or ownership or non-ownership of the means of production that has been analysed rather than women's. This is because women were assumed to be dependent upon men within the household and their participation in paid employment was assumed to be intermittent and secondary to men's and to their domestic role. This is not particularly problematic when aggregates are being dealt with such as the working class or the middle class. But when studies attempt to allocate individuals who live in households to an occupational class problems arise. Until a feminist critique was mounted it had been practice to classify family-households on the basis of the male, head of household's occupation. This was the case regardless of whether or not there were women working in paid employment in the household. Women's occupations simply did not count. And, after all, most women were housewives, weren't they? If women lived on their own or without an adult male in the household, however, their occupation was taken into account and their household was classified accordingly. Feminists pointed out that this is not consistent. In one context women's occupations are ignored and in another they are taken as the basis for classification. And, secondly, it is the household and not individuals that are being classified, and yet it is the occupation of one individual within that household which is taken to define the household's class. Feminists have taken exception to this mode of classification for various reasons, but there is almost as much disagreement within the feminist camp as there is between feminists and those who support the 'conventional' method of classification such as Goldthorpe (1983, 1984). For instance, some argue that women and men should simply be classified on the basis of their own occupation and that the family-household should no longer be used as the basic unit of stratification (Stanworth, 1984; Marshall *et al.*, 1988). This is problematic as, despite demographic and other changes, most people live in households for significant parts of their lives and social mobility still occurs through marriage (Delphy & Leonard, 1986). In recognition of this, others argue that a combination of individual and household classification should be developed so that living arrangements are not ignored but neither are women's occupations (Heath & Britten, 1984; McRae, 1986). And some argue for accepting housewifery as an occupation in its own right which would mean that housewives should be classified in a class of their own (Delphy, 1981; Walby, 1986).

The debate continues about the ways in which gender can be incorporated into definitions and measurements of class (for a useful summary, see Charles, 1990). But what has become clear is that the occupational structure is gendered (Marshall *et al.*, 1988). For instance, gender and associated notions of masculinity and femininity affect the type of job an individual is likely to get. Manual work is dominated by men and is associated with particular forms of masculinity while non-manual office work is dominated by women and associated with particular forms of femininity (Willis, 1977). And caring work, both within and outside the home, is almost universally assumed to be a feminine speciality (Stacey, 1981). The gendering of jobs leads to an occupational structure where men occupy the top and bottom levels of the hierarchy while women are clustered in the middle (Marshall *et al.*, 1988). Similarly, the domestic division of labour is associated with definitions of masculinity and femininity, with child care and housework being almost by definition part of the feminine role. Male participation in these tasks may undermine their masculinity, despite the advent of the so-called new man.

Gender divisions of labour within the home also affect the jobs available to women and men. Because of women's responsibility for child care and domestic labour their participation in the labour market is limited. Conversely, men who have their children looked after by their wives and do not have to concern themselves with the daily routines of domestic life are free to get on and achieve in the world of employment; this affects the relative positions of the genders in the occupational hierarchy (Delphy & Leonard, 1986; Crompton, 1986; Marshall *et al.*, 1988). This is discussed more fully in Chapter 2.

Feminism is, however, divided, not only in ways that are discussed below but in terms of its epistemology. Within social theory and philosophy there is an opposition between theoretical positions which are materialist (that is, which assume that material reality exists independent of human thought and is knowable) and positions which are idealist (that is, assume that social and material reality is constructed within human thought). The idealist position is captured in the following limerick, the response to which points up one of the problems with idealism:

There was once a man who said, 'God
Must think it exceedingly odd
If he finds that this tree
Continues to be
When there's no-one about in the quad.'
(Attributed to R. Knox)

REPLY

Dear Sir, your astonishment's odd:
I am always about in the quad.
And that's why the tree
Will continue to be
Since observed by, yours faithfully, God.

This timeless philosophical distinction between idealism and materialism is represented within feminism. The idealist form of feminism has mounted a critique of the objectivity of sociology and of social science in general. This critique is not peculiar to feminism and did not originate with it, but a powerful strand of feminism has appropriated it as its own and has elided objective with masculine and subjective with feminine. Thus objectivity, as well as being impossible to achieve, is nothing more than male subjectivity. The critique is an epistemological one because it questions the nature and status of the knowledge produced by sociological investigation and, indeed, questions the possibility of producing an objective knowledge of the material world. Thus, some feminists argue that all knowledge is subjective, and as it has been men who have produced this knowledge then existing knowledge is based on male experience and is a product of male subjectivity (Spender, 1985). The task for feminism is to produce a specifically and equally valid female knowledge. There is no means of assessing which knowledge is more accurate, although some feminists argue that women's interpretations of the world are more complete than men's because women constitute a subordinate group (Spender, 1985). However, all knowledge is condemned to being partial because it is the product of gendered subjectivities.

This discussion is part of a much wider debate which has exercised philosophers for centuries: about the nature of reality; whether it exists objectively 'out there' or whether it is a construction of the human mind (it is the gender of that mind which is of particular concern to feminists); and whether it is possible to produce an objective knowledge of that reality, if it exists, or whether all knowledge is subjective. This is a debate between idealism and materialism and this strand of feminism has opted for idealism.

A related issue is the way in which knowledge is produced; as well as a critique of theory this also involves a discussion of methodology and data collection. This discussion was initiated within ethnomethodology and phenomenology rather than within feminism. But the recognition that researchers are also social actors who may influence the data produced and the virtual impossibility of being an 'objective' observer have been taken up by feminists. It is argued that certain methods of data collection are aimed at producing objective knowledge while others are much more suited to the understanding of subjective realities. Again there is an elision between objectivity and masculinity, on the one hand, and subjectivity and femininity, on the other. Thus, large-scale, statistical surveys are supposedly more masculine than small-scale, unstructured interviews or participant observation because they attempt to be objective. In order to be feminist, research must recognise the impossibility of achieving objectivity and incline more to those research methods which are oriented towards the subjective worlds of individuals (Graham, 1986; Oakley, 1981; Roberts, 1981). There is a problem here. Feminists mobilise

Western stereotypes of masculinity and femininity in their definitions of objectivity and subjectivity. They then define as *feminist*
those methods which are more associated with stereotypically
feminine attributes. Thus we have come full circle.

The tendency within feminism to question the very project of
understanding the material social world upon which sociology is
engaged is not shared by all feminists, although the argument that
all knowledge is relative and that there is no means of measuring
the validity of different interpretations of reality has become more
widespread with the advent of discourse analysis, post-
structuralism and post-modernism. This renders the whole notion
of women's subordination problematic because it is argued that
the significance of gender divisions and the nature of relations
between women and men can be interpreted only in terms of the
categories mobilised by specific societies and social actors. As
different societies have different ways of understanding gender
divisions, and different social groups and actors within the same
society also differ in their understanding of gender divisions, the
possibility of comparing women's status becomes remote. This is
particularly apparent with regard to cross-cultural comparisons of
gender divisions of labour, as I discuss in Chapter 1, and, it could
be argued, is a necessary antidote to the assumptions of early
feminist research that women shared a common oppression no
matter what their social circumstances and what type of society
they were living in. It is important to recognise the cultural
specificity of sociological and anthropological analysis, as the
feminist critique of social theory has demonstrated, but it is also
important not to retreat into such cultural relativism that
meaningful comparison becomes impossible.

A reliance on subjective accounts and interpretations of gender
that are socially and culturally specific marks much recent feminist
anthropology. Such analysis focuses on cultural constructions of
gender and gender symbolism without necessarily relating these to
gender divisions of labour, much less to the wider social and
economic structure of society (Moore, 1988). An alternative
approach, which I adopt here, is to focus on production and
reproduction and the gender divisions of labour with which they
are associated in different societies. Such an approach of necessity
relates gender divisions of labour to the social and economic

structure of society. These approaches should not be mutually exclusive and a full account of gender requires that material and ideological relations are analysed.

THE BOOK

Given the enormous upsurge of interest in gender and the increasing amount of material available on it, a book of this size cannot hope to cover every aspect of the topic. I have chosen to explore gender divisions of labour in different types of society in an attempt to understand the mechanisms that lead to change while, at the same time, evaluating theories which purport to explain women's subordination. Such a focus is important for those who are interested in changing gender divisions of labour in order to bring to an end women's oppression.

In Chapter 1 I look at explanations of gender divisions of labour which link them to biology and nature and discuss whether the seeming universality of gender as a social category means that it has to be explained by recourse to another universal, biology. The possible ways in which gender divisions of labour which subordinate women might have emerged are explored and I demonstrate that it is possible to explain women's apparently universal subordination without arguing that it is programmed into our genetic make-up. I also question the validity of assuming that gender divisions inevitably and everywhere subordinate women. Important issues are raised here such as the emergence of male control over female labour and the association of women with reproduction as well as production. These themes recur in later chapters as does the relation between gender divisions of labour and the economic organisation of society or mode of production.

In Chapters 2 and 3 gender divisions in capitalist industrial societies are discussed and explanations for them evaluated. Chapters 4 and 5 focus on socialism and gender divisions. This focus requires some explanation given the collapse of socialism as it existed in the Soviet bloc and its apparent consignment to the dustbin of history. I explore the relation between socialist economic development and gender divisions in order to clarify the links between social and economic change and changing gender divisions of labour, both in the paid workforce and within the domestic sphere. What the chapters on capitalism and socialism show is that, despite the greater ideological commitment of socialist regimes to gender equality, the outcomes of capitalist and socialist industrialisation are surprisingly similar. Women are involved in paid and domestic work while men are involved in paid work and politics. Again women's responsibility for reproductive activities within the home emerges as a factor militating against gender equality. And although industrialisation and women's participation in wage-labour give women the freedom to sell their labour power and reduce male control over female labour, this freedom is limited by women's responsibility for domestic labour within the home. I therefore look at the experience of socialist societies not to provide a descriptive account of gender divisions but to assist in theorising the relationship between gender divisions and economic change.

Chapters 6 and 7 explore the impact of colonialism and capitalist development on gender divisions of labour in the Third World. It is shown that both processes increase the potential for male control of female labour and that women's responsibility for subsistence or reproductive activities renders them 'disadvantaged' in the development process. Socialist development strategies, although not eradicating gender divisions of labour which subordinate women, benefit women in ways that capitalist development does not. However, in certain circumstances, socialist development may also undermine women's autonomy and increase the potential for male control over their labour. It is suggested that modernisation and industrialisation in the Third World, whether capitalist or socialist, transform pre-existing gender divisions of labour but that their effects upon women are complex and contradictory.

Chapter 8 looks at women's attempts to transform gender divisions of labour in Western, capitalist societies. It traces the emergence and decline of the women's liberation movement and evaluates the effects it has had on the social position of women in these societies. Both this chapter and the chapters on gender divisions and socialism illustrate that policies which are aimed at greater gender equality do not necessarily achieve their aims, and that their major impact may be to facilitate economic change rather than to liberate women. Thus gender divisions may be changed, but these changes may relate to the requirements of the economy as much as they do to demands of women for liberation. The relation between economic change and the form taken by gender divisions is of central importance in the pages which follow.

/ 1 /

THEORISING ORIGINS: BIOLOGY VERSUS CULTURE

In this chapter I evaluate theories which attempt to explain the origins and apparent universality of gender divisions of labour in which women are subordinate to men. The search for origins is an impossible task as we can never know how close theoretical speculations get to the way in which real human societies emerged and developed. And the search for a universal explanation for women's subordination has become unfashionable; indeed, the question is no longer posed in these terms by feminists within sociology and anthropology (Rosaldo, 1980). Instead, we are asked to consider the difference between women in different social circumstances and in different societies, to acknowledge the immense divergence in their experiences and to accept the futility of attempting to explain the mechanisms which have led societies to evolve gender systems which, apparently, endow men with power over women and result in women's subordination and oppression. There is reason to be wary of universal explanations, as there is reason to be cautious of accepting uncritically accounts which posit a shared experience of oppressed womanhood throughout societies and history. Even so, the creation of universalistic explanations and the assumption of essential and unchanging gender characteristics continue to emerge and capture public attention however much the practice is eschewed by feminist academics. It is important to explore such explanations, not only because of their popular currency, but also because they explain gender divisions by recourse to biology and thus legitimate social inequalities by ascribing to them the immutability of nature. And thirdly, many feminist explanations of women's subordination are based on similar assumptions and are therefore tarred with the same brush of universalism and essentialism.

The mobilisation of biological science in the cause of legitimating social inequalities has a long history. It is not only inequalities of gender that have been 'proved' to be rooted in biology but also 'racial' inequalities and class inequalities (Sayers, 1982; Lowe & Hubbard, 1983; Bleier, 1984). If such inequalities can be defined as natural then they are neither the proper object of sociology or anthropology nor can they be politically contentious. After all, what is natural is unchangeable. The role of science as legitimator of the social order is addressed by Steven Rose:

> The consequence of Darwin's theory of evolution was to finally change the form of the legitimating ideology of bourgeois society. No longer able to rely upon the myth of a deity who made all things bright and beautiful and assigned each to their estate . . . the dominant class de-throned God and replaced him with Science. The social order was still to be seen as fixed by forces outside humanity, but now these forces were naturalistic rather than deistic. (Rose, 1987: 25)

Within biology itself various theories have been put forward specifically to justify inequalities between women and men, ranging from women's lesser brain size to the threat posed by overindulgence in intellectual work to their capacity for childbearing. These were arguments advanced in the nineteenth century to justify exclusion of women from higher education and the professions (Sayers, 1982; Hubbard, 1983). The modern variant of such theories can be found in the works of sociobiologists who argue that certain behaviours are genetically programmed and differ according to sex (Wilson, 1975; Tiger & Fox, 1974; Barash, 1978). The most recent argument to be made and popularised is contained in a book called *BrainSex* (Moir & Jessel, 1989). It was heralded in the popular press as revealing 'Why the sexes will never be equal' and purportedly demonstrates that women and men 'behave differently because their brains are, quite simply, different' (*Daily Mail*, 23 Oct. 1989). It has been written by a geneticist and a journalist, a woman and a man, and provides 'scientific' evidence to support the inevitability of – surprise, surprise – women's subordination and male dominance. The difference in the brains of women and men are to be found in their 'wiring', the newspaper article explains. These sorts of arguments have tremendous currency because they mesh with the dominant ideology of Western capitalist societies that defines gender divisions as natural. Indeed, the power of biology as explanation has ensnared many who have been consciously attempting to avoid it.

In what follows I intend to evaluate different explanations of gender divisions, beginning with those that seek to prove they are biologically determined. I shall then move to a discussion of various feminist explanations of gender divisions. Throughout I shall attempt to clarify the conceptual frameworks that are being used and the place of biology in the different explanations. Finally, I shall look at recent attempts to theorise gender divisions which claim to take account of biological difference without falling into the trap of biological determinism.

SOCIOBIOLOGY

Sociobiology is the most recent attempt to renaturalise gender divisions in face of the challenge posed to this view by feminism and the women's liberation movement. Indeed, many sociobiologists construct their arguments as an explicit refutation of feminist claims (see, for example, Goldberg, 1979). However, they share certain questions and assumptions with some feminists. They seek to explain an apparently universal phenomenon, male dominance, by one single cause despite the diversity of human societies and the almost infinite variation in gender roles, both of which have been well documented by anthropologists (Mead, 1935, 1970; Oakley, 1972; Friedl, 1975). However, for sociobiology the variation in form conceals a common essence as is clear in this now-notorious statement by E.O. Wilson:

In hunter-gatherer societies, men hunt and women stay at home. This strong bias persists in most agricultural and industrial societies and on that ground alone appears to have a genetic origin. (Wilson, 1975)

It is extremely hard to imagine what there is in common between factory work in an industrial society and hunting animals for food in a subsistence economy. Moreover, the assumption that women stay at home is a myth whatever type of society is examined. Women in advanced capitalist societies make up almost half the workforce and women in hunter-gatherer societies, which appear to provide Wilson with his model, provide the bulk of the foodstuffs for themselves and other adults and children by foraging away from the home base (Lee, 1982; Draper, 1975; Rosaldo & Lamphere, 1974; Slocum, 1975). However, for Wilson these behaviours are essentially the same and indicate that men and women are genetically programmed to behave in different ways. Similarly, Dawkins argues that behaviour is governed by the self-interest of genes which leads individuals to act so as to maximise the chances of their genes surviving (Dawkins, 1976). They do this by maximising their reproductive success and the strategies differ for women and men. The battle of the sexes arises from attempts by women and men to try to get each other to invest more, parentally, in their offspring. Nature places men at an advantage in this battle because women, by virtue of becoming pregnant and carrying a child for nine months, have to make a greater initial biological investment. Men do not suffer from this disadvantage. On the contrary, they ensure that their genes are spread about as much as possible by developing a strategy of philandery. The more women they impregnate the more successful their genes are. Women are bound to be the primary caretaker because of their greater biological investment in the child, but they develop a strategy of 'coyness' in order to persuade the man to make an investment in a child by forming a more permanent union and contributing to parenting. Thus Dawkins explains the division of labour in child rearing, the sexual double standard and the battle of the sexes, all of which are supposedly universal features of human society, as arising from a gene's instinct for survival (Dawkins, 1976). Rape is also explained as a strategy to maximise the chances of survival of genes. Barash, for instance, states:

Perhaps human rapists, in their own criminally misguided way, are doing the best they can to maximise their fitness. (Barash, 1978: 55)

This argument employs the language of Darwinian evolutionary theory to endow genes with an urge to ensure their own survival. Never mind that evolution takes place precisely because genes mutate and hence do *not* survive in the same form. It also seems to endow genes with the characteristics of the twentieth-century conception of the 'maximising' individual. This is paradoxical, as individuals are denied the possibility of behaving in ways which will 'maximise' their potential precisely because of the selfish activity of the 'maximising' gene. They exist simply as a means of ensuring genetic continuity. Thus, language and concepts which are familiar to us are put to work in ways which are unjustified and unjustifiable but which sound credible precisely because of the familiarity of their assumptions.

Critiques of this approach to human behaviour have been mounted by sociologists and natural scientists alike (Sayers, 1982; Lowe & Hubbard, 1983; Rose, 1987). Sociobiologists have been taken to task for ignoring anthropological data (Leacock, 1981a), for presenting only partial evidence from studies of animal, particularly primate, behaviour (Liebowitz, 1983; Bleier, 1984), for using a teleological methodology which assumes that which it is attempting to prove (Sayers, 1982; Bleier, 1984) and for imputing ethnocentric and androcentric conceptions of human behaviour to animals and then using the 'discovery' of these behaviours among animals to 'prove' that they must be biologically based and therefore an inevitable feature of human society (Bleier, 1984; Rose, 1987; Sayers, 1982). It is extraordinary that, given their evident lack of scientific method or ability to recognise and explain the massive evidence that contradicts their assumptions, anyone takes them seriously at all. Unfortunately, they do, as is evidenced by the glee which greeted the publication of *BrainSex*. What is more alarming is that their prescriptions for human behaviour and the pseudo-scientific gloss they put on them are taken up and used by politicians of the New Right and by such neo-fascist organisations as the National Front to justify a reactionary politics of sexism and racism (Rose, 1987; Bleier, 1984).

The protagonist of sociobiology that I wish to look at in some detail is Steven Goldberg. In his book *Male Dominance: The inevitability of patriarchy* (1979) he takes up the feminist challenge. His project in the book is to demonstrate that male dominance is universal and exists in all societies. He differentiates between patriarchy, 'any system of organisation (political, economic, industrial, financial, religious, or social) in which the overwhelming number of upper positions in hierarchies are occupied by males' (29); male dominance, which is a 'psycho-physiological reality' expressed in 'authority in familial and dyadic relationships' (29); and male attainment, 'in every society males attain the high status (non-maternal) roles and positions and perform the high status tasks, whatever those tasks are' (50).

He begins his argument by asserting what he is trying to prove, that throughout history hierarchical authority has always been associated with men. He takes account of figures such as Margaret Thatcher and the Queen by saying that they are the exceptions that prove the rule. He then illustrates his contention by providing figures on the number of women in positions of authority in various capitalist and 'socialist' societies. Indeed, many feminists marshal similar sorts of evidence to demonstrate that patriarchy exists worldwide and that it persists under 'socialism'. However, he then argues that the reason for this is a 'physiological factor that renders a non-patriarchal society impossible to achieve'. This 'physiological factor' derives from the neuroendocrine system and, although he is not explicit about this, it can be assumed he is referring to an interaction between stimulation of the nervous system and production of hormones which differs in women and men. So much for patriarchy. His second factor, male dominance, is always evident at the level of feelings. He defines it thus:

a *feeling* acknowledged by the emotions of both men and women that general authority in dyadic and familial relationships, in whatever terms a particular society defines authority, ultimately resides in the male. (Goldberg, 1979: 41)

So patriarchy is a structural feature of societies whereas male dominance is apparent at a subjective, experiential level. And they are both universal. He justifies this claim by a discussion of anthropological data which show that men are dominant no matter what type of society you look at or what particular form the gender division of labour assumes. This position is not so far removed from some feminist arguments as I discuss below.

The third aspect he looks at is male attainment and here he quotes Margaret Mead in support of his argument. She wrote:

In every known human society the male's need for achievement can be recognised. Men may cook, or weave or dress dolls or hunt humming-birds, but if such activities are appropriate occupations of men, then the whole society, men and women alike, votes them as important. When the same occupations are performed by women, they are regarded as less important. (Mead, cited in Goldberg, 1977: 50)

This is precisely the problem that has, and still does, exercise feminist anthropologists and many would accept that men's tasks – whatever they may be – are universally valued more highly than women's (see, for example, Collier & Rosaldo, 1981). However, as I discuss below, the explanations they offer for this phenomenon differ from those put forward by sociobiology. For Goldberg the reason that males attain high status positions is that the high status attached to them motivates men to achieve. It does not have this effect on women because such behaviour arises from the action of a specific part of the neuroendocrine system present in men and absent in women. Goldberg is interesting in that he takes account of – in order to dismiss – sociological and anthropological evidence of the immense variety of gender roles in human societies, but having done that he slips into an ethnocentricity which regards the gender roles typical of white, middle-class North American society as typical of women and men in every society.

He also assumes that hierarchical organisation is a universal feature of human existence. It is interesting that, according to his argument, without hierarchies male dominance behaviour would not be triggered off. Their presence, however, makes men feel competitive and leads them to sacrifice all sorts of benefits in order to achieve positions of status in the public world and dominance over women in the public and private world. Thus, for Goldberg, male biology in the form of neuroendocrinology, in combination with a social factor, hierarchies, triggers off male dominance behaviour.

He also takes on the argument that gender appropriate behaviour and roles are not innate but learnt through a process of socialisation. He argues that this is not the case. On the contrary, socialisation is in conformity with behavioural patterns rooted in biology. Thus, boys are socialised to play with guns and to fight because they have a greater biological predisposition to do this anyway. Socialisation merely responds to physiological tendencies rather than causing gender differentiation. Here his ethnocentrism is apparent. There are extant societies where children of both genders are socialised into non-aggressive behaviour such as the !Kung hunter-gatherers of Southern Africa and the Mbuti pygmies in north-eastern Zaire (Turnbull, 1982; Draper, 1975; Lee, 1982). This reversion to ethnocentrism is surprising given his care earlier on in the book to stress that there are no universal male characteristics – not even aggression which is so beloved of sociobiology – apart from the tendency to dominate and occupy high level positions. However, he does pose a problematic question for those feminists who accept that male dominance is a feature of all human societies but who explain gender roles as a product of socialisation. And that question is why is it males who in every society are socialised to exhibit dominance behaviour (Goldberg, 1977: 117)? Goldberg's argument is tautological; that is, he starts off by assuming what he is trying to prove. He assumes the universality of patriarchy and male dominance ('it conform[s] to the nature of man' (Goldberg, 1979: 166)) and the universality of hierarchical social organisation. To support his argument he misuses biological evidence, he ignores historical and ethnographic evidence of non-hierarchical and egalitarian societies (Leacock, 1981a) and he ignores biological evidence suggesting that male dominance is a learned response to specific material environmental conditions and is not a universal feature of primate behaviour (Bleier, 1984; Liebowitz, 1975; Sayers, 1982).

From this brief discussion of sociobiology it is clear that sociobiologists conceptualise gender divisions as arising from biological differences between women and men, whether these differences be in aggression, brain construction, genetic programming or neuroendocrinological make-up. The message is that biology is natural and unchangeable and, as gender is biologically caused, inequalities between women and men and male dominance are an inevitable and unavoidable feature of human existence.

Feminists have taken issue with this position and argue that patriarchy is not inevitable, although it may be universal and not easily amenable to change, and in their attempts to explain gender divisions they have been at pains to distance themselves from biological determinism. Ann Oakley, for instance, argues that gender is socially constructed and is separable from biological sex. She draws on ethnographic evidence from a wide range of societies to show that gender divisions take on an almost infinite variety of forms, many of which contradict the stereotypical notions of masculinity and femininity which exist in Western capitalist societies. She draws on biological and behavioural sciences to demonstrate that gender roles are learned rather than innate and argues that the process by means of which gender is learned is socialisation. Thus, gender is culturally determined and, as Oakley puts it, although gender divisions may have a biological basis, the cultural elaboration of gender makes that basis invisible (Oakley, 1972).

This sort of evidence puts a question mark over notions of aggression or passivity being universally associated with either women or men. However, the issue that is not tackled by Oakley, nor by other feminists who argue that gender divisions can be explained through differences in socialisation processes, is that of men's power over women. Socialisation theory denies any effectivity to biology, thus seemingly avoiding the pitfall of biological determinism. But it cannot answer the question raised by Goldberg and by many feminists; that question being how to explain the apparently higher value attached to men's activities. Additionally, the difference in socialisation processes between women and men is itself in need of explanation. Socialisation theory remains at the level of description rather than offering a theory with the power to explain why gender divisions take the form they do in different societies, why they appear to exist universally, and why it appears that male dominance and women's oppression, no matter what form is taken by gender divisions, are universal features of human society. These are the questions to which sociobiology provides an answer. Feminists ask the same questions and, apparently, provide different answers. But, as we shall see, the answers turn out to have considerable similarities to those provided by sociobiology.

FEMINISM AND UNIVERSAL MALE DOMINANCE

Patriarchy has been defined from within feminism as follows:

Patriarchy is the power of the fathers: a familial–social, ideological, political system in which men – by force, direct pressure, or through ritual, tradition, law, language, customs, etiquette, education and the division of labour, determine what part women shall or shall not play, and in which the female is everywhere subsumed under the male ... Under patriarchy I may live in *purdah* or drive a truck ... I may serve my husband his early morning coffee within the clay walls of a Berber village or march in an academic procession; whatever my status or situation, my derived economic class, or my sexual preference, I live under the power of the fathers ... (Rich, 1984: 57–8, cited in Eisenstein, 1984).

The terminology is different, but what is being described here, and what is in need of explanation, bears a very close resemblance to Goldberg's definition of patriarchy and male dominance.

Many theories have been advanced from within feminism to

account for this state of affairs and most operate within the
essentialist paradigm that is also the hallmark of sociobiologists
(Smith, 1983). Thus, no matter what form is taken by gender
divisions of labour the essence is male domination–female subordination which remains the same throughout history and across
different types of society. What has to be explained, then, is the
essential male trait – or the essential female trait – which leads to
this relation of domination–subordination. This trait varies
depending on the analysis that is looked at. For some it is male
aggression (Brownmiller, 1986), for others it is the fact that
women bear children (Firestone, 1971) or that they mother
(Chodorow, 1978) and are thereby seen as closer to nature
(Ortner, 1974) and are confined to the private, domestic (as
opposed to public) sphere (Rosaldo, 1974; Ortner & Whitehead,
1981). Others look to the exchange of women by men (Rubin,
1975) or the control of female labour by men (Hartmann, 1986).
Some of these explanations are more clearly linked to biology than
others and I shall explore them first. But, as Joan Smith has
pointed out, they share with sociobiology the assumption, first,
that all societies are characterised by male domination and female
subordination and, second, that there must therefore be one
universal feature of human society which can explain this universal
phenomenon (Smith, 1983).

Shulamith Firestone analyses the causes of women's oppression
in her book *The Dialectic of Sex*. She argues that the division of
labour in biological reproduction, specifically the fact that women
give birth, is the material basis of patriarchy. She argues that the
first class division is that between women and men and all other
social divisions are based upon this. She imitates the language of
Marx and Engels to make her point:

Historical materialism is that view of the course of history which seeks the
ultimate cause and the great moving power of all historic events in the
dialectic of sex: the division of society into two distinct biological classes
for procreative reproduction, and the struggles of these classes with one
another; in the changes in the modes of marriage, reproduction and child
care . . . in the connected development of other physically-differentiated
classes (castes); and in the first division of labour based on sex which
developed into the (economic–cultural) class system. (Firestone, 1971: 12)

The logic of her argument forces her to the conclusion that the only way of overcoming the biological basis of women's oppression is to develop reproductive technology such that women no longer need to become pregnant and thereby dependent on men for the species to be reproduced. Her vision is reminiscent of Aldous Huxley's *Brave New World* with its rows of test-tube babies. While Firestone saw technology as liberating women, feminist analyses of the development of medical technology and its control by men should ring alarm bells about the unalloyed progress that new reproductive technologies represent, particularly for women.

However, the argument to which I wish to pay slightly more attention is that which links the emergence of patriarchy to male violence towards women. This argument is put most clearly by Susan Brownmiller in *Against Our Will* (1986) and has been very influential in the thinking of feminist sociologists and anthropologists. Many now regard it as axiomatic that male violence towards women, whether it is actual or potential, is an important means of social control of women and reinforces female dependency on men and, hence, patriarchy (Hanmer & Maynard, 1987; Collier & Rosaldo, 1981; Walby, 1986).

Brownmiller's argument is that rape, or the possibility of it, is the main way in which male dominance over women is perpetuated. She argues that male violence towards women has a long history, that in the dawning of pre-history it led to the establishment of patriarchy and that its continuation and the continual threat of it maintains patriarchy. A similar position is taken by Kate Millett and is based on the existence of myths in more than one society which attest to the violent overthrow of matriarchal society by men and the subsequent establishment of patriarchy (Millett, 1971). Brownmiller adopts this position despite a considerable amount of work that argues against the existence of a matriarchy, suggesting that mythical representations of powerful women depict not so much matriarchal as egalitarian societies (Saliou, 1986; Leacock, 1981a; Webster, 1975; Coontz & Henderson, 1986a). However, what concerns me here is the ultimately biological basis of her case. The construction of her argument depends on anatomical biological difference. She regards rape as physiological in origin because, firstly, human females can be sexually receptive at any time during the oestrus cycle, which marks humans off from all other species, and secondly, the fact that men have a penis means that they are physiologically equipped to rape. The argument (myth) that she constructs goes as follows: in some primeval past men collectively discovered they could rape women and so proceeded to do so and by so doing they maintained all women in a state of fear, the only protection for women being provided by a man. Thus, women became dependent on individual men for protection from men in general and the individual man would avenge any attack on her by other men. She explores the history of rape to show that it has, until relatively recently, been regarded as a crime, not against a woman, but against the man whose property, as wife or daughter, she is. However, she also analyses the power relations that are played out in the use of force and, by looking at homosexual rape in prisons, demonstrates that forcible sexual conquest indicates the existence of an unequal power relation between those concerned, whatever their gender. This is undoubtedly the case, but whether it can then be argued that the power emanates from force or whether force can be used by those whose power originates from other sources is a moot point. Moreover, there is evidence to suggest that male sexual violence may stem from powerlessness rather than from power (Sanday, 1986). What is at issue here is not the validity or otherwise of her observations of the effects of potential male violence on the lives of women, but the fact that her argument is based on a biological difference between the sexes. She writes:

In terms of human anatomy the possibility of forcible intercourse incontrovertibly exists. This single factor may have been sufficient to have caused the creation of a male ideology of rape. When men discovered that they could rape, they proceeded to do it. (Brownmiller, 1986: 14)

Once rape was 'discovered' it was used as a means of controlling women because all women fear being raped. Thus women are kept in a 'state of fear' by the possibility of rape. This possibility, whether it is indulged in by all men or not, acts as a form of social control by men over women.

Perhaps another myth is also at work here for Brownmiller and her Western readers; that of the prehistoric caveman wielding an enormous club (symbolising what?), dragging 'his' woman by her hair to subdue her through physical violence. These images abound in children's comics and are current in Western society. But the question that needs to be asked is whether this represents a real

prehistoric past or a myth created by male dominated capitalist societies (a myth not dissimilar from the more respectable 'Man the Hunter' one) in order to legitimise male domination by making it appear rooted in 'primitive man' and not, in any way, linked to the hierarchical and stratified nature of Western capitalist society.

However, for Brownmiller and other feminists who locate the origins and maintenance of male domination in male violence and, ultimately, in biology, the way to transform it is for women to organise collectively and challenge the power of men. Even though that power has a biological source, society, more particularly women, can collectively challenge and control it. Thus, feminists might locate the problem of women's oppression in biology, but they do not then accept it as being unchangeable. This does not appear to make logical sense and appears achievable only by substituting female power for male power. Male power remains a potential source of male dominance requiring collective control by women. Thus, feminists differ from sociobiologists in the prescriptions they offer for society, but what they share with sociobiologists is the essentialist construction of their argument: biology – whether the penis or neuroendocrinology – is directly responsible for male dominance and patriarchy, in every society and throughout history. The assumptions underpinning these essentialist arguments are that patriarchy and male domination exist in all societies and therefore a universal explanation has to be found. The only common denominator between different societies is biology, therefore biology must cause women's oppression. Such arguments do not take account of the complexities of different societies, nor do they allow for meaningful historical change. They in fact reduce these complexities to a single, often biological, essence (Smith, 1983; Sayers, 1982).

FEMINISM AND UNIVERSAL FEMALE SUBORDINATION

In an attempt to distance feminist theorising from biological determinist or essentialist conceptual frameworks other explanations for the apparent universality of women's subordination have been put forward. These explanations bear the influence of two opposing theoretical traditions. One seeks to explain women's position in society by an appeal to apparently universal systems

and symbolic representations; that is, it analyses the gender
ideologies of societies in order to unearth the ways in which gender
is experienced and understood. The other looks to the way
material production is organised in order to understand the
specific form taken by gender divisions in specific societies (Moore,
1988). The former takes as its theoretical heritage Freud, Lévi-
Strauss and, ultimately, an idealist epistemology deriving from
Western philosophical traditions. The latter's heritage is Marx and
Engels and a materialist epistemology and conception of history.
Both traditions have been and continue to be very influential in
attempts to understand and explain the forms taken by gender
divisions. I shall first explore the main arguments put forward by
those who focus on belief systems and ideologies and then go on to
look at the explanations of those who begin from an analysis of
the material basis of societies.

The most well-known and influential analyses of gender which
concern themselves with the question of the universality of
women's subordination are probably those put forward by Sherry
Ortner and Michelle Z. Rosaldo. The former argues that women
are everywhere devalued in relation to men because all societies
construct women as being closer to nature than are men (Ortner,
1974). The latter argues that this devaluation of women stems
from their universal assignment to the domestic sphere (Rosaldo,
1974). Both authors were heavily influenced by the arguments put
forward by Simone de Beauvoir in her classic, *The Second Sex* (de
Beauvoir, 1972).[1] This path-breaking work, which was published
in 1949, was extremely influential on feminist writers of the late
1960s and early 1970s. In this work she presents an analysis of
woman's second class status in relation to man in which she argues
that women are seen as 'other' by men. Because of women's
otherness men are enabled to be active subjects, transcending the
physical and biological basis of life in which women are confined
and which women have to reproduce in order that men may be
transcendent. At one point she writes that women's life 'is not
directed towards ends: she is absorbed in producing or caring for
things that are never more than means, such as food, clothing and
shelter. These things are inessential intermediaries between animal
life and free existence' (de Beauvoir, cited in Spelman, 1988: 59).
This analysis forms the basis of Ortner's discussion and many of
its problems are reproduced by her. Particularly important are

de Beauvoir's generalisations about women on the basis of the experience of white, Western middle-class women and her assumption that there are universal features of womanhood. (For a useful critique of her analysis, see Spelman, 1988.)

Ortner argues that every known human society differentiates between nature and culture, seeing them in a relation of opposition to each other and assigning to culture a higher value than that assigned to nature. In addition, all human societies see culture as controlling nature. Alongside this there is the 'pan-cultural fact' of women's secondary status (Ortner, 1974). Ortner is seeking an explanation of this 'pan-cultural fact' and is therefore, on her own admission, not seeking to understand any particular society but the general features of social life which are common to all societies. Thus we see her asking the same question as the sociobiologists and looking for a global, essentialist answer. The explanation that she comes up with is that all cultures symbolically construct an opposition between nature and culture and that women are seen as being closer to nature. This arises because of women's physiology which ensures that they are involved for much of their lifetime with 'the natural processes surrounding the reproduction of the species' (Ortner, 1974: 75). This analysis and ideological valuation of women's physiology owes much to de Beauvoir, to her view of woman's 'enslavement to the species' in contrast to man's ability to engage in culturally creative activities. In de Beauvoir's words, woman is immanent and man is transcendent 'for it is not in giving life but in risking life that man is raised above the animal; that is why superiority has been accorded in humanity, not to the sex that brings forth but to that which kills' (de Beauvoir, cited in Ortner, 1974: 75).

Ortner develops the argument to say that women occupy a place within culture but they are seen as mediating between nature and culture, and, hence, are seen as closer to nature. Thus they transform raw into cooked food and transform children, through socialisation, from natural into cultural beings. These transformations take place in the domestic sphere, the sphere of 'the family'. She writes:

The family (and hence woman) represents lower level, socially fragmenting, particularistic sorts of concerns, as opposed to interfamilial relations representing higher level, integrative, universalistic sorts of concerns. Since men lack a 'natural' basis (nursing, generalised to child care) for a familial orientation, their sphere of activity is defined at the level of interfamilial relations. (Ortner, 1974: 79)

Thus, the domestic sphere is of a lower order than the public sphere and Ortner agrees with Rosaldo's argument that the 'domestic is always subsumed by the public' (Ortner, 1974: 79).

Despite her effort to distance herself from Lévi-Strauss's position, that the domestic unit or the family is identified with nature and is a biological group, and despite her attempt to argue that 'seeming' to be closer to nature is distinct from 'being' closer to nature, it is difficult to avoid the conclusion that women are constructed in this way by all human societies because of their involvement in biological reproduction. Indeed, Rosaldo, in a later discussion, herself points out that both formulations – that woman is seen as closer to nature and that women are confined to a domestic sphere – arise from the seemingly inevitable social consequences of women's ability to bear children and become social as well as biological mothers. Thus they are accounts that suggest:

how 'brute' biological facts have everywhere been shaped by sociological logic. Reproduction and lactation have provided a functional basis for the definition of a domestic sphere, and sex asymmetry appears as its intelligible, though non-necessary, consequence. (Rosaldo, 1980: 399).

Unfortunately, the insertion of 'non-necessary' in this statement is not altogether convincing if these consequences are taken as being universal, as Ortner and Rosaldo argue. Rosaldo's solution to the problem is to change the terms of the debate and retreat from asking questions about why women are everywhere subordinate to men. Instead the concern of feminist anthropologists, in particular, should be to analyse gender divisions as part of a system of inequalities which are specific to different types of society (Rosaldo, 1980). An example of this type of analysis can be found in an article she wrote with Jane Collier (Collier & Rosaldo, 1981). However, before looking at the implications of this sort of development it is important to explore the debate which was stimulated by Ortner's argument.

CRITIQUES OF UNIVERSALISM: IDEALIST

Ortner's article has spawned a plethora of ethnographic writings which have taken issue with her main argument (see, for example, MacCormack & Strathern, 1980). They criticise her on two points: first, that her statement that all societies have symbolic systems which oppose culture and nature in a relation of hierarchy and that woman is always associated with the term of lesser value, usually nature, cannot be substantiated; and, second, that the nature:culture dichotomy is rooted in the Western philosophical and ideological tradition and she is therefore guilty of ethnocentrism when she assumes that it is a cultural universal. Similar criticisms have been levelled at the domestic:public dichotomy and at the notion that women everywhere are defined as mothers (Chodorow, 1978; Collier & Rosaldo, 1981). Ethnographic material provides convincing evidence that different societies have different ways of interpreting the material and social worlds within which they exist. Thus, not only is there no universal association at the symbolic level of woman with nature, but there is also no evidence of a universal tendency to interpret the world in terms of hierarchies (MacCormack & Strathern, 1980; Strathern, 1987). Thus, the universal cause for women's subordination cannot lie in a universal evaluation of women in relation to men or nature because such a universal symbolic construction does not exist. Similarly, the domestic:public dichotomy is totally irrelevant to pre-state societies where there is no differentiation of spheres in this way (Leacock, 1978; Sacks, 1979). If a universal explanation is still being sought it would seem not to lie in universal symbolic systems.

The second point on which Ortner and others have been criticised is on their ethnocentrism. It is interesting to look at this in some detail as in recent years anthropology has become acutely aware of the difficulties of understanding other cultures and of making cross-cultural comparisons and generalisations. The way in which Western categories of explanation are constructed can have, and certainly has had, profound implications for the type of data that have been produced within anthropology. And many of these data have been used to support arguments demonstrating the universality of male dominance.

The nature:culture dichotomy mobilised as explanation by

Ortner has been severely criticised for its cultural specificity. Indeed, Ortner's reliance on de Beauvoir, an existentialist philosopher, is strongly indicative of the provenance of this dichotomy. It gained currency, within Western thought, during the seventeenth and eighteenth centuries but has its roots in classical times (Bloch & Bloch, 1980). Bloch and Bloch discuss the varying ways in which the relationship between nature and culture has been conceptualised within Enlightenment thought.

According to some Enlightenment philosophers, culture is differentiated from nature and is in a hierarchical and controlling relationship with it. Culture, or society, is elaborated by human beings, in fact usually men, in opposition to and arising out of nature. But nature is also mobilised as a category of challenge in Enlightenment thought. Specifically, it is part of the ideological challenge to the legitimacy of a social order whose authority came from 'God through monarch and church . . . the accepted original source of "right" is replaced by an antecedent and therefore superior basis for morality and society: "nature" ' (Bloch & Bloch, 1980: 31). Thus, in the context of the Enlightenment the concept of 'nature' was appealed to as a way of challenging conceptions of divine right. It was part of the ideological revolution asserting rationality, equality and democracy and was mobilised to provide an alternative source of goodness and right. Nature, in this context, carried positive connotations.

These varying meanings attached to 'nature' posed a problem for Enlightenment thinkers when they turned their attention to the relation between the sexes because women were categorised as being closer to nature than men. As Bloch and Bloch point out, there is an inconsistency in arguments which, on the one hand, define nature as a positive and superior realm in relation to corrupt society (culture) but, on the other hand, regard women as inferior and to be excluded from the political domain, explaining this exclusion as necessary because women are closer to nature than are men. This latter association has more in accord with the view that nature must be controlled by culture than that nature is the source of positive values. However, nature is again brought in to explain this apparent contradiction. According to Rousseau, for example, women and men are different and complementary and nature has made them thus. Nature has endowed men with strength and made them active while women are weak and passive.

Woman's natural role is motherhood (Bloch & Bloch, 1980). So nature has decreed the gender division of labour specific to emerging bourgeois societies, and, as 'nature knows best', this is the way things ought to be. This contradictory interpretation and mobilisation of 'nature' perhaps provides an insight into the dual images of women that abound in Western thought – that women are at one and the same time guardians of morality but also dangerous and potentially disruptive; the madonna–whore dichotomy.

Ortner is not the only social scientist to work within the categories provided by Western philosophical traditions. She is in good company. Durkheim, Marx, Engels and Weber were also confined by this perspective when discussing women, Lévi-Strauss elevated the nature:culture dichotomy to a human universal and Talcott Parsons' reliance on 'nature' to explain gender roles within the modern family is abundantly clear (Kandal, 1988; Rosaldo, 1980; Stacey, 1981).

One of the outcomes of the problems associated with the search for a universal explanation of women's subordination and the realisation that, ultimately, all such arguments resort to essentialist and usually biologistic or naturalistic explanations, has been a turning away from these questions altogether. Instead, feminist anthropologists have begun to ask questions about the ways in which gender systems interlock with other systems of difference and inequality (Collier & Rosaldo, 1981; Strathern, 1987a). As Collier and Rosaldo put it:

The alternative proposed in this essay requires a suspension of earlier, evaluative questions in favour of an approach that treats gender as a particularly salient aspect of social personhood, and assumes that personhood itself is ultimately bound up with economic and political processes that give rise to and help reproduce social relationships and inequalities . . . such a model should permit the delineation of structurally significant similarities and differences in the construction of gender in diverse social groups . . . (Collier & Rosaldo, 1981: 277–8)

However, although the detailed knowledge, the production of which it is implied is necessary for this sort of enterprise, is essential to develop a fuller understanding of gender divisions, it is not so clear that this process will provide anything more than a description of gender divisions in different societies and the ways in which they articulate with other social divisions. This project is of itself valuable, but is a precursor of explanation rather than an explanation in and of itself. The problem I am pointing to is clear in the following passage:

The kind of understanding developed here is ultimately circular: social relationships of production, marriage, politics and gender are construed not in linear fashion but as mutually determining aspects of a complete social whole. (Collier & Rosaldo, 1981: 279)

It is unclear how it is possible or, indeed, whether it is possible, to move beyond this sort of analysis or detailed description to the development of an explanation that might be valid not only within a particular society or culture but cross-culturally. Indeed, the problems of this sort of project are high on the agenda of anthropologists who are interested in the study of gender (Strathern, 1987a). However, before moving on to a consideration of this debate it is important to explore the ways in which gender divisions have been studied by anthropologists in recent years.

As I have already indicated, there has been a move away from posing universal questions about the nature of gender relations towards a recognition of the biased nature of information that has been produced, hitherto, by anthropologists asking questions of male informants and taking their view as representative of the views of the society being studied. Ardener highlighted the possible difference between a dominant group's interpretation of social reality and the interpretation of a muted group (Ardener, 1975, 1975a). This could, of itself, result in the overvaluing of a dominant group's activities and the undervaluing of those of the muted group by the researcher. It was assumed that the dominant group in most societies studied by anthropologists was constituted by men. However, even if men are not dominant, Ardener's discussion introduced the view that not all social groups may understand their social reality in the same way; indeed, their social realities may differ substantially. Thus anthropologists have begun to provide ethnographies which give space to women's voices as well as to men's (Keesing, 1987; Shostak, 1983; Messick, 1987) and to re-examine the ethnographic record in an attempt to develop an unbiased analysis of women's status. An example of this re-evaluation is provided by a reinterpretation of menstrual taboos. An ethnography which relies on women's accounts as well as men's can provide a different interpretation of the same social practices. Thus in Kwaio society in the Solomon Islands both women and men are considered taboo when they are in seclusion. Men are secluded 'to confine the dangerous manifestations of sacrifice and ancestral power' while women are secluded to 'confine the dangerous emanations of menstruation and childbirth' (Keesing, 1987: 45). This has been interpreted as a contrast between the pollution surrounding the creation of infants and the sanctity surrounding the creation of ghosts. However, Keesing interprets the seclusion of both women and men as a way of maintaining boundaries and recreating cultural order: 'It is not menstrual blood that emanates danger; it is menstrual blood in the wrong places' (Keesing, 1987: 46). Leacock argues similarly that menstrual taboos might have developed for perfectly good, commonsense reasons such as avoiding dripping blood on a trap (Leacock, 1981a: 168). Attributing fear of menstruation and notions of female pollution to other cultures may in fact be a product of Western, androcentric bias.

However, the escape from male bias is not easy. Collier and Rosaldo themselves, while providing a detailed analysis of bride-service societies based on the !Kung of southern Africa, the Australian aborigines and the Ilongots of the Philippines which are all classified as egalitarian or pre-class societies, and while writing specifically about gender, often appear to be writing about men and from a male perspective. Thus they write:

In a world where acquiring a wife is the most important – and most problematic – goal to which one can aspire, social relationships among adults will have a good deal to do with claims to women. (Collier & Rosaldo, 1981: 291)

This is not to detract from their work but rather to indicate the enormously problematic nature of discussing gender relations when the data which is being relied on are at best partial and at worst distorted (Mukhopadhayay & Higgins, 1988). The problem is not avoided, it seems to me, by simply stating, as some authors do, that ethnographies are based on male informants but then proceeding to use this 'biased' material to discuss the nature of gender relations or gender symbolism in a particular society (Werner, 1987).

The direction now being taken by anthropologists working within the idealist/structuralist[2] tradition is to pose as problematic the whole project of cross-cultural comparison (Strathern, 1987a). This is an important discussion and raises many profound methodological issues, not only for anthropology. An example of the difficulties of meaningful cross-cultural comparison is the attempt to compare women's status in different societies. The first problem with such attempts is that there is no agreed universal indicator of women's status that can be invoked, either at an experiential or theoretical level. Added to this, women's status is a result of many different social processes and may not be uniform across all areas of social life. Thus a woman may have higher status in the domestic sphere than in the occupational sphere or she may enjoy sexual autonomy only at certain stages in her life cycle (Sacks, 1979). Women's status is, thus, variable and dependent on social context. Further problems arise if women's own subjective assessment of status is taken into account in attempts at measurement. As Mukhopadhayay and Higgins point out, in an extremely interesting overview of developments within feminist anthropology:

If we are to continue making cross-cultural assessments, we must acknowledge that what we consider valuable – what confers high status – may not be what other societies find good and desirable. What confers status elsewhere or is desired by women may not be autonomy, control over production or formal political power. (Mukhopadhayay Higgins, 1988: 468)

One might add that, even in our own society, it is not possible to assume a unity of interests between women and it would be patronising and domineering to assume that 'our' agenda ought to set the priorities for women from other ethnic groups, social classes and cultures (Bujra, 1978). Thus, at the level of social action, perceptions and experiences of status are problematic, what one woman perceives as oppression may be perceived as privilege by another. This is a different order of problem, however, from developing an objective, theoretically informed measure of women's status which would allow meaningful comparisons between different types of society.

The very real problems associated with cross-cultural comparison have led some anthropologists to argue that such comparisons are invalid and that each society must be studied on its own terms (Strathern, 1987a). Symbolic representations of gender and the attribution of value are therefore discussed as self-contained systems; gender asymmetry is not assigned any meaning apart from the meaning which is assigned to it by the social actors within each particular society. Strathern argues that the meaning of gender for people in a particular society cannot be comprehended without an understanding of the ways in which personhood and agency are understood. For instance, she argues that in many 'egalitarian' societies the notion of personhood is distinct from the Western concept of the individual. The concept of individual implies a unique self with unique experiences who intervenes as an actor in the social world and acts as a subject on an object or objects. In contrast, the notion of person in, for instance, Chambri society is defined as being the 'product of a social position' rather than the 'product of a set of unique experiences' (Errington & Gewertz, 1987: 83). It is argued that gender is an aspect of personhood and that it also affects agency, a social actor's ability to act in ways which are regarded as meaningful or worthwhile in that society. Such agency may also be gendered; to be a 'woman of worth' (that is, a female person who is acting in a socially meaningful way) may not involve the same processes as being a 'man of worth', for instance (Errington & Gewertz, 1987; Strathern, 1981, 1987a). Thus, it may not make sense, in the terms of a particular society, to interpret difference between the social roles of women and men as implying inequality or domination/subordination. Thus, our notion of inequality may simply be incomprehensible to a person in Chambri society and this renders invalid an interpretation of difference in that society as representing hierarchy or inequality. This discussion is complex, but what is at issue is the possibility of any relation between concepts which are culturally specific, or, indeed, the possibility of elaborating concepts which are *not* culturally specific.

An interesting illustration of the problem is provided by Errington and Gewertz who return to Margaret Mead's ethnography of the Tchambuli (Chambri) in Papua New Guinea and reassess the meanings that she and the Chambri assign to dominance. They argue that Mead's understanding of the relations of domination/subordination in that society was a misinterpretation based on a specifically Western notion of dominance. She understood Tchambuli men to be dominated by women by virtue of their economic activity. However, this definition of dominance has no meaning in Chambri society and instead dominance is seen as occurring if people are prevented from becoming 'persons of worth' as defined by that culture (Errington & Gewertz, 1987: 64). They discuss a particular event, the remarriage of Yebiwali, a widow, and show that although it could be interpreted as being arranged by men and preventing her from marrying her lover, in fact the marriage was in her best interests as it allowed her to attain a culturally valued gender-specific position within Chambri society. Through the marriage she could become 'a woman of worth'. Men arranging her marriage could be conceived of as dominating her in Chambri terms only if they had arranged a marriage which had not been in her best interests (Errington & Gewertz, 1987: 85). Thus, notions of dominance/subordination, like notions of status, cannot simply be transferred from one society to another in order to understand the meanings attached to social events.

This argument seems to imply that the concept of dominance is culturally specific precisely because it relies on a concept of the individual whose entitlement to specific rights – legal, social, political – is curtailed in some way. This concept has developed only with the advent of bourgeois society. Women in such societies have organised to fight for their rights and for an end to male domination. Perhaps imputing male domination to other cultures and other historical epochs is a misguided exercise, particularly as an assessment of domination involves not only objective but also subjective factors – it is much easier to demonstrate that men predominate in positions of power than that this predominance is subjectively experienced as domination. However, it can be argued that even if women do not feel themselves to be dominated by men this does not mean that women's subordination is not a feature of that society. It may be that the way in which such domination is legitimated is through a set of ideas and values that masks such domination and affects the ways in which women and men experience it. It is important to probe beneath commonsense interpretations of social reality in order to be able to understand and explain social relationships. If a society characterised by male domination was immediately experienced as oppressive by all women then it is likely that it would be marked by severe conflict and it would be unlikely to last very long. Here a concept of ideology is useful and enables a distinction to be made between immediately given, subjective experience of social relations and an analytical understanding of the nature of those relations. Everyday experience is interpreted and understood through ideology and ideology, it is argued, is a partial representation of social reality and, in particular, masks dominant social interests (Ramazanoglu, 1989: 146–7). Thus social relations which are characterised by domination and subordination may not be immediately experienced as such. It may be that the problems of cross-cultural comparison are compounded by analyses that concentrate on the realm of subjective experience and interpretation. An analysis of the material and objective realities of such societies and the ideologies which are part of them and shape people's experience is also necessary.

If the argument that it is not valid to assess other societies by our own cultural standards is taken to its logical conclusion, then it is hard to see how a judgment can ever be made about the existence of male domination, or anything else, in societies other than the one in which you live and whose values you share. There is a danger that this retreat towards cultural relativism may render impossible the whole project of cross-cultural analysis and the generation of explanations of gender divisions because it is defined as invalid. Even within Western societies differences of ethnicity and class may render judgments about women's oppression invalid if relativism is taken to its logical conclusion. This sort of position renders the whole feminist project of ending women's oppression totally untenable because there can be no common ground on which to unite and no assessment of women's subordination in other cultures is permissible (Lovibond, 1989; see also Ramazanoglu, 1989, especially 142–4, for a useful discussion of this issue).

A significant consequence of this tendency is that the issue of women's subordination has been lost to view and in its stead gender, a politically neutral term, has become the object of study. There is a danger that cultural relativism will lead to the abandonment of any effort to evaluate gender differences other than in the terms available to the actors themselves.

The problem of cross-cultural comparison needs to be put in perspective, however. Non-class societies in Melanesia or southern Africa or North America are often studied as if they existed in isolation from international capitalism and as if the people were unaware of the existence of inequality and exploitation in the world economy. This is not of course true of all anthropologists, but it is surprising how systematically these cultures are represented as if they existed in isolation (see especially Strathern, 1987; MacCormack & Strathern, 1980). As Leacock comments:

> . . . the societies studied by anthropologists are virtually all in some measure incorporated into the world economic and political systems that oppress women, and most have been involved in these larger systems for centuries. Anthropologists know this historical reality well, but commonly ignore it when making generalisations about pre-class social–economic systems. (Leacock, 1978: 247)

This surely holds significance for an evaluation of women's status and needs to be incorporated into any realistic discussion of gender divisions.

CRITIQUES OF UNIVERSALISM: MATERIALIST

As we have seen, for anthropologists located within the theoretical tradition stemming from Lévi-Strauss there seems to be a retreat from asking questions about women's oppression, either into the development of more accurate, gender-sensitive ethnography, which is to be applauded, or into a position of cultural relativism (Redclift, 1987). This is not the case for anthropologists whose theoretical heritage derives from marxism. Here the debate has been conducted on different terms. Instead of accepting that male dominance is a universal feature of human society and attempting to generate a universal explanation, it has been conceptualised as a historically specific and bounded phenomenon produced by specific combinations of factors relating to the socio-economic organisation of societies (Engels, 1972; Leacock, 1972 and 1981a). This theoretical position has been complemented by studies of specific societies which have revealed that egalitarian gender relations have existed and still do exist in some relatively isolated non-class societies (Leacock, 1981a; Draper, 1975; Sacks, 1979; Turnbull, 1982), that not all societies are patrilineal and patrilocal (contrary to Lévi-Strauss' assumptions) (Leacock, 1981a) and that in some extant cultures women occupy social positions which are valued within their societies (Sacks, 1979;

Redclift, 1987; Strathern, 1987). What has *not* been discovered is any evidence for the existence of a matriarchal society in which women are dominant and men subordinate.

Perhaps the best place to begin a discussion of the contribution made to the understanding of gender divisions and women's subordination by those working within the marxist tradition is with Engels. In *The Origin of the Family, Private Property and the State* Engels locates the emergence of women's subordination in the transition from non-class to class societies; specifically it is linked to the emergence of private property. Basing himself on Morgan he traces the development of the family from prehistoric times to the nineteenth century when he was writing. The crucial part of his analysis lies at the point where the pairing family gave way to monogamy in which women were subordinate to men. He argued that in subsistence economies gender relations were equal, no surplus was accumulated and the only division of labour was that based on the 'natural' divisions of age and sex. He cites evidence from Morgan on the Iroquois which demonstrates that women held positions of power in that society and were regarded as the equals of men, and indicates that there was no conception of the domestic sphere being 'private' and subordinate to the 'public'. In his words housework had a 'public character' (Engels, 1972: 137). This assessment of Iroquois society has been supported by later work such as that by Leacock – she found similar egalitarian relations between women and men among the Montagnais-Naskapi of Labrador – and Brown. Both of these authors base their findings on historical record as well as contemporary observation. They are thus able to document the impact colonialism has had on present-day 'egalitarian' societies and demonstrate that at the moment of contact with colonial powers social relations were non-hierarchical in those societies and the people had no conception of a public as opposed to domestic domain (Leacock, 1981; Brown, 1975; Anderson, 1985). Similar evidence has been provided by ethnographies of the !Kung bush people (Lee, 1982; Draper, 1975), the Mbuti pygmies (Turnbull, 1965) and the Aboriginal peoples of Australia (Bell, 1983).

The precise mechanism Engels pinpoints that set in motion the emergence of class society and women's subordination is problematic and has come in for substantial criticism (Sacks, 1979; Rubin, 1975; Sayers, 1982; Humphries, 1987). Feminists have criticised him for assuming a 'natural' division of labour such that women stayed at home cooking and caring for children while men went out hunting. This division of labour sounds remarkably similar to the ideal of bourgeois family life in nineteenth-century England, except, of course, that men were not out hunting. Additionally, it is not an accurate representation of the actual division of labour which is thought to have existed. Women's foraging activities outside the camp or home base provide around two-thirds of the food needs of a band (Draper, 1975; Lee, 1982) and families are not discrete social units but live as part of a cooperating group whose composition may vary (Sacks, 1979). There is also evidence that the product of men's hunts is distributed according to complex rules, it is not necessarily handed over to their wives in a way analogous with the wage packet of industrial workers (Collier & Rosaldo, 1981). Thus Engels' representation of this 'natural' division of labour is problematic. However, it is not critical to his theoretical formulation (Sayers, 1982). His argument is that when subsistence economies, which had previously relied on hunting and gathering for their food supplies, began to grow crops and domesticate animals, a surplus was produced for the first time which made production for exchange a possibility. The division of labour between women and men was such that men looked after the animals from which the surplus arose; the surplus product was therefore in the hands of men. Men wished to hand the surplus on, in the form of private property, to their biological descendants. However, because maternity is much more certain than paternity, and because relations between the sexes were egalitarian and women were in control of their own sexuality, men had no guarantee which children were biologically theirs. They, therefore, instituted monogamy, for women only, to ensure their biological paternity and enable the inheritance of private property. This Engels terms 'the world historic defeat of the female sex'.

There is, of course, a problem here as there is no reason why men should 'naturally' wish to hand on private property to their biological descendants. Again, Victorian familial ideology seems to be governing Engels' conception of men's 'natural' desires. However, despite these problems with the precise mechanisms which brought about women's subordination, Engels' linking of it to the emergence of private property, stratification, class societies and the state is theoretically significant and seems to be supported by empirical evidence (Draper, 1975; Leacock, 1972 and 1978; Sacks, 1979). Further, his theoretical framework allows the biological fact of women's capacity to bear children to have some influence on their social position without resorting to biological determinism (Sayers, 1982). Thus, in egalitarian non-class societies a gender division of labour existed and still exists, but was neither hierarchical nor did it deny women's autonomy. With the transition to a mode of production which made accumulation and therefore private property possible, women's reproductive capacity assumed a different significance and had an impact, *in combination with specific social and historic factors*, on their position in society. Thus, biological difference is, for Engels, part of the material basis of society and, in combination with the mode of production, affects women's status (Sayers, 1982). The important theoretical point is that Engels links the emergence of gender inequalities to the emergence of other social inequalities based on differential access to the means of production. Most feminist anthropologists working within the marxist theoretical tradition take this as their starting point.

Leacock, for instance, argues that it is the emergence of production for exchange which sets in motion the processes which lead to women's subordination. Where societies produce use-values solely for their own common consumption women occupy positions equal in status to those of men, though it should be noted, equality does not necessarily imply identity. In addition, Leacock argues that for many foraging societies it is the process of colonialism which has resulted in women's subordination, though in this case also it is often trading and exchange with the colonial powers which is the mechanism whereby stratification, hierarchical social relations and women's subordination are stimulated (Leacock, 1978, 1981a and 1986).

The link that Engels proposed between the adoption of a sedentary mode of existence, the domestication of animals and the subordination of women is supported by recent ethnography. The !Kung of southern Africa are undergoing a process of transition between a nomadic hunter-gatherer society and a society which is sedentary and based on cultivation and domestication of animals.

Draper's research shows that !Kung women in the former societies enjoy autonomy and gender relations are egalitarian whereas, in the latter, women stay within the domestic sphere more than men and participate less in the decision-making that affects their lives (Draper, 1975). It should also be noted that amongst the nomadic !Kung, women space their pregnancies such that their reproductive capabilities are subordinate to the requirements of production, specifically foraging, in their society (Draper, 1975; Sacks, 1979). As we have already noted, in hunter-gatherer societies it is women's foraging activities which provide the bulk of the food supply. They carry their infants with them on foraging expeditions, older children either accompanying them or remaining in the camp with other adults (Turnbull, 1982; Draper, 1975; Lee, 1982). As Sacks comments:

Women adopt a family planning policy that fits reproduction to the demands of their productive activities rather than the other way round. In this case, motherhood is subordinated to the productive relation of food provider. (Sacks, 1979: 70–1)

Thus, even in so-called primitive societies women are not at the mercy of their biology as popular mythology would have us believe.

Although evidence from !Kung ethnography supports Engels' broad schema, Draper does not discuss the development of production for exchange rather than use which Leacock points to as the key element in Engels' argument (Leacock, 1978). The effect of transforming production for consumption into production for exchange is that the social division of labour becomes more complex resulting in stratification which eventually leads to divisions between producers and non-producers. This creates the conditions for the emergence of class society and for the loss of control of women over their production, and their eventual subordination both as producers and as reproducers (Engels, 1972; Leacock, 1978; Coontz & Henderson, 1986).

Following Engels, feminists have looked more closely at production, reproduction and the relation between the two, in order to understand the precise mechanisms of women's subordination. Some argue that production and reproduction form two distinct systems and need to be analysed separately (Harris & Young,

1981; Rubin, 1975), while others argue that the organisation of production itself influences the ways in which biological reproduction is organised (Leacock, 1986; Sacks, 1979; Coontz & Henderson, 1986). Here I want to look at those arguments which give analytical primacy to the organisation of production and to assess the place given to biological factors in this type of argument.

Central to marxist analysis is the view that the relation of the direct producers to the means of production structures relations of exploitation and oppression within societies. This notion is developed by Sacks, who argues that women's relation to the means of production is crucial in determining their position in society. She argues, further, that this relation is mediated through the way in which societies organise marriage (Sacks, 1979). Sacks compares two types of society, one characterised by what she terms a communal mode of production and the other by a kin corporate mode of production.[3] In the communal mode of production there is no private property. The band collectively owns the means of production – hunting nets, cooking pots, gathering bags and so on – and each individual controls the product of their labour. The land is a common resource. In the kin corporate mode of production, however, property is owned by the kin corporate group, access to land and other means of production is dependent on membership of this group. In the communal mode of production, women's status in terms of their access to the means of production is not affected by marriage, but in the kin corporate mode of production, it is. This is because ownership rights are invested in the kin corporate group which collectively owns land and on which it grows food and rears domestic animals. Women have ownership rights in the group they are born into but they do not enjoy the same rights in the kin corporate group they marry into. Their status as wives, therefore, differs from their status as sisters; their relation to the means of production is determined by kinship relations. As Sacks points out, in contrast to the communal mode of production, where women's status is not affected by marriage because their relationship to the means of production remains constant, in a kin corporate mode of production 'spouses stand in different relations to the productive means' (Sacks, 1979: 118). Sacks is discussing patrilocal societies, where women marry out of their kin corporate group into that of their spouses, and their access to the means of production of their husband's corporate kin group is mediated through him. Thus, in their own corporate kin groups, women maintain rights to means of production and to products by means of their status as sisters, and they have rights to the labour of *wives* of that group, but at the same time their position as wives in the kin corporate group of their husband, where they are producers but not owners, is secondary (Sacks, 1979: 119). This status is not fixed, however, and as wives become mothers, and particularly mothers-in-law in the kin corporate group of their husbands they gain some independent access to the means of production.

Sacks illustrates her theoretical point, that women's relation to the means of production affects their status, by detailed case studies of several societies in Africa: the Mbuti, Lovedu, Mpondo and Buganda. In all she demonstrates that the more women are defined as wives rather than sisters and the less direct access they have to the means of production the lower is their status. She links a decline in women's status to the emergence of class societies which was prefigured by emerging inequalities in the kin corporate mode of production. For her the most significant measure of women's status is their access to the means of production although in her discussion of specific societies she recognises the multi-dimensional nature of status. However, without access to the means of production women's status in other areas of their lives is likely to be reduced.

One of the interesting features of her case studies is the incidence of woman–woman marriage. Among the Lovedu it was a means by which women could enhance their status and prestige and accumulate wealth; Evans-Pritchard noted its occurrence amongst the Nuer (Sacks, 1979: 77). Wealth was used in these societies to build a following. Establishing a household by obtaining a wife, even if you are a woman, gives you the status necessary to translate 'private wealth into social standing' (Sacks, 1979: 79) and also gives women access to children and through them to the status of 'ancestress' after their death. Thus, women's social status in many African societies is not limited to that of wife, or even sister, but they can also become husbands and the social father of their wives' children. They may, at the same time, be married to men (Sacks, 1979).

Sacks' argument is important because it has contributed to a sophisticated theoretical reconstruction of the possible origins of women's subordination, explicated by Coontz and Henderson (1986). The question that they ask is why male dominance – although not biologically determined and not inevitable – 'was a likely outcome of processes associated with socio-economic expansion and increasing social complexity?' (Coontz & Henderson, 1986a: 26). They acknowledge that the question of the origins of women's oppression cannot be definitively resolved, but they take the view that it is important to be able to provide a convincing theory in order to counter assertions of the inevitability and universality of male dominance. Thus they seek to provide a concrete reason for the appearance and spread of male dominance in ancient cultures. Like Leacock, they link the emergence of male dominance with that of commodity production, stratification and classes, but the contradiction within kin corporate groups that enables this process to be set in motion is derived from Sacks' analysis of the differential positions occupied by owners and producers in kin corporations: the distinction between sisters and wives. Their analysis avoids the problem of arguing either that male dominance is a result of external, colonial pressures on previously egalitarian societies (Leacock, 1978) or that it is a product of a biological drive on the part of men to endow their sons with property (Engels, 1972). Instead, they see male dominance as arising from two processes: the emergence of ranking internal to many pre-class societies and the type of property that preceded individual private property (Coontz & Henderson, 1986: 110).

They assume the existence of a patterned, cross-cultural sexual division of labour 'whereby women perform subsistence, manufacturing and processing tasks that are closer to home base, while males take on more long-distance and risky pursuits that require sudden, sustained and unplanned periods of activity and are thus difficult to reconcile with pregnancy or nursing' (Coontz & Henderson, 1986: 113). It appears that in this assumption they are relying on an underlying reproductive model in their analysis (Mukhopadhayay & Higgins, 1988: 478). Liebowitz has argued that such a division of labour is not inevitable but is the result of complex processes involving changes in technology, specifically the development of projectile weapons, and increasing fertility which accompanied changes in diet amongst the early hominids (Liebowitz, 1975, 1983, 1986). Thus, this division of labour, given certain social and technical arrangements of society, is related to women's reproductive capacity but is not inevitable. In this way they recognise that biology has some influence on the social roles of women and men. This patterned division of labour was flexible and non-hierarchical; difference did not imply inequality, dominance or a differential valuing of male and female tasks. And women who were not performing a reproductive role could be and were involved in activities such as hunting and warfare (Albers, 1989: 136,142). For example, Canadian Indian women who were childless were involved in hunting and the female warriors of Dahomey were required by the king to remain celibate (Coontz & Henderson, 1986: 114). Indeed, as Sacks comments, fatherhood is no more compatible with warrior status than is motherhood (Sacks, 1979: 69). This is an important point because it emphasises that women's involvement in certain tasks can and does change depending on the stage of the life cycle; this is clear from many ethnographies.

This flexible gender division of labour had some implications for the ways in which the products of women's and men's labour were distributed. Women's foraging or cultivation activities produced the daily means of survival. Men's hunting or trading activities or, less frequently, involvement in warfare, could produce a lot or nothing at all. This produces a situation where the rules for redistribution of men's products are likely to be more complex than those for the redistribution of women's products. Women's products could be consumed by women and their close associates and as all women were involved in this type of productive activity on a daily basis it was unlikely that any would go without (Collier & Rosaldo, 1981: 281–3; Coontz & Henderson, 1986: 115).

Coontz and Henderson argue that the processes that could transform such a flexible division of labour into the exploitation of female labour arise from the transformation of communal societies into those based on kin corporate property owning groups. This corresponds to the distinction made by Sacks between the communal and kin corporate modes of production. The transition from foraging societies into societies producing food by cultivation and domestication of animals led to a need to manage resources; one of the resources to be managed was labour. In communal societies, as we have already seen, access to resources is equal and everyone has control over his or her means of production and the products of their labour. Generalised reciprocity[4] characterises this type of society (Draper, 1975; Lee, 1982). In kin corporate groups, however, access to the means of production and the products of labour are controlled through kinship. Hence, Sacks' distinction between sisters and wives, a distinction that can just as easily be made between brothers and husbands in kin corporate groups with matrilocal rules of residence; that is, where men move to live with the women they marry. The mechanism of the emergence of male domination is located in the contradiction between owners in a kin corporate group and those who move into the group on marriage as producers. Those who move are at a disadvantage, in terms of access to and control over the means of production, in the group they move into, while retaining ownership rights in their group of origin. The means of production, most importantly land and tools, are held in common by the kin corporate group. Property rights are therefore invested in the group but are not available, at least not on an equal basis, to those moving into the group on marriage.

An important result of kin corporate groups having to manage labour and the distribution of commodities is that balanced reciprocity and the circulation of spouses become the means by which these processes are ensured. It has long been assumed by anthropologists that exchange of women by men, together with the incest taboo, is what marks off human society and the emergence of culture from a purely biological phenomenon (Lévi-Strauss, 1969; Meillassoux, 1972; Rubin, 1975). However, the exchange of women is precisely what needs to be explained, it cannot be taken as a universal given of human society. And recent discussions suggest that even where it appears to Western observers that women are being exchanged by men, it does not necessarily follow that they are being treated as objects, the passive pawns in men's active negotiations (Strathern, 1987a). The development of this type of exchange is, therefore, problematic and in need of explanation. This Coontz and Henderson attempt to provide by looking at the processes of differentiation which may have created an incentive for corporate groups in patrilocal societies to control women's labour.

They argue that within societies based on kin corporate groups there is the potential for development of inequalities between groups. This can initially be because of differences in fertility of land, different access to raw materials such as metals and differential success in exchanging with other groups. Goods acquired in this way can be redistributed through feasting and so on, but the rules of reciprocity characterising kin corporate groups require that generosity is reciprocated. If a kin corporate group does not have access to sufficient products to be able to do this a situation develops where labour is pledged in return for gifts. Sacks describes such a situation in her analysis of the Mpondo where cattle are required by young men for bride-wealth payment and, in order to obtain cattle, they pledge their labour to a group who own cattle (Sacks, 1979: 176–7). This control over labour can lead to ranking as clearly had happened in Sacks' example. As labour produces more wealth which can then be redistributed, thus enhancing the prestige of the lineage or kin corporate group still further, there is likely to be an incentive to accumulate labour in these groups. And, due to the gender division of labour, women's labour and men's labour is valuable in different ways.

Coontz and Henderson argue that in patrilocal societies the incentive to exert control over labour was greater than in matrilocal societies for several reasons (Coontz & Henderson, 1986: 129). Firstly, men produced variable wealth, by means of hunting, exchange and warfare, and their obligations were to their residential group. In matrilocal groups men's obligations were not only to the group they married into but also to their natal group. Their wealth was therefore dispersed whereas in patrilocal groups it could be accumulated. Female products, on the other hand, were not subject to elaborate redistribution rules and were produced on a regular daily basis, being mainly food. Secondly, for redistribution of male products, such as a large animal killed in the hunt, feasts were necessary for which women's labour was essential. These factors in combination could have led to a situation in which men in patrilocal kin groups had control over women's labour and could therefore intensify women's production while, at the same time, being better able to accumulate their own products within the lineage. In matrilocal societies, in contrast, men's products were divided between their mothers, sisters and wives, which meant that they were dispersed between kin corporate groups, and as the women were the owners in the group, the men were not in a position to control women's labour and intensify their production. In patrilocal societies, men's involvement in exchange, hunting and warfare and their control over female labour within their kin group came together to give them an advantage over matrilocal societies in terms of the ability to accumulate, gain prestige and thereby create even greater inequalities between themselves and other kin corporate groups.

Coontz and Henderson pinpoint the mechanism leading to women's subordination as arising from the control exercised over female labour by men in patrilocal societies. They thus locate women's subordination as arising from men's need/ability to control their labour, as incoming wives, rather than with a desire to control their sexuality or reproductive potential. However, the more women that were available in a society the greater the potential for a new generation of labourers. They therefore see men's control over women's reproductive powers as arising from their control over women's labour; productive relations are given analytical primacy over relations of reproduction:

... patrilocality, with its greater possibilities for the appropriation of wives' labour, could more easily set into motion the kind of social, political and psychological processes that could culminate in the full-fledged control of all women's lives and bodies. (Coontz & Henderson, 1986: 142)

Thus, kin corporate property creates the possibility of a contradiction between the rights of producers and owners within lineages. This contradiction, in combination with patrilocal rules of residence, balanced reciprocity and differential access of groups to men's products, produces both ranking *and* the incentive for men to control women's labour. Thus, Coontz and Henderson link the emergence of male dominance to a certain form of property ownership and the development of ranking. In turn, increasing control over female labour facilitates processes of stratification and eventually the development of class society. Thus, the emergence of inequalities of gender and class are linked in this analytical framework as mutually dependent and reinforcing. What is also significant is that the eventual development of class society presupposes control of labour, and one form of labour that is controlled is that performed by women. This control develops from kin corporate property and the potential this creates for ranking. However, without the flexible, previously developed gender division of labour described by Coontz and Henderson, such development would not have occurred. Thus, in this analysis, women's role in reproduction produces a gender division of labour which provides part of the material basis allowing for the subsequent possible development of male domination. What needs to be remembered, though, is that it is this patterned gender division of labour *in combination with* social factors such as private property and ranking that explains the emergence of male domination, not the gender division of labour on its own. In turn, private property (in the form of kin corporate group property) emerges from the change from a communal mode of production to one based on kin corporate groups, which is itself a result of a transformation in the way in which groups organised production. Communal or egalitarian societies are hunter-gatherers or foragers while societies based on kin corporate groups are sedentary and rely on cultivation of crops and domestication of animals (Leacock & Lee, 1982: 8–9; Etienne & Leacock, 1980). The contradictions inherent in the kin corporate mode of production pave the way for the emergence of ranking and, although this type of society is often characterised as egalitarian it should strictly be seen as transitional in terms of this typology (Etienne & Leacock, 1980: 12). The societies of Melanesia described in Strathern's collection (1987) fall into the latter category while the foraging !Kung and the Mbuti pygmies fall into the former (Draper, 1975; Lee, 1982; Sacks, 1979).

The analysis provided by Coontz and Henderson, then, suggests that, although the mechanisms proposed by Engels for the 'overthrow of mother right' were biologistic and open to criticism, his theoretical schema which linked the emergence of women's oppression to the development of production for exchange, private property and class societies is largely supported, both empirically and analytically. And, although Engels and Coontz and Henderson give some explanatory power to biological factors, for male domination to emerge there have to be very specific social and economic developments. This analysis, therefore, suggests the possibility of future changes in social and economic relationships leading to a transformation in the effect that women's repro-ductive capabilities have upon their social status. In other words, women's subordination is not an inevitable effect of female biology and is therefore amenable to change. And although biology is given a place in this analytic framework, it is not seen in deterministic or essentialist terms.

This type of explanation, therefore, allows biology, as part of the material conditions of existence, to have some effect on gender divisions, without assigning to biological differences a determinant role in any explanation of gender divisions and women's subordination. It also points to the need to analyse the specific forms taken by gender divisions in different types of society. Given that there is no essence to the diversity of gender divisions, it is possible to understand the ways in which specific gender divisions emerge and are reproduced only by analysing them in concrete societies. Different societies combine social relations of production and the biological difference between women and men in different ways to produce different forms of gender divisions, which may or may not involve female subordination. This implies that no generalisations can be made across societies and different historical periods about the essential nature of the relation between the genders and that, in order to understand gender divisions, the relation of gender to social inequalities, particularly the relation between gender and control over the means of production, needs to be analysed. Such an approach moves away from notions that all women share a common experience of oppression and, therefore common interests, to a more complex position that women in different societies, and in different classes and social groups within the same society, may be subordinated in different ways. Indeed, it may be that even in societies marked by male dominance some women may not be oppressed as women because of the status and control they enjoy by virtue of their membership of other social groups. These issues will be explored in the following chapters which focus on the form taken by gender divisions in capitalist, 'socialist' and 'developing' societies. I look first at gender divisions in industrial, capitalist societies using Britain as an example of such a society.

NOTES

1. De Beauvoir was an existentialist philosopher profoundly influenced by Jean-Paul Sartre with whom she had a life-long relationship.

Existentialism assumes that 'each human being is a subject reaching towards transcendence and there is no other justification for existence than this movement towards an empty future. The worse evil is to fall into objectness' (Nye, 1988: 82). In terms of her analysis woman is object to man's subject; she is immanent, he is transcendent.

2. Structuralism and structuralist analysis derive from linguistics. Structuralism has been very influential within anthropology, where it is associated with Lévi-Strauss, and in the analysis of culture. Structuralist approaches argue that human thought and language are systems of signs which derive their meaning from the relationship of the signs to each other rather than from their reference to the material world. Indeed, the material world is given meaning and interpreted through these systems of signs rather than having any intrinsic meaning itself. Structuralism is not necessarily idealist but is more commonly associated with an idealist rather than materialist philosophical position.

3. The kin corporate mode of production has been variously termed the lineage mode of production; the domestic mode of production; the simple or complex community mode of production; and, confusingly, the communal mode of production. What is important is that, whatever the terminology, kinship is conceptualised as the basis of production relations, the kin corporation (lineage or clan) owns land which is the chief means of production and there are no classes (Stamp, 1986: 36).

4. Generalised reciprocity differs from balanced reciprocity in so far as the latter refers to exchange and the former refers to gift giving. Both involve reciprocity, but the expectations in societies characterised by balanced reciprocity are that the exchange will be of equivalent items or services and will take place simultaneously; debts are incurred if this does not happen. In societies characterised by generalised reciprocity, the expectation is that if someone needs what you have then it is given to them and vice versa. Everyone gives to everyone else when they are able and receives when they are in need.

/ 2 /

GENDER DIVISIONS AND CAPITALISM

Advanced capitalist societies are characterised by a very specific gender division of labour. In the workforce men's jobs are skilled, women's are unskilled, men receive higher pay than women, their work is of higher status, they are in a majority in the professions and in the skilled manual occupations. Within families men are the primary breadwinners and women are their dependants. Although married women may be involved in paid work outside the home they have as their first priority the care of their husbands and children. How have these divisions become institutionalised within advanced capitalist societies? How are they maintained? Is capitalism undermining or perpetuating them? Are they functional to capitalism or is capitalism as a system of exploitation utterly sex blind? What is the relation between capitalism and gender divisions? These are the questions which I want to explore in this and the following chapter. In order to do this I shall first discuss the gender division of paid work and gender divisions within the household, exploring the ways in which they are mutually reinforcing. I shall then briefly discuss the role of the state in relation to the gender division of labour, concentrating specifically on the development of social and economic policies. Finally, I shall evaluate the major explanations of gender divisions within capitalist societies and suggest that a historical perspective is essential for a proper understanding of the relationship between gender divisions and capitalism. Most of the empirical material will be drawn from Britain although where appropriate comparisons will be made with other capitalist societies. The theoretical arguments, however, are clearly not limited in application only to one country.

GENDER DIVISIONS AND PAID WORK

In 1984 an official survey of women's paid employment in Britain was published which served, yet again, to dispel the myth that women, particularly married women, do not work outside the home (Martin & Roberts, 1984). It was not the first survey to have done this (Hunt, 1968), but the idea that women do not have the same commitment to the workforce as do men, or indeed have a choice as to whether or not they take up paid employment, is very hard to overcome. Contrary to popular belief, women have always been an important part of the workforce. The figures for 1901, for instance, a period when married women's formal participation in employment was at its lowest in Britain (Tilly & Scott, 1987), show that women constituted around 30% of the workforce (Myrdal & Klein, 1968). In the USA at the turn of the century there were just over twenty women workers for every hundred men working and the picture was similar in Sweden. In France women constituted over a third of the workforce (Myrdal & Klein, 1968). These figures, of course, exclude women's activities in the 'informal' economy and are therefore bound to be an under-estimate of women's economic activity. However, if we look at women's participation in the formal economy, it is clear that in all these countries there has been an upward trend in female participation rates during this century which is still continuing (Bakker, 1988). For instance, in Britain female employment increased by 1.6 million (17%) between 1979 and 1989 (Equal Opportunities Commission, 1991: 13) and similar trends are apparent in most advanced capitalist societies (Bakker, 1988). The percentage increase in women's economic activity rates during the 1980s in Europe is shown in Table 2.1.

In their survey, Martin and Roberts found that 69% of women between the ages of 16 and 59 were economically active, 63% being in paid work and 6% unemployed and looking for work (Martin & Roberts, 1984). As a comparison the male economic activity rate in 1984 was approximately 74%; there is, therefore, not a huge disparity in women's and men's involvement in the workforce (*Employment Gazette*, August 1986). In fact men's economic activity rates are decreasing while women's are increasing, a phenomenon sometimes referred to as the 'feminisation' of

Table 2.1 Economic activity rates of women aged 25–49 years in the European Economic Community

	Economic activity rate 1989 (%)	Annual growth rate between 1983 and 1989 (%)
Ireland	45	2.77
Spain	47.9	7.74
Luxemburg	51.6	2.42
Greece	54.3	3.14
Italy	55.8	2.43
Netherlands	58.2	4.23
Germany	63.4	1.44
Belgium	65.5	1.81
Portugal	69.9	2.61
UK	72.7	2.39
France	73.2	1.14
Denmark	87.9	0.29

Source: Marnani, 1992: 4.

the workforce. Organisation for Economic Cooperation and Development figures show that, between 1950 and 1985, female economic activity rates in the advanced industrial nations increased from 38.2% to 55.9% while male economic activity rates declined from 87.4% to 84.3% (Bakker, 1988: 19). There is, however, an enormous difference in the types of jobs women and men do, the pay they receive, the hours they work, the skills they acquire and their patterns of employment over a lifetime (Dex, 1985; Feminist Review, 1986; Breugel, 1983; Beechey & Whitelegg, 1986; Martin & Roberts, 1984; Marnani, 1992). Detailed descriptions of the gender division of paid work can be found elsewhere (see, for example, Lewis, 1984; Dex, 1985; Beechey & Whitelegg, 1986; Jenson, Hagen & Reddy, 1988). Here I want to paint an overall picture rather than going into the finer detail.

Occupations within capitalist economies are largely either women's or men's and within occupations men tend to occupy the higher, more prestigious positions and women the lower ones; this is known as horizontal and vertical segregation (Hakim, 1979). This is the case even in so-called women's occupations; for instance, in nursing 9% of nurses are men but they hold 45% of the top nursing jobs (Stamp & Robarts, 1986) and in factories men are the chargehands and supervisors while women work on the assembly line (Pollert, 1981; Glucksmann, 1986). Where men and women work at the same jobs, in the professions for instance, women still tend to be concentrated in the less prestigious areas. In medicine they tend to specialise in areas such as paediatrics and child and adolescent psychiatry whereas men are in the higher status areas such as neurosurgery and forensic psychiatry (Oakley, 1983: 122; Leeson & Grey, 1978). Jobs are therefore divided into men's work and women's work. The boundaries are not fixed, they can and do change, but what is significant is that where men take over a woman's occupation, as with healing in the eighteenth and nineteenth centuries, its status increases, and where women take over a man's occupation, as with clerical work and teaching at the beginning of this century, its status decreases (Oakley, 1979; Lewis, 1984; Tilly & Scott, 1987; Lowe, 1987). Workforces in advanced capitalism are therefore divided along lines of gender, with 'women's work' being of lower status than men's.

As well as being clearly demarcated, men's and women's work is valued differently; men's is consistently more highly valued than women's and is regarded as requiring a level of skill which most 'women's work' does not. In Britain, for instance, Martin and Roberts found that women workers think men would be able to do 'women's work' but would not want to, whereas men simply think women are incapable of doing 'men's work' (Martin & Roberts, 1984). This valuation is reflected in the low pay attached to 'women's work' and partly explains the failure of equal pay and equal opportunities legislation to alter radically the gender division of paid work (Dex, 1985; Showstack Sassoon, 1987).

This rigid gender segregation of the workforce makes it difficult for women to achieve equal pay with men (Snell, 1986). When the Equal Pay Act (EPA) was first introduced a woman had to be doing 'the same or broadly similar' work to a man before she could claim equal pay. It has recently been made slightly easier for women to claim equal pay as it is now the value of women's and men's jobs which is to be compared and the jobs are no longer required to be identical. Despite this, however, women's pay is on average 70% of men's, the exact disparity depending on whether you take hourly or weekly earnings in manual or non-manual occupations (Dex, 1985; Marnani, 1992). Despite the so-called equality legislation within the EEC, the earnings gap between men and women has not been significantly eroded. Thus, in Britain there has been no change since 1983; in some countries, such as Italy, Denmark and Portugal, the gap has widened and in only a few has it narrowed slightly (Marnani, 1992: 52).

Skill is also divided along lines of gender. Men occupy the skilled sectors of the manual workforce: they are the skilled tradesmen – carpenters, bricklayers, electricians; they are the fitters and mechanics. Men are much more likely than women to have received some training, either on or off the job (Martin & Roberts, 1984). Women's work is, almost by definition, unskilled (Lewis, 1984; Cockburn, 1985; Phillips & Taylor, 1980). It has been suggested that male workers have been able to define their jobs as skilled and protect them in the face of mechanisation and undercutting (Lewis, 1984; Hunt, 1986; Cockburn, 1985). In contrast, women's skills, such as dexterity which is important for fiddly electrical assembly work, and caring which is important in nursing, are not recognised as such. It has been suggested that this is because they are learned outside the production process, often within the home, and are regarded as innate and natural requiring no monetary reward (Dex, 1985; Elson & Pearson, 1986). Men's skills, on the other hand, are acquired through apprenticeships and on-the-job training and men have organised to ensure that they are recognised and rewarded; the craft unions provide an example of this (Tilly & Scott, 1987; Lewis, 1984; Dex, 1985).

Men's and women's hours of work also differ, with far more women than men working part-time (Martin & Roberts, 1984; Beechey & Perkins, 1987). In fact the provision of part-time work, particularly in the service sector of the economy which has expanded since the Second World War, has been seen as a way of enabling married women to combine paid employment with their domestic responsibilities. Policy makers after the Second World War and facing an acute labour shortage recognised the provision of part-time work as a way of encouraging married women to enter paid employment while still being able to fulfil their domestic duties (*Economic Survey 1947*). Thus the 'twilight' shift was introduced in 1950 in factories to enable 'housewives' to work for four hours in the early evening (Lewis, 1984: 153). Trade unions have also encouraged part-time work for women (Charles, 1979). It is significant that neither government nor trade unions suggested that men's hours of work might also be adjusted to fit in with the demands of child care.

The increase in part-time working is marked in Britain. Over a million part-time jobs were created during the 1970s and by 1988 part-time working was much more widespread amongst married women employees in the UK (53%) than in the rest of the European Community (37%) (Equal Opportunities Commission, 1991: 23). In Britain over 90% of part-time workers are women and almost one half of women's jobs are part-time (Beechey & Perkins, 1987). In addition, most part-time women workers are or have been married. In 1984 the figure was 98% compared with 68% of women working full-time. However, marriage does not seem to be the relevant factor affecting women's hours of work; it is rather whether or not they have children and the age of their youngest child (Martin & Roberts, 1984). For instance, in a study of women shift workers it was found that women with pre-school-age children worked a twilight shift while women with older children worked full-time but on shifts which fitted in with their partners' hours of work. So women whose partners worked days worked night shifts while other women worked 'back to back' with their partners on double-day shifts, one working the morning shift the other the afternoon shift (Charles & Brown, 1981). What most women with children find themselves unable to do is work full-time days if their partner also is. In that situation they have to take up paid work that fits in with their children's school hours, and industries relying on female labour adapt their hours of work accordingly. Such work is usually part-time (Beechey & Perkins, 1987; Jephcott, Seear & Smith, 1962).

Although there is a strong correlation between the increase in married women working in paid employment and the increase in part-time jobs in Britain, this is not the case throughout the whole of the advanced capitalist world. Many countries have experienced a marked increase in women's economic activity rates during the latter half of this century whether or not part-time work is available. This is true of Australia, Canada, Belgium, Finland, Spain, Sweden, Britain and the USA (Beechey & Perkins, 1987). Although part-time work is increasingly available and is replacing full-time employment in many of these societies, this is not true for all of them (Bakker, 1988; Marnani, 1992). In Finland, for instance, women's participation in the workforce is extremely high and most women work full-time (Beechey & Perkins, 1987). So although in Britain the rationale for the expansion of part-time work for women is to enable them to combine paid employment with their domestic responsibilities, this is not the only route to increased numbers of women working outside the home. Provision of child-care facilities also enables women to work outside the home. In France there is a higher level of full-time working among married women than in Britain; women in France also enjoy better provision of child-care facilities and maternity benefit than women in Britain (Beechey & Perkins, 1987).

It has long been assumed that family responsibilities have an impact on women's participation in the workforce, particularly their hours of work, and the opposite assumption has been made about men's hours of work. However, men are likely to work more overtime than women, particularly when children are small, and may even have to work at two jobs to support their families. Thus, men's hours of work are also affected, though in different ways from women's, by the stage in the life cycle of the family (NBPI, 1970; Henwood *et al.*, 1987; Melhuish & Moss, 1991).

Part-time work, although fitting in with women's domestic responsibilities has disadvantages. It tends to be lower paid than normal full-time work and is much lower paid than overtime and shiftwork. This enlarges the gap between men's and women's earnings. Terms and conditions of employment are also usually worse for part-time than full-time employees, another factor disadvantaging women in the labour market.

However, not all women in paid employment work part-time, and those who work full-time in non-manual occupations are likely to have better opportunities and conditions of employment than the majority of women workers (Martin & Roberts, 1984). This means that they may be able to resolve the contradiction between full-time paid employment and domestic commitments by paying someone else to undertake their child care, either in their own or someone else's home or in a day nursery, and perhaps their household tasks as well. This is an option which is not open to most women who usually have to resolve the contradiction by taking paid employment that will fit in with the needs of their children and the hours of work of their husbands. This restricts the choice of jobs open to them and is reflected in the fact that a substantial proportion of women, when returning to work after the period of childbearing is completed, take jobs which are lower in pay and status than those they held prior to the birth of their first child (Martin & Roberts, 1984). Shouldering responsibility for children and domestic work therefore handicaps women in a job market which is structured on the assumption that workers do not have time-consuming domestic responsibilities. The workers that fit this model are men.

Lastly, women's and men's patterns of employment differ. For instance, while men's patterns of employment have remained relatively stable throughout the period of capitalist domination of the economy, women's patterns of employment have undergone considerable change (Tilly & Scott, 1987; Lewis, 1984; Pinchbeck, 1981). In contemporary Britain men's paid work takes them out of the home for eight, or more, hours a day throughout their working lives. In contrast women enter the workforce on leaving school and withdraw from it, temporarily, if and when they have their first baby. They tend to return to paid employment between the birth of each child, albeit usually to lower status, lower paid and often part-time work, before returning permanently to the work-force once their youngest child reaches school age (Martin & Roberts, 1984). At the beginning of this century the pattern was different. Married women tended to leave paid work on marriage (there was a marriage bar in operation in many occupations) and to participate in some form of waged work when the needs of their family required it (Tilly & Scott, 1987; Lewis, 1984). Before restrictions were placed on child labour in the last quarter of the nineteenth century women continued in paid employment while their children were too young to go out to work themselves; as soon as their children were able to earn a wage women could afford to withdraw from the workforce (Tilly & Scott, 1987). Earlier still, during the period of industrialisation, women did not withdraw from paid employment except for the time necessary to give birth to a baby (Engels, 1969). Thus women's patterns of employment have varied greatly throughout the period of indus-trial capitalism and, throughout, women's economic activity has been vital, both for the economy at large and for the domestic economy of their households. The changes in women's economic activity have been linked to varying demands for female labour, the economic strategy of the household unit to which they belong, industrial and economic development and gender ideologies; these issues are explored below.

THE EXPERIENCE OF PAID WORK

Large-scale surveys such as that carried out by Martin and Roberts, along with census data and periodic government surveys, provide valuable data on the overall distribution of women and men within the workforce (Hunt, 1968; Department of Employment, 1974; Martin & Roberts, 1984). However, they give us little indication of how individual women and men experience paid employment and the significance of it in their lives. This gap is filled by studies of women workers which have appeared in recent years, complementing the many studies which have focused on men as workers (West, 1982; Pollert, 1981; Sharpe, 1984; Cavendish, 1982). Interestingly, though, studies of women workers have replicated studies of men workers in that they have tended to focus on women in manufacturing industry (Pollert, 1981; Cavendish, 1982; West, 1982). By far the greatest number of women are employed in the service sector of the economy, working as sales assistants, waitresses, clerks and typists (Dex, 1985). The narrow focus of studies is now beginning to be rectified (see, for example, Pringle, 1988). An important theoretical concern in studying women as workers is the relationship between gender and class; more specifically, how and in what ways gender affects class consciousness (Pollert, 1981; Cavendish, 1982; Porter, 1982; Hunt, 1980). Most of these studies point to women's 'fragmented and contradictory' consciousness. As Beechey puts it in an interesting review article, 'They all reveal elements of what might be called a work consciousness among the women, but in every study this is shown to coexist with a primarily familial definition of the women's consciousness' (Beechey, 1983: 38). However, it is important to ask whether this distinguishes women from men and sets them apart, or whether men's consciousness too may not be 'fragmented and contradictory'. Perhaps the familial dimension of men's consciousness has been missing in studies of men as workers just as the worker dimension of women has been missed in studies of women as wives and mothers? The relation between gender and class is of continuing concern within sociology (see, for example, Goldthorpe, 1983 and 1984; Britten & Heath, 1983; Charles, 1990).

As well as pointing to women's 'fragmentary and contradictory' consciousness these studies provide important data on women's experience of paid work and what it means to them. Money is clearly important in motivating both men and women to take up paid employment, and women's earnings are crucial in keeping families out of poverty. If women did not work, 40% of households would fall below the poverty line (Mack & Lansley, 1985); women's pay is therefore important to the household budget. However, women are motivated to work not only by money but for other reasons as well; this is also true of men as has become clear from studies of male unemployment (Sharpe, 1984; Fineman, 1987). Paid work is important for women because it provides relief from the isolation of the home, companionship and the creation of an individual identity apart from being someone's mother or someone's wife. For many women paid employment is an escape from the boredom, isolation and confinement of housework and child care in a house on your own all day (Sharpe, 1984). Indeed, it has been shown that full-time housework and child care can predispose women towards depressive illness and that participation in paid employment may restore a woman's mental health (Brown & Harris, 1978; Sharpe, 1984).

These studies also show that class affects women's experience of paid employment. Most working-class women regard their paid employment as temporary; even though paid employment is something that the majority of working-class women are involved in for most of their lives. In contrast, women in jobs with a career structure, usually middle-class and often professional women, regard paid employment differently; for them motherhood is a temporary interruption to paid employment rather than paid employment being a temporary interlude before the real job of wife and mother begins (Pollert, 1981; Sharpe, 1984). The 'temporariness' of women's employment does not appear to be a recent development and was apparent at the turn of the century when factory work for women was more positively regarded than it is now:

It is a significant fact that whereas large numbers of factory girls cannot be prevailed upon to give up their factory work after marriage, the majority of shop assistants look upon marriage as their one hope of release and would, as one girl expressed it, 'marry anybody to get out of the drapery business'. (Holcombe, 1973: 117 cited in Tilly & Scott, 1987: 184)

However, most young girls, even those with factory work, regarded it as temporary (Tilly & Scott, 1987: 184), perhaps with more reason then than today as most women did not continue to work in paid employment after marriage.

Many women, therefore, experience their paid work as temporary, whatever its duration, and this has been seen as differentiating their work experience from that of men. However, this difference may not be so great if we begin to consider the number of working-class men who would welcome an escape from the daily grind of wage-labour; perhaps an indication of this is the popularity of football pools and national lotteries. Having said that, however, the possibilities of 'escape' are much closer to hand for women and it is the domestic division of labour which ensures that this is so.

For girls and women brought up to see their primary role as that of mother and housewife with paid employment as a secondary role there always seems to be the possibility of doing one thing or the other. If paid work is boring they can 'escape' into marriage and motherhood, if motherhood is boring they can 'escape' into paid work. However, women's identity comes from both roles and the contradiction between them produces tension and stress (Sharpe, 1984; Wilson, 1977).

Additionally, women's domestic role conflicts with their paid employment and women feel this conflict as guilt. If they are going out to work they are not fulfilling their maternal role properly; if they meet all their child's needs adequately (including when they are sick and their mother needs to take time off work) they are not doing their paid work properly. This contradiction between women's domestic work role and paid work role is not felt by men. The domestic division of labour assigns to men the role of breadwinner and paid employment is a constituent part of it rather than being in contradiction with it.

The domestic division of labour also defines women as financially dependent upon men, and this situation is reinforced by the fact that women's work is generally lower paid than men's. This contributes to women's ambivalence about issues such as equal pay. Many women feel that men 'need' more pay than women because they have families to support but in terms of the work women can see them doing they do not necessarily deserve it

(Barrett & McIntosh, 1980; Charles, 1986). This contradiction can produce ambivalence:

> I believe women doing the same work as a man should have equal pay, but men will feel downgraded. I expect to be supported by my husband if I'm married, but if I was earning as much as him – he wouldn't feel he was supporting me he'd be downgraded. And, if men do women's work and women do men's, it'll also put women out of work. (Pollert, 1981: 85).

This is interesting because it indicates that equal pay between men and women is seen as undermining men's position as head of household and main breadwinner. Men are reluctant to encourage this, as evidenced by the long history of trade union opposition to equal pay for women (Walby, 1986; Lewenhak, 1977; Boston, 1987), but it is not clear that all women are totally in favour of it either. If they look at it from the point of view of the rate for the job, they are; if they look at it from the point of view of wives – that is, dependants of men – they feel that men should earn more than women.

The gendering of jobs is another factor which affects women's and men's experiences of them differentially (Willis, 1977; Pollert, 1981; Bradley, 1989). Women often have difficulty identifying with manual jobs which are seen as masculine; the job contradicts their gender identity (Pollert, 1981). On the other hand, office work confirms their gender identity (Willis, 1977; Griffin, 1985). Griffin found that girls regarded office work as 'good' and factory work as 'bad'. She comments that office work meshes with an idealised form of femininity whereas factory work does not (Griffin, 1985). Similarly, unskilled manual labour is identified by the working-class 'lads' of Willis's study with masculinity; it is part of the masculine identity. For young women, on the other hand, unskilled manual work does not confirm or mesh with their femininity, they cannot identify with it in the unproblematic way in which young men are able to (Pollert, 1981; Willis, 1977).

All these factors produce ambivalence in women's work consciousness. They produce the fragmentation and contradiction referred to earlier and indicate that gender divisions within households and the ideologies which are associated with them, specifically familial ideology, have important effects on the way women (and men, although research still needs to be done in this area) experience and understand their paid employment.

GENDER DIVISIONS WITHIN THE HOME

Many writers, feminists and non-feminists alike, have attributed the different participation of women and men in the workforce in capitalist economies to the gender division of labour within the home. More particularly women's maternal role has been seen as the primary obstacle and some see it as positively preventing even the possibility of equality in the world of work (Firestone, 1971; Goldberg, 1979; Sharpe, 1984; Millett, 1971). Undoubtedly, gender divisions within the workforce are closely bound up with gender divisions within the home; but the precise ways in which they relate to each other is a subject for debate. Tilly and Scott, for instance, argue that with the separation of production from the domestic sphere which occurs with capitalist industrialisation, women's participation in paid work is circumscribed by the need to attend to child care and housework. However, if the 'family economy' needs the wages of the mother she will seek paid employment, if it is available. The availability of suitable work for women in turn depends on economic developments. They also link women's participation in paid work to demographic changes and argue that a reduction in family size together with a demand for women workers is conducive to women's participation in paid work (Tilly & Scott, 1987).

That domestic commitments affect women's participation in the workforce seems startlingly obvious; it is after all accepted wisdom that women put their families first. However, the relation is not that simple. While in Britain it is assumed that women with children will be unlikely to work in full-time paid employment, in other parts of the advanced capitalist world they manage to combine full-time work with domestic commitments, and studies of ethnic minority women in the USA show that black women expect to work full-time whether they have children or not (Beechey & Perkins, 1987; Stack, 1975). It is therefore not *only* domestic commitments which affect women's participation in the workforce. Factors such as a demand for female labour, the availability of other sources of child care (whether kin or state-run day nurseries), hours of work and the gender division of labour within the household are also important. Here I wish to concentrate on the gender division of labour within households, and particularly to ask if the increased participation of married women in the workforce over the past fifty years or so has led to any changes in the domestic division of labour. First, though, it is important to establish what exactly we are discussing.

'The family' was defined in the 1851 census as consisting of 'husband, wife, children and servants, or, less perfectly but more commonly, of husband, wife and children' (quoted in Hall, 1982: 24). The role of housewife is also historically specific. It was in the 1881 census that women's 'household chores' were defined as unproductive; previously women who were engaged on work within the home had been considered economically active:

Thus in 1881, for the first time, housewives were classified as 'unoccupied', although uncertainty as to the proper classification of wives' and daughters' domestic work persisted until after the 1891 census. In 1911, enumerators were firmly instructed that no entry was to be made for wives or daughters wholly engaged in domestic labour at home. (Lewis, 1984: 146)

Thus, the notion of 'the family' consisting of husband, wife and children, where the wife and children are financially dependent on the husband, is historically specific (Oakley, 1985). In fact it is argued by many that it is specific to capitalism and/or functional for industrial societies (Secombe, 1974; Oakley, 1985; Parsons, 1949). These arguments will be explored below. Here I want to suggest that the realities of most households do not conform and never have conformed to this ideal type of family.

Within British society only 29% of households actually contain a man, a dependent woman and dependent children (Henwood *et al.*, 1987). It is often argued that this is a new phenomenon, 'the family' is on the decline (Berger & Berger, 1984). However, historical studies indicate that the majority of households have never conformed to this 'perfect English family' and that the composition of households has varied enormously (Tilly & Scott, 1987; Lewis, 1984; Gittins, 1985). Indeed, it is only amongst middle-class households in late Victorian England that this pattern predominated (Lewis, 1984; Branca, 1976). The majority of working-class households have never been able to afford to conform to this pattern even if it was aspired to, and sometimes achieved, by the labour aristocracy (Lewis, 1984). Since the 1920s and 1930s the increase in opportunities for female employment has made this form of household even less common (Tilly & Scott,

1987). In addition, if households do conform to this ideal type it is usually for only a few years while children are very young and women are occupied full-time with their care (Charles & Kerr, 1988).

As well as assuming that families consist of a man, a dependent woman and 2.4 (or 1.9) children, it is also assumed that within family-households resources, such as money and food, are distributed equally and that the same standard of living is shared by all household members. Much research has been published recently which seriously questions these assumptions, showing that households cannot be unproblematically treated as an undifferentiated unit (Pahl, 1983, 1989; Land, 1976; Brannen & Wilson, 1987). They demonstrate that within most households women have less access to all resources than do men and are more likely to experience poverty; they may even experience poverty in households where the husband's income is a long way above the poverty line (Glendinning & Millar, 1987; Kerr & Charles, 1986; Brannen & Wilson, 1987). Thus households are internally divided and within them men have power over women and children. Similar studies were carried out as part of so-called poverty studies around the turn of the century demonstrating how women sacrificed themselves for the well-being of their husbands and children (Pember Reeves, 1979; Oren, 1976). These studies often bring out class differences between households; however, they have mainly focused on white households, and studies of ethnic minority households remain few and far between (Thorogood, 1987). Thus any conclusions that are drawn about gender divisions within households must be recognised as ethnically as well as class specific.

These assumptions about families and what goes on inside them can be understood as part of familial ideology. Indeed, this ideology affects what people think 'ought' to go on in families and influences the ways in which they interpret women's and men's participation in paid employment and the domestic division of labour. For instance, Martin and Roberts found that a quarter of the women in their survey, and a higher proportion of the men, agreed that 'a woman's place is in the home' and over 50% agreed that 'a husband's job is to earn the money; a wife's job is to look after the family' (Martin & Roberts, 1984). In addition, 14% of women working in paid employment felt that their partners would prefer them not to; this compares with 54% who felt their partners were pleased they worked outside as well as inside the home.

Qualitative studies provide more data on men's attitudes towards women working outside the home and it seems that most men are reported as 'not minding', as long as family life does not suffer. The implications of this are that women are expected to be able to cope with two jobs: paid employment and running a home. If this happens, men are generally happy with the situation. However, one study reports that one in ten men disapproved and they often made their disapproval felt. For instance, one man, whose wife worked a twilight shift, took half her wages from her as payment for looking after their children while she was at work (Sharpe, 1984).

This data would suggest that women's paid employment is undertaken in addition to their domestic responsibilities and, indeed, that many men tolerate their wives' or partners' employment only if it does not disrupt domestic routines. This is borne out by evidence on the relationship between women's paid employment and the domestic division of labour.

The majority of women work in paid employment whether or not they are living with a man and only about a third of women in Britain are financially dependent on a man (Martin & Roberts, 1984). Women's participation in paid employment and whether it is full or part-time appears to affect the distribution of household tasks. For instance, women in paid employment are less likely than full-time housewives to carry the entire burden of housework, and there seems to be a difference between women with full-time and those with part-time paid employment. Thus, 52% of women in full-time jobs do the shopping compared with 64% of women with part-time jobs (Jowell & Witherspoon, 1985). In comparison, 43% of women with full-time jobs share this task with their partners whereas this is true of only 32% of women with part-time jobs. This difference is also apparent in a more egalitarian distribution of resources and a tendency towards 'pooling' incomes which has been observed amongst middle-class households where women are more likely to be in full-time employment (Pahl, 1989; Charles & Kerr, 1988).

Despite this, a very clear gender division of labour is maintained. Women are largely responsible for cooking, cleaning, shopping, washing and ironing while men's domestic tasks consist of repairs (Henwood *et al.*, 1987). Martin and Roberts defined a 'houseworker' as the person with major domestic responsibility and they found 99% of the married women in their survey were houseworkers. However, where women are in full-time employment there again seems to be a difference, with a lower proportion (54%) of women with full-time paid work being the houseworkers in their households (Martin & Roberts, 1984). They comment that most women seem happy with this state of affairs, it is as it should be, and only 20% of the women thought their partners should do more in the house (Martin & Roberts, 1984).

It seems, then, that women's full-time participation in paid employment may affect the domestic division of labour, but what does not seem to alter is the view that domestic tasks are women's responsibility. This is illustrated by the 'subtle but consistent differences' between women's and men's reports of men's contribution to domestic tasks (Henwood *et al.*, 1987: 15). Men view the extent of their participation as greater than do women. And if men *do* take a more active role in the home, it is defined as 'helping' their partners, the underlying assumption being that the responsibility for household tasks is women's (Oakley, 1985; Henwood *et al.*, 1987; Charles & Brown, 1981).

The unwillingness of men to be seen to be doing 'women's' work has its amusing side:

He comes shopping with me for the simple reason that he drives and I don't, so he takes me to the supermarket, but he won't have anything to do with the washing and the ironing. In fact, I can tell you something very funny about that. I said to him, 'I'm going to wash some pots so could you get the vac out and run it round the floor for me?' So I was in the kitchen and I dashed in and he was on his knees, pushing the vacuum cleaner round himself, and I said, 'What *are* you doing?' He said, 'I'm doing it so nobody sees me through the window ...' He was actually on his knees turning round in circles ... And something else, he won't go out and get washing off the clothes line – it's really funny – in case somebody saw him doing it! (Sharpe, 1984: 181–2)

As Sharpe comments, some men seem to see it as a slur on their masculinity to do, or worse to be seen to be doing, 'women's work'. The association of domestic labour with an undermining of masculinity may also explain the resilience of the domestic gender division of labour in the face of male unemployment (Morris, 1990, 1990a). Oakley's evidence also points to a lack of equality within marriages which puts a question mark over Young and Wilmott's conclusion that we have arrived at a stage of the 'symmetrical family' (Young & Wilmott, 1973; Oakley, 1985).

Work that involves caring within households is also carried out disproportionately by women, as it is in the world of paid work. Child care is the most obvious example, but increasingly elderly or disabled relatives are being cared for by women in the home (Finch & Groves, 1983; Walker, 1982). It has been estimated that child-rearing tasks for a child still in nappies take up seven hours a day (Piachaud, 1984). These basic tasks take up more time than most men's jobs and men's participation in them is minimal (Henwood *et al.*, 1987). If men *are* involved in child care it is not in the basic routine tasks of feeding, dressing, washing and so on, but in the more enjoyable parts of child rearing such as playing with children or taking them out (Henwood *et al.*, 1987; Charles & Kerr, 1988). Even leisure is divided by gender; women who work in full-time paid employment enjoy 2.1 hours of leisure on a weekday and 7.2 hours per day at weekends; for men the figures are 2.6 hours and 10.2 hours. Men have access to more leisure than do women (Henwood *et al.*, 1987).

Clearly there is a gender division of labour within households which allocates the majority of household and caring tasks to women and also affects the distribution of resources such as money, food and leisure. It is tempting to look no further than this for an explanation of the gender division of labour within the workforce, and it is certainly used as a justification for women's secondary status. Piachaud concluded from his study of child care:

It is mothers who bear the brunt of basic child care tasks. This in turn leads to the self-perpetuation of sex inequalities. Since women commonly interrupt employment to look after children, they are given less training and acquire less experience than men, which results in their lower pay. If a family is then faced with the issue of whether the mother or father should reduce their paid work, it may make financial sense for the mother, with a lower hourly pay, to stay at home – and this then reinforces the vicious circle of sex inequalities still further. (Piachaud, 1984, quoted in Henwood *et al.*, 1987).

It makes perfect sense – or does it? Why are women's childbearing capacities used as a reason for not training them? Particularly when they are only temporarily absent from the workforce during the early years of their child's life? Men may equally be lost to the employer who trains them; in the last century men were much more likely to emigrate than women for instance, but this did not make employers reluctant to employ them or train them (Lewis, 1984). Additionally, the domestic gender division of labour seems to be affected by women's participation in paid employment, particularly if it is full-time (this may itself be linked to social divisions of class and 'race'), to men's employment status (whether they are unemployed, for instance) and to the demands of the economy (Wheelock, 1990; Morris, 1990). It seems that gender divisions within the workforce cannot simply be explained by women's responsibility for child rearing. This in itself is not a natural phenomenon but is socially constructed, as is the gender division of the workforce (Oakley, 1972). Explanations of both aspects of the gender division of labour need therefore to be sought; one cannot be explained by the other, although at the level of daily experience they are clearly mutually reinforcing as Piachaud's comments indicate.

Before looking at explanations, however, I want briefly to explore the role of the trade unions and the state in relation to gender divisions.

TRADE UNIONS

Trade unions are significant in the world of paid employment. Martin and Roberts found that women in trade unions were likely to enjoy better terms and conditions of employment and better training facilities than women in jobs that were not unionised (Martins & Roberts, 1984). Membership of a union is therefore important for women workers as it is for men. However, it is relevant to explore the way trade unions operate in a gender divided society. Do they further the interests of their women members as impartially as those of their men members? Do their policies and practices have any effect on the gender division of labour in the workforce?

As with workers' consciousness trade unions' policy and practice seem to be contradictory in relation to their women members. On the one hand, negotiations are often couched in terms of men needing to earn a wage adequate to support their wives and families, and on the other, statements at national level commit unions to a policy of equal pay for their women members. As Barrett and McIntosh point out, the two positions are mutually exclusive (Barrett & McIntosh, 1980). This tension – between the notion of a family wage to be paid to men (with the implication that women are dependent upon men either because they work only for pin money or because they do not work in paid employment at all) and the idea of equal pay for women (which implies a non-dependent relation between men and women) – has marked much of the history of the relation between the trade union movement and women; indeed it is still apparent today (Lewis, 1984; Walby, 1986; Charles, 1986). Support for a family wage to be paid to men has been so extensive within the trade unions, particularly in the second half of the nineteenth and early twentieth century, that many analysts argue that the struggles waged over pay and conditions by the working classes have been a major contributory factor in the institutionalisation of gender divisions within the workforce and within the working class (Walby, 1986; Hartmann, 1986; Barrett, 1980; Barrett & McIntosh, 1980; Humphries, 1977a and b, and 1981). These arguments are examined in Chapter 3. Here I wish to look at trade union policies and practices and their relation to gender divisions.

At the level of policy there seems to be a commitment on the part of the trade unions, particularly at national level, to women's equality if not to women's liberation. A working women's charter was drawn up in the 1970s which included demands for contraception, abortion and day care provision as well as for more traditional union demands such as equal pay (Boston, 1987). There was a recognition of the importance of encouraging women to join unions. However, national policy cannot always be taken as an indication of practice at local level; indeed it may simply be worthy rhetoric. An illustration of this is provided by the fact that the TUC first committed itself to equal pay for women in 1888. But in 1975, when the Equal Pay Act (EPA) was finally introduced, many unions, who were themselves employers, were not paying equal pay to their women employees and, as negotiating bodies, were still negotiating for men's rates and women's rates. To be fair this problem is recognised by the TUC, that is, at national level:

If trade unions are going to successfully negotiate positive action for women, they must promote genuine equality for women within their own structures. (TUC, 1982, quoted in Boston, 1987: 327)

But there is no guarantee that such statements will necessarily be put into practice as the following example indicates. The general secretary of SOGAT, Mr W.H. Keys, presented to the 1979 TUC the charter *Equality for Women within Trade Unions*. This document included ten points to be observed by unions in order to eliminate discrimination on grounds of gender from their own structures. His own union was taken to task by the Equal Opportunities Commission (EOC) in 1986, seven years later, for continuing to operate two branches, one exclusively male, the other exclusively female. As Sarah Boston comments:

The exclusively male central London branch had reserved for its members the higher paid jobs. (Boston, 1987: 329)

Some trade unionists clearly do not practise what they preach.

There are three issues which I wish to explore in relation to trade unions and the gender division of labour. These are: women's participation in trade unions at local and national level; union attitudes towards so-called women's issues; and union policies towards women's employment.

During the 1970s quite a lot of unions began to be concerned about women's participation in unions. The decade was marked by a high profile for issues of gender equality. The Equal Pay Act and Sex Discrimination Act (SDA) became law, the Equal Opportunities Commission was established and the Employment Protection Act (1975) gave women who had been continuously employed by the same employer for two years rights to maternity leave, maternity pay and reinstatement after maternity leave, as well as protecting them from dismissal because of pregnancy. Several unions produced reports on gender divisions within their own organisations (NALGO, 1975; ACTT, 1975). It is useful to look at the findings of the NALGO report as it is not an unusual union and there is little evidence that the situation has altered in the intervening period (Boston, 1987; Rees, 1992).

NALGO's membership is drawn from non-manual workers in government services. At the time of the survey 8% of their men members and 35% of their women members were earning less than the TUC low pay target. Women made up 40% of the membership in 1975; however, they were not proportionately represented in the higher ranks of the union, nor even at local level in the branches. On executive committees at local level men outnumbered women by four to one; at national level 8% of the executive committee were women. This is not unusual. Research carried out in 1982 found that COHSE, with a female membership of 78%, had no women on their executive committee, USDAW, NUT, NALGO and the TGWU had one or two women on their executives but they were vastly under-represented, and NUPE and the CPSA were the only unions to have representation of women at national level which was *almost* proportional to the number of women members. Trade union officials are similarly usually men, even in unions such as NUPE, USDAW, and the NUT where the majority of members are women (Boston, 1987); and so are shop stewards (Pollert, 1981; Charles, 1986). Gender stereotyping is also apparent. The only post which was held by women on the local NALGO committees was that of assistant secretary. The report comments:

Posts like assistant secretary are presumably held by women so that they can do the branch typing work. 41.5% of assistant secretaries are female but only 5.3% of chairmen [*sic*]. (NALGO, 1975: 30)

So, as with the occupational hierarchy, the trade union hierarchy is monopolised by men.

This situation is often blamed on women's domestic responsibilities. Women's lack of participation in the organising and running of unions is seen as stemming from their responsibilities within the home; something which unions are powerless to do anything about. But are they? Or do the ways in which unions are organised actively reinforce women's lack of participation? If close attention is paid to the way unions operate at local level it becomes clear that they make it difficult for women to participate. For instance, meetings, if they are held at all, are held in the evenings or at weekends (NALGO, 1975; Charles, 1986; Pollert, 1981). This makes it very difficult for women who have children to care for to attend. Similarly, despite TUC recommendations, there are not often crèche facilities at meetings (Charles, 1986; NALGO, 1975). If meetings were held during working hours these problems would not arise, and in workplaces where this does occur women are as good attenders as men. These sorts of practices serve to put obstacles in the way of women's attending, obstacles which men do not experience and which they are, therefore, as trade union organisers and officials, unlikely to be aware of unless women bring it to their attention. Women's participation in trade unions is clearly not as high as the proportion of the membership that is female would suggest it might be.

The second area of importance is the attitude of unions towards issues which are seen as 'women's issues' – issues which usually tend to have more to do with working conditions than rates of pay. Union attitudes may also have some bearing on women's enthusiasm for participating in unions. An indication of these attitudes is given by events at a recent Trade Union Congress. One of the delegates, a man, said:

The hall was crowded and totally silent when we discussed the miners' dispute – quite rightly so – but look at it now. Just look at it, it is half empty and delegates are talking to each other because we are discussing something we do not necessarily want to hear. (TUC, 1984, quoted in Boston, 1987)

What they were discussing was the Report of the Equal Rights Committee. This sort of situation is not unusual. The TUC expects its women members to support struggles which are regarded by everyone as important, such as the miners' strike of 1984–5 and opposition to the Industrial Relations Act of 1971. And support is forthcoming. However, when women ask for support in return it very often fails to materialise. Similarly, again at national level, there is a women's TUC where 'women's' issues are debated and discussed (by men as well as women). A report goes from the women's TUC to the TUC, but the issues are not debated. If they *are* debated, as the example above indicates, the (mainly male) delegates are not interested.

If equal rights are not seen as something which should be supported by the whole trade union movement, how much less likely it is that issues such as child care, abortion and contraception will be. There are some exceptions to this. For instance, in 1979 the TUC organised a demonstration against the Corrie bill which was an attempt to restrict the 1967 Abortion Act (see Chapter 8). However, this sort of support is very unusual and marks a very real departure from the previous reluctance of the TUC to become involved in issues other than 'strict trade union issues'; uncomplicated issues such as pay and hours of work. Again, there is a disjuncture between positions adopted at national level and what happens at local level. At local level issues such as child care are generally regarded as *individual* problems to be solved by women outside of work. They are not regarded as needing collective solutions which trade unions can press for. Indeed most trade unions at *local* level regard them as not the business of trade unions at all. When women are at a place of work they are expected to behave as if they were men. As one woman put it:

Well, you're classed as a man so I would say you're all the same, you know, you're all classed as brothers. (Charles, 1986)

The concern to increase female membership of unions noted earlier is guided as much by self-interest as concern for women workers. As long ago as 1966 the TUC voiced concern that non-unionised workers, a large proportion of whom were women, might be used by employers to undercut terms and conditions that had been hard fought for by the unions:

... the degree of organisation in many occupations may be seriously prejudiced if a solution is not found to ways of bringing women into unions. The position could become more acute if an employer finds it expedient to utilise machinery more efficiently through two or three part-time shifts rather than one full-time shift. While part-time women remain unorganised the committee believes they constitute a threat both to the effectiveness of union machinery and to the security and working conditions of other workers. (*TUC Report*, 1966: 144)

Two decades later this has a prophetic ring to it: part-time jobs are increasing at a phenomenal rate while full-time ones are decreasing; it is women who are taking the part-time jobs and mostly men who are losing their full-time ones (Beechey & Perkins, 1987). This process can be viewed as a restructuring of the labour market in which non-unionised labour, in this case part-time women workers, is used to undermine the terms and conditions of employment which go along with the provision of full-time work. In the past women have been used by employers in many deskilling processes to facilitate the introduction of new machinery and to lower wages and break the resistance of skilled workers (Lewis, 1984; Lewenhak, 1977; Hunt, 1986; Walby, 1986).

In this context it is particularly illuminating to examine trade union policies towards part-time work because it shows how attitudes towards women as workers not only reinforce gender divisions, but also create disunity and divisions within the trade union movement.

Part-time working for women has been welcomed by the trade unions as a way of enabling women to combine their child-care responsibilities with paid employment. However, what this 'solution' does is ensure that women, rather than men, continue to carry the burden of domestic responsibilities. The trade unions *en bloc* have not accepted that there is a need to tackle the structural causes of gender divisions within the workforce (Lewis, 1984), let alone tackle the gender division of labour within the household. Thus, encouraging part-time work for women ensures that the domestic gender division of labour is unchallenged and that women remain disadvantaged within the workforce. Some have argued that this is conscious policy on the part of unions and is part of a strategy to maintain patriarchal power relations within the workplace and within the home (Walby, 1986; Hartmann, 1986). Others, however, point to the strength of familial ideology and its effect on the positions and strategies adopted by the trade unions, an effect which is equally felt by women and men and thus cannot be viewed as a male conspiracy to further their own interests (Barrett, 1980). However these policies are understood, it is clear that they do not challenge gender divisions either within the workforce or within the home. Until very recently, unions have not been in the forefront of campaigns for social facilities such as day nurseries to relieve women of some of their domestic burden, or campaigns to restructure the working day so that either parent could parent. For instance two or three part-time shifts (at full-time rates of pay) would be much easier to combine with child care than an eight-hour working day. Such alternatives have been advanced by feminists but have not yet been incorporated into trade union strategy, despite their professed interest in gender equality.

In addition to seeing part-time work as the ideal solution for married women workers, part-time workers are regarded as second-class workers by trade unions (Charles, 1979 and 1986). They often negotiate different rates of pay for part-time work; indeed, they tolerate the existence of part-time work as long as it is not a threat to full-time work. In an electronics factory, for instance, which employed a twilight shift which was totally female one of the shop stewards voiced the opinion that they would tolerate part-timers so long as the full-time jobs were protected; the latter were priority as far as the union was concerned (Charles, 1986). As Beechey and Perkins suggest, this fear of part-time work being a threat to full-time work is not unfounded; but the unions' own attitudes and practices towards part-timers have contributed to a situation where part-timers are cheaper to employ than full-timers, easier to hire and fire, and therefore can be used by employers more flexibly and for less of an outlay than can full-timers (Beechey & Perkins, 1987). The policy of encouraging part-time work for women while not being over-enthusiastic about organising part-time workers (despite the delegates' warning quoted above) ensures that women workers remain unprotected and therefore provide a cheap, flexible source of labour for employers. Trade unions are officially committed to a policy of equality for their women members. Unfortunately many women workers are not in unions and therefore do not enjoy the advantages which undoubtedly accrue from a union's protection. In addition to this, union organisation is characterised by gender divisions and trade union policies towards 'women's issues' and women's employment generally tend to reinforce rather than challenge gender divisions. Most unions have not yet taken on board the structural constraints which contribute towards the continuance of gender divisions, let alone begun to develop policies which might challenge rather than reinforce them.

THE STATE AND GENDER DIVISIONS

State policies are also implicated in the maintenance and reproduction of gender divisions. As with trade union policies state policy is based on the assumption of women's financial dependence on men and a domestic division of labour which assigns to women primary responsibility for housework and child care. That is, they assume the existence of a 'normal' family with which people are encouraged to conform (Wilson, 1977; McIntosh, 1978; Doyal, 1981; Lewis, 1984). Thus the social security system treats married or cohabiting couples as a unit. If both partners are unemployed only the breadwinner may claim on behalf of that unit. In theory, since 1983 when the EEC Directive on Equal Treatment for men and women in social security took effect, either the woman or the man can be the designated breadwinner. In practice it is the man who claims for his dependent wife or cohabitee and their children (Wilson, 1977; Dale & Foster, 1986; Pascall, 1986; Ungerson, 1985). The Beveridge report which was central to the setting up of the post-war welfare state in Britain and, in particular, to the social security system, defined the tasks expected of married women very clearly:

In any measure of social policy in which regard is had to facts, the great majority of married women must be regarded as occupied on work which is vital though unpaid, without which their husbands could not do their paid work and without which the nation could not continue . . . the plan for Social Security treats man and wife as a team. (Quoted in Wilson, 1977: 150)

In return a woman's husband was to provide for her, and her entitlement to benefits was through his contributions. Married women were assumed to be financially dependent on their husbands and this assumption still underpins the social security system. One of the policy changes sought by feminists and others interested in gender equality is that income should be disaggregated and men and women treated as individuals whatever their living arrangements (Dale & Foster, 1986). This already happens in some other advanced capitalist societies (Showstack Sassoon, 1987).

Employment policies are also premised on the assumption that married women will be financially dependent on their husbands and responsible for housework and child care. After the Second World War, for instance, there was a severe labour shortage and married women constituted the only untapped pool of labour. The government appealed to married women to enter the workforce and suggested that industry would have to be prepared to adjust hours of work accordingly:

Industries will need to adjust their conditions of work to suit, as far as possible, the convenience of women with household responsibilities and to accept, as they did in the war, the services of women on a part-time basis. (*Economic Survey 1947*: 28)

Thus, women's entry into paid work was to take place without threatening gender divisions within the home. Part-time employment was seen as the ideal way of enabling married women to enter the workforce. Jephcott, Seear and Smith studied the implementation of these policies in Peek Freans which, until the war, had employed only single women, dismissing them on marriage. Labour shortages during and after the war forced them to offer part-time work to women as, according to the authors, women were refusing to work full-time. This resulted, by the mid-1950s, in 46% of their workforce being part-time women workers whereas before the war there had been none (Jephcott, Seear & Smith, 1962).

In a survey carried out immediately after the war recommendations as to how to encourage more women to enter paid employment were made. It was estimated that there was:

A total of 900,000 women who might be persuaded to take up work if part-time as well as full-time jobs were available, and if a sufficient number of nurseries could be provided. (Thomas, 1948: 4)

It is significant that the option that was acted upon most decisively was the provision of part-time work; nurseries were provided only in textile areas where women *had* to be employed as no men could be induced to work for such low wages (Charles, 1979). The option that was taken was therefore of low cost to employers and the state and ensured that gender divisions were not altered. Provision of child-care facilities would have been a recognition that the responsibility for child care shouldered by women was an obstacle to their participating in the workforce and that other ways of organising it were possible. Clearly women were to continue to enter the workforce on a different basis from men; government employment policies therefore took as read the gender division of labour within the home.

It must be pointed out that there are contradictions at the level of state policy. For instance, the EPA and SDA are measures aimed at ensuring greater equality between women and men. They do not, however, tackle the structural causes of inequality and are therefore likely to have only a marginal impact on gender divisions. This is particularly clear when it is noted that most other state policies undermine gender equality by assuming that married and cohabiting women are not committed to paid employment in the same way as are men and are available, for instance, to care for the growing number of elderly people at home (Finch & Groves, 1983; Walker, 1982). Indeed, these policies may create the situation they assume already exists. For instance, many women are forced to give up paid employment because of the difficulties of combining it with full-time caring and thus become dependent, either on their partner or on the state (Glendinning & Millar, 1987). This affects an increasingly significant number of women. Martin and Roberts found that 13% of women are responsible for sick or elderly dependants and the EOC has found that 75% of carers of elderly or handicapped people are women. This is likely to be a growing problem as state policies on community care assume that women are available to take on the task of caring (Finch & Groves, 1985).

State policies, both social and economic, are imbued with assumptions about the gender division of labour which reflect and therefore support existing gender divisions within the workforce and within the home. But how can these gender divisions of labour be explained? Are gender divisions in advanced capitalist societies due to capitalism or patriarchy or both or neither? In the next chapter I explore the various attempts that have been made to explain gender divisions of labour in capitalist societies.

NOTES

1. When discussing women's economic activity it is important to consider not only the work for which they are paid wages but all the work that they do in exchange for payment. This is particularly important when looking at women's economic activity in developing societies, as I discuss in Chapter 7. A loose definition of the difference between the formal and informal economy is that in the formal economy people work within the capital–wage labour relation in factories or offices for instance. They are employed and their employment is regulated by the state. In the informal economy economic activity is unregulated and work often takes place outside the capital–wage labour relation. It may take the form of petty commodity production within the home, for instance, or selling services, such as cleaning shoes or washing clothes. Historically women have been over-represented in the informal sector and thus their economic activity rates have been seriously under-estimated.

/ 3 /

EXPLAINING GENDER DIVISIONS
IN CAPITALIST SOCIETIES

In this chapter I wish to explore various alternative explanations of gender divisions in capitalist societies and to suggest firstly, that gender divisions cannot be explained without a concept of gender ideology; secondly, that to understand fully the way in which gender divisions have become institutionalised a historical analysis is necessary; and, thirdly, that the form taken by gender divisions is linked to economic development.

Explanations of gender divisions within capitalism can be split into four groups, depending on their main explanatory variable. These variables are industrialisation, capitalism, patriarchy and social reproduction. Many of the explanations use several of these in combination but usually lay stress on one in particular. I shall look briefly at examples of each of these types of explanation, beginning with those that see industrialisation as the key to gender divisions in capitalist societies, before going on to assess the historical evidence.

INDUSTRIALISATION

Those who explain gender divisions by recourse to the concept of industrialisation argue that before industrialisation productive economic activity was carried out within the family-household and that all members of the household participated in this production including the smallest children. In Britain spinning and weaving were the major form of domestic productive activity (Pinchbeck, 1981; Charles & Duffin, 1985; Tilly & Scott, 1987; Oakley,

1985). The economy was primarily agricultural and, until the enclosure movement, most of the rural population had access to land to grow food and tend livestock as well as working for large, increasingly capitalist landowners and/or engaging in domestic production of one form or another organised by merchant capital (Pinchbeck, 1981; Tilly & Scott, 1987; Charles & Duffin, 1985). In the pre-industrial economy, therefore, production was largely centred on the household; there was no separation between domestic work and productive activity and women were able to combine child care with economic production (Oakley, 1985; Tilly & Scott, 1987; Pinchbeck, 1981). It must be remembered, however, that childhood as a concept did not exist in the form we know it today. There were high infant mortality rates and, indeed, mortality rates in general, and children were regarded as small adults and put to work as soon as they were physically able (Tilly & Scott, 1987; Aries, 1962). A prolonged period of childhood therefore did not exist. A second point to be made is that a gender division of labour existed prior to industrialisation, a point sometimes glossed over by authors wishing to present industrialisation as the source of gender inequalities (Oakley, 1985). Pinchbeck's analysis of the capitalist transformation of agriculture in the eighteenth century demonstrates this. Prior to the 'agricultural revolution' she writes:

Among the cottagers as a class, the family income was made up of the wages of the man, the profits from the stock on the common, which depended mainly on the wife's industry, and earnings from any by-employment in which either the cottager or his wife, or the farm as a whole was engaged. (Pinchbeck, 1981: 24)

It could be argued that this division of labour was already due to the development of capitalist relations of production in the countryside; however, other historical evidence points to the existence of a similar, albeit flexible, division of labour prior to capitalist development (Charles & Duffin, 1985).

Capitalist industrialisation, by concentrating production in factories removed it from the home and, it is argued by Oakley and others, that this made it increasingly difficult for women to combine economic activity with their domestic duties of housework and child care. Oakley points to the emergence of the 'housewife' as evidence of the deterioration in the position of women and argues that industrialisation, because of the separation of home and work, created gender inequality where before there was little or none (Oakley, 1985). The elaboration and extension of women's responsibility for housework and child care and the obstacles this put in the way of participation in paid employment, given the separation of home and work, are seen as explaining gender inequalities in industrial societies (Oakley, 1985).

Pinchbeck's view is similar, although in contrast to Oakley, she regards women's exclusion from production in a positive light as it enables them to fulfil the roles of mother and wife without the stresses and strains of attempting to combine them with the role of paid worker (Pinchbeck, 1981). Her analysis of the way in which women's work changed during the industrial revolution is interesting as it shows that for most of this period it was assumed that women would work and their contribution was essential to the family economy. Indeed, much concern was expressed during the eighteenth century at the effects of capitalist development on women's work and the lack of 'suitable' employment for women (Pinchbeck, 1981). This notion of work being 'suitable' is interesting because it indicates that there was a cultural definition of work appropriate for women and men which was adhered to by women and men alike.

Middleton has commented that many of these analysts look upon the pre-industrial period as a golden age for women, where production could be combined with domestic activity and all the family worked together (Middleton, 1985). Christa Wolf puts this view in context with a description of contemporary Greek rural life:

The way of life in the villages remains stable in face of the political excesses of this century. There are two sides to that: the underside is (among other things) that the working life of women has continued to be restricted. It is far more difficult here than in Central Europe to see the villages as an escape and round-up point for civilisation-weary towns-people. The deceptive family peace that arises from the women's total attachment to the fate of the men (or rather to the fate of being a woman), as well as from the indissoluble attachment of the sons to their families, erupts again and again into bursts of barbaric behaviour. Or a hint of despair over lifelong silent endurance and suffering. Those who dream today of turning the clock back to the benefits of agrarian societies have never lived in one. (Wolf, 1984: 209)

I do not wish to enter into the debate over whether capitalist industrialisation has improved or worsened women's position (see Bradley, 1989 for a useful summary of the arguments). The main point made by these authors is that the organisation of paid employment outside the home created problems for the way child care was organised; and as it was women who undertook the necessary child care it created problems for women's ability to combine child care and productive employment.

ʼ The functionalist view also explains gender divisions as arising from industrialisation, arguing that the gender division of labour is functional for industrial societies. For functionalism women are central to the family and they are assumed not to work in paid employment. Their main role within the family is to socialise children and to provide a stable emotional environment to cushion the male worker from the psychological damage of an alienating occupational world; their role is expressive. Men's role, on the other hand is instrumental: they work in the world of paid employment in order to earn money to support their wife and children; within the family they maintain discipline (Robertson Elliot, 1986). This gender division of labour also enables men to move as and when the job requires; this is important for industrial production to be able to function smoothly. If women also worked in paid employment this function would be impaired as the family unit would not be so mobile. This view of the family has been criticised on many counts, not least of which is that it seems to be an analysis of the white, middle-class American family, the very family which led Betty Friedan to write a book on 'the problem that has no name', an analysis of the situation of white middle-class American women who were not satisfied with being the ideal wife and mother and blamed themselves for the unhappy predicament in which they were placed (Friedan, 1965). However, what is interesting about functionalism, and about Talcott Parsons in particular, is that he recognises that this gender division of labour may be problematic for women (Parsons, 1954: 194; Harris, 1983: 61); he nevertheless argues that it is a functional prerequisite of industrial societies. Thus the gender division of labour is seen as arising from the 'needs' of an industrial economy.

THE CAPITALIST MODE OF PRODUCTION

The next set of explanations bears some similarity to the functionalist position despite the fact that it emerges from the marxist tradition. During the 1970s a number of different authors put forward the view that capitalism produced a split in the process of production such that domestic labour was separated from wage labour (Secombe, 1974). Domestic labour remained within the family and was carried out by women; wage-labour was removed to the factory and was carried out by men. In Marx's analysis of capitalist production he argued that the wage labourer sold his or her labour power to the capitalist who then put it to work in combination with the other means of production which were also owned by the capitalist. The important aspect of labour power is that it is conceptualised as a commodity with the ability to create value when it is put to work within the capitalist production process. The value created by the wage labourer is appropriated by the capitalist, part of it (equivalent to necessary labour-time or value) is returned to the wage labourer in the form of a wage, the other part (equivalent to surplus labour-time or value) is retained by the capitalist (Marx, 1974). Latter-day marxists attempted to integrate domestic labour into this analysis by arguing that domestic labour carried out by women in the home contributed to the creation of surplus-value by keeping down the value of labour power and, hence, the value of the wage. The crux of all these arguments is that domestic labour within the home, far from being unproductive in the marxist sense, actually contributes to the creation of surplus-value by lowering the value of labour power and thus keeping wage levels down. It does this by producing use-values within the home – food, clothes and so on – which would otherwise have to be bought on the open market with the wage and the wage would therefore have to be higher (Secombe, 1974). This argument has been presented in many different forms (Dalla Costa, 1973; Secombe, 1974, 1975; Gardiner, 1976) and is usefully criticised by Humphries (1977a), Molyneux (1979) and Barrett and Hamilton (1986). The question raised by the domestic labour debate is whether domestic labour creates value, thereby contributing to the creation of surplus-value, and whether it is appropriate to analyse it as part of the capitalist mode of production. Indeed, Secombe argues that the capitalist mode of production is split into two, the domestic sphere and the industrial sphere, the private and the public. And women are confined to the former. The similarity with the functionalist model presented above is apparent. It is argued that capital 'needs' domestic labour to be carried out in the private realm of the family because it reduces the value of labour power and thereby increases profits.

A major problem with this argument is that it does not take account of the historical fact that this model of the family is an ideological construct. As many authors have pointed out, within the working class a family wage earned by a man to support a dependent wife and children has never been the norm (Lewis, 1984; Barrett & McIntosh, 1980). In Britain the only class and historical period where it has been the norm has been the middle class in Victorian England. In addition, women's participation in the economy is always underestimated because of the nature of much of their paid work which is informal (Breugel, 1983), and until relatively recently little research had been carried out in this area. It was assumed, as the proponents of what has come to be known as the domestic labour debate assume, that most married women's sole occupation under capitalism was that of housewife.

A third problem with this analysis is that it offers no explanation of why it is that women should carry out domestic labour. It is left unspecified and the only conclusion that can be drawn from this is that it in some way flows naturally from women's childbearing capacity. Thus biological determinism, ahistoricism and functionalism are all charges that can be levelled at this type of explanation.

PATRIARCHY

The third major set of arguments explain the existence of gender divisions under capitalism by recourse to a notion of patriarchy (Hartmann, 1986; Walby, 1986; Delphy, 1984). Patriarchy is notoriously difficult to define but it is usually taken to mean the dominance of all men over all women or the dominance of older men over women and younger men (Beechey, 1979; Barrett, 1980; and see Chapter 1). These authors argue that patriarchy predates capitalism, and exists also in socialist societies; and it is patriarchy that produces gender divisions. Within capitalist societies patriarchy exists in articulation with capitalism. The precise mechanisms of this articulation vary. Delphy proposes the existence of a domestic mode of production in which men as a class exploit women as a class. In each household the husband extracts surplus labour from his wife. The capitalist mode of production is entirely separate (Delphy, 1984). Hartmann suggests that patriarchy exists in articulation with capitalism and that men have organised to ensure that they maintain patriarchal power, both within the workforce and within the home (Hartmann, 1986).

Walby's is perhaps the most sophisticated analysis in this tradition. She argues for the existence of a patriarchal mode of production based within the household which is articulated with the capitalist mode of production within the economy. The patriarchal mode of production consists of a producing class, housewives or domestic labourers, and a non-producing class, husbands. The housewife produces labour power in the form of her husband and children by looking after them and bringing them up. She does not, however, sell the labour power that she has produced. It is sold in exchange for a wage by her husband within the capitalist mode of production. He thereby receives payment for a commodity, labour power, that has been produced by his wife; a process analogous to the extraction of surplus labour from the wage labourer by the capitalist (Walby, 1986). This argument has many similarities with the domestic labour debate and similar criticisms can be advanced. Firstly, it is problematic to assert that labour power is produced by domestic labour; labour power is the ability to work and many factors enter into its production such as education, training and so on (Althusser, 1971). Secondly, while Walby derives gender divisions from a patriarchal mode of production and Secombe and others derive them from the capitalist mode of production, their concepts of the domestic are similar in that, for both, the domestic labourer creates value (Walby, 1986; Secombe, 1974).

Walby continues her argument by postulating that the patriarchal mode of production is articulated with the capitalist mode of production through the husband entering the capitalist mode of production where he sells his labour power. And to ensure that women continue to serve their husbands and to create value in the patriarchal mode of production, men exclude women from paid work on the same basis as themselves. Thus men organise in trade unions and in the state, and by this means ensure that they monopolise the positions of power. They hold the best paid and most prestigious jobs, they occupy the highest posts in the state and they maintain patriarchal authority within the household. She accompanies her theoretical analysis with a very detailed historical analysis of how men have systematically excluded women from positions of power and/or status within the workforce in the process of resisting and accommodating to capitalist exploitation (Walby, 1986).

Thus her main conclusion is that women's access to paid work is controlled by patriarchal relations at work and in the state as well as by those in the household (Walby, 1986). Now her historical analysis is very convincing; there is ample evidence to show that men have organised and attempted to reduce competition for jobs and minimise the threat of undercutting posed by women's low wages by excluding women from certain jobs. But this is by no means the whole story as we shall see below, and these processes can be explained by concepts other than that of a patriarchal mode of production.

Analyses that explain gender divisions by recourse to a notion of patriarchy are often seen as 'dual systems' explanations. There is another author who has been accused of taking a 'dual systems' approach to the question of gender divisions and capitalism and that is Barrett (1980). Brenner and Ramas criticise her for assigning to gender ideology rather than capitalism the cause of gender divisions and say that in this respect she is no different from analysts who posit patriarchy, a system separate from capitalism, as the cause of gender divisions (Brenner & Ramas, 1984).

SOCIAL REPRODUCTION

The fourth set of arguments hinge on the concept of social reproduction, more specifically the reproduction of labour power which Marx suggested could be left to the labourer to ensure (Marx, 1974). Before looking at these arguments, however, it is necessary to discuss what is meant by reproduction.

Within feminist analysis the concept of reproduction is used in various different ways and the precise sense often remains unclear.

Here I am taking it to mean the reproduction of labour power. Clearly biological reproduction has to occur for labour power to be reproduced but in an advanced capitalist society the reproduction of labour power involves more than this. Labour power needs to be literate, have a certain level of health and accept the values of a capitalist society. Harris and Young (1981) suggest that there are three aspects to the reproduction of labour power: firstly, the reproduction of individuals with a specific relation to the means of production (that is, owner or non-owner); secondly, the reproduction of adequately socialised labour; and, thirdly, the day-to-day maintenance of people. The second and third categories are conceptualised as the ideological and material reproduction of labour power. Clearly women's domestic labour is vital to the day-to-day maintenance of people. However, although women within the family are important to the process of socialisation, within capitalist societies various other institutions enter into this level of reproduction of labour power, institutions, such as education, the health service, the media and so on. Women may therefore be involved in the reproduction of labour power both as domestic labourers within the home and as employees within the welfare state.

The concept of social reproduction includes more than the reproduction of labour power, however, referring also to the reproduction of a particular society through time. But within much marxist-feminist analysis it is usually the importance of women's domestic labour to the reproduction of labour which is emphasised and used to explain gender divisions which subordinate women (Harris & Young, 1981; and see Chapter 6). It is often forgotten that much besides women's domestic labour enters into the reproduction of labour power and, in advanced capitalist societies, many of these processes, such as the production of food, may take place in the capitalist sector, may involve men and may be defined as 'productive' rather than 'reproductive' activity.

The development of this line of argument owes a great deal to Althusser's analysis of ideology and the state (Althusser, 1971) and underpins much marxist analysis of the welfare state. It is argued that the development of state intervention in welfare ensures the continued social reproduction of the working class (McIntosh, 1978; Wilson, 1977; Burton, 1985; Gough, 1983; Ginsberg, 1979). It is important that a capitalist welfare state does this because the reproduction of the working class is one of the conditions of existence of capitalist production; without a working class with the requisite skills, attitudes and values, capitalism would be unable to exist. Early variants of this position hold that women are central to the reproduction of the working class because women's domestic labour both reduces the cost of labour power and ensures its reproduction on a daily and generational basis. This latter process involves looking after their husbands and giving birth to, rearing and socialising healthy children, the next generation of wage-labourers (Wilson, 1977). This argument is similar to those put forward by proponents of the domestic labour debate and to those holding that women's domestic labour creates the labour power of their husbands (Walby, 1986; Secombe, 1975). There is also a similarity with the functionalist analysis of the gender division of labour in so far as women are viewed as the agents of socialisation of the next generation of workers and givers of emotional support and succour to their husbands. The difference, however, lies in the explanatory power given to the notion of class struggle and the rejection of the assumption that all women are primarily housewives.

The argument has developed in two directions. The first is that the cheapest way of ensuring the reproduction of the working class for *capital* is the institutionalisation of a gender division of labour within the working class in which men are the main breadwinners and their wives and children are dependent upon them. During the nineteenth century women's and children's hours of work were reduced and protective legislation was introduced, all of which extended the period of dependence of children upon their parents and reduced, but did not eliminate, women's participation in the workforce. This coincided with a reduced demand for labour after the initial labour-intensive stages of capitalist industrialisation. It is argued that these developments were important in ensuring the reproduction of the working class because, prior to state intervention limiting hours of work, even the *biological* reproduction of the class was under threat (Humphries, 1977a and b, and 1981; Brenner & Ramas, 1984). However, they were not inevitable and were only one solution to the problem of maintaining production and reproduction. This solution came about through a process of class struggle in which the working class fought for improved living and working conditions, while adopting the gender ideology of the bourgeoisie which defined a woman's place as the home. This process of class struggle, combined with the reforming zeal of the philanthropists, meant that a specific gender division of labour became institutionalised within the working class as well as the bourgeoisie from whence it originated (Barrett, 1980; Wilson, 1977). This gender division of labour is seen as arising from a gender ideology which had its roots in bourgeois ideals of family life and it both shaped the aspirations of the working class and guided the moral sensibilities of the nineteenth-century reformers. The resulting gender division of labour is seen to benefit capital because it reduces the costs of reproduction of the working class and because it creates social and political stability by dividing the working class along lines of gender (Barrett, 1980).

The second variant of the argument sees the gender division of labour as being a product of the working class ensuring its own reproduction under conditions of capitalist exploitation (Humphries, 1977a, b; Brenner & Ramas, 1984). Here the gender division of labour is considered to be of advantage to the working class, because women's unpaid labour in the home raises the living standard of the whole of the class and, at the same time, the ability to withdraw women from the workforce gives the class some bargaining power over the value of labour power (Humphries, 1977a, b). A similar argument suggests that, in the context of capitalist exploitation, women's role in biological reproduction and high levels of fertility during early industrialisation determine the form taken by the working-class family. Constant pregnancies and nursing are seen as incompatible with the demands of capitalist production. These material conditions produce the specific gender division of labour associated with capitalism. As Brenner and Ramas argue:

When women spent much of their married life bearing and nursing children, as they did throughout the 19th century, the logic of the sexual division of labour embodied in the family household system was overwhelming. (Brenner & Ramas, 1984: 52)

Thus, the gender division of labour is related both to the organisation of production and to the material reality of biological reproduction.

The institutionalisation of this gender division of labour has also been conceptualised as the outcome of a struggle between the working class and the capitalist class over which class will bear the costs of the reproduction of labour power (Vogel, 1983). Given conditions of capitalist exploitation and the biological fact that women bear children, it is argued that capital is able to extract surplus-value from men at a higher rate than from women who are 'incapacitated' from time to time by pregnancy and childbearing. During their 'non-productive' periods women have to be supported, and a struggle is waged between the capitalist and working class over whether this support comes from the wage and takes the form of individual men supporting women who are dependent upon them, or whether it comes from profits taking the form of social facilities such as child-care provision, paid maternity leave and so on (Vogel, 1983). This argument links the gender division of labour both to the nature of capitalist exploitation and to the material reality of biological reproduction rather than to gender ideology. In this sense it is similar to the second variant of explanations relying on notions of social reproduction. Its difference lies in that it sees this gender division of labour as benefiting the capitalist class while, at the same time, ensuring the reproduction of the working class.

Although criticisms can be and have been made of these arguments (Barrett, 1984; Barrett & McIntosh, 1980), the historical evidence that is marshalled to support them is important. What emerges from this evidence is that it is not possible to argue that gender divisions arose *simply* because men wished to exclude women from the workforce, a point which is important in relation to Walby's position. Secondly, the point is made that the family household was a unit and the members of that household very often worked together as a team, often literally in the early stages of capitalist industrialisation (Humphries, 1981; Tilly & Scott, 1987). Thus men's interests cannot be seen as being opposed to those of women in any simple way. Thirdly, the contemporary sense of individualism and of the rights of individuals in opposition to the family household of which they are part is historically specific. This ideology originates from the bourgeoisie and depends on a conception of individual rights and freedom which developed with the bourgeois revolutions in Europe during the eighteenth and nineteenth centuries (Tilly & Scott, 1987; Humphries, 1977a, b).

The analyses which link gender divisions to the reproduction of the working class are differentiated not only by their assessment of the class dimension of gender divisions within capitalism – that is, whether they are of benefit to the working class or the capitalist class – but also by the importance they attach to ideology. Humphries, Brenner and Ramas, and Vogel give more weight to women's reproductive role and levels of fertility whereas, for Barrett, gender or familial ideology is essential to the institutionalisation of gender divisions within capitalism. They all agree, however, that a gender division of labour, which assigns the main responsibility for reproductive tasks to women within the domestic sphere, became institutionalised though a historical process of class struggle. Indeed, the relation between gender divisions and class struggle is central to their analysis. Walby adopts a similar position although she approaches the problem from the point of view of patriarchy and gender struggle rather than social reproduction and class struggle (Walby, 1986). The growth in amount and sophistication of historical research on gender divisions in recent years allows us to assess the merits and demerits of these arguments and to draw some conclusions about the relation between gender divisions and capitalism.

HISTORICAL EVIDENCE

Recent feminist historical research into the development of the textile and mining industries and the printing trade shows how gender divisions were transformed and reconstituted within the capitalist production process through the resistance and accommodation of the working class to capitalist exploitation. What is evident from these studies is that capitalism developed within pre-existing social divisions which became rigidified and in some cases transformed in the process of capitalist development (Hall, 1982; John, 1986; Scott & Tilly, 1982; Lown, 1983). It is not possible to argue, as some have, that gender divisions were simply transferred from the home to the factory (Alexander, 1979). This was sometimes the case, but the process of constitution of gender divisions within capitalist society was not as straightforward as that, men and women did not simply do what they had previously done at home in a factory (Charles & Duffin, 1985; Osterud, 1986).

Prior to the emergence of capitalism Europe was largely feudal and the labouring class was the peasantry. Femininity and economic activity were not held to be mutually incompatible amongst the peasantry; indeed, everyone was expected to participate in production. The notion of femininity being in contradiction with productive employment emerged amongst the middle classes in the nineteenth century (Scott & Tilly, 1982). Scott and Tilly suggest that as early industrial workers were rural in origin it is the values of a peasant household economy which would have guided their behaviour even though economic changes were creating a totally new situation (Scott & Tilly, 1982). As they point out, a division of labour based on age and gender existed within peasant societies and pre-industrial societies. Women and children were legally subordinate to the male heads of household, although this subordination certainly did not imply exclusion from economic activity. The salient features of this for gender divisions in capitalist societies is that all members of the family household contributed economically in whatever way they were able and the household was a productive unit. These features of family organisation were incorporated into capitalist production in various ways. Firstly, industrialisation did not mean that women and children were suddenly no longer expected to contribute economically to the family household; quite the reverse. In areas of textile production, for instance, all members of the family entered the factory (not necessarily the same one) and in mining the system continued whereby whole families worked together underground, the men hewing coal, the women transporting it and the children opening and closing ventilation doors (Humphries, 1981; Hall, 1982; Osterud, 1986; Lown, 1983). However, pre-industrial divisions of labour were often transformed in this process. For instance, prior to industrialisation, cotton textile manufacturing was organised on a domestic basis. Men wove, women spun and children assisted by picking the 'cotton wool' clean. Each weaver could absorb the production of several spinners. Pinchbeck describes it as follows:

The cotton worker's cottage was indeed a miniature factory, in which the father superintended the weaving, and the mother was responsible for all the preparatory processes and the training and setting to work of the children. (Pinchbeck, 1981: 113)

However, industrialisation transformed this gender division of labour:

By 1830, cleaning, carding, roving and spinning had been taken from the cottage into the factory, and spinning, for so many centuries a woman's industry, was now performed by a class of skilled workmen on complicated machinery. Weaving, on the other hand, as far as the power loom was concerned, was largely performed by women and girls although there was still a large class of men and women handloom weavers. (Pinchbeck, 1981: 113)

This is explicable in terms of men, used to a supervisory role when production was carried on in the home, maintaining this position when technological change and developments in the capitalist production process associated this supervisory role with work which had previously been women's. Hall explains:

The early factory spinners, who were women and children, needed no auxiliaries. As the machines became more complex, however, each spinner employed two or three assistants over whom he had direct authority. He usually paid them out of his own gross wages . . . the moment at which the spinners took on a supervisory role was the moment at which male spinners established their dominance. (Hall, 1982: 21)

Thus, it was the authority relations of the family and family-based production which were carried into industrial production rather than the specific gender division of labour which actually changed its form (Hall, 1982). This can be understood in terms of a gender ideology which sanctioned male authority (Lewis, 1985). This authority, deriving from pre-industrial family relations, was retained through men's adoption of supervisory roles within industrial production; capitalist production was organised in a way which reflected family authority relations. Interestingly, in many cases the employer paid the father for the labour of his assistants who were often his own family; a similar system operated in coal mines (Hall, 1982; Humphries, 1981). As Humphries points out, work discipline was therefore enforced by parents over children rather than directly enforced by the capitalist or agents of the capitalist (Humphries, 1981). However, there was no hint that women should not work to earn a wage; on the contrary, their contribution was necessary to the survival of the family unit. Men expected their wives to work and often they worked in separate establishments and were paid individually, albeit at a lower rate than men (Humphries, 1981; Osterud, 1986; Lown, 1983). Even though women's wages were lower than men's, again something which predates industrialisation, in many areas men did not apparently fear competition from their wives nor see them as posing a threat to their wage rates. They were all contributing to the family economy and, as long as gender boundaries remained clear, women were not likely to pose a threat to male employment (Osterud, 1986).

It is also apparent that certain occupations were regarded as suitable for women and others were not. Work which required physical strength was, for example, regarded as more suitable for men than women (Pinchbeck, 1981; Humphries, 1981; Osterud, 1986). However, this does not mean women never undertook such work, they clearly did in the mines and in nail and chain making, for example (Humphries, 1981; Pinchbeck, 1981). However, such cultural attitudes meant that employers contributed to the maintenance of gender boundaries by employing women on work seen as suitable for them. But for employers there was also a countervailing tendency. The lower wages paid to women meant that they were cheaper to employ. There was therefore an incentive to substitute female for male labour. This substitution became critical with changes in the labour process which led to the introduction of machinery requiring unskilled operatives. It then became possible for unskilled workers (often women) to take the place of skilled labourers (who were usually men) and seems to have become a major source of conflict during the latter part of the nineteenth century (Osterud, 1986). Attempts to introduce cheaper female labour were, unsurprisingly, resisted by male workers as it threatened their jobs and their wage rates.

Another legacy of pre-industrial production was that skilled workers were highly organised in craft unions which developed out of the medieval guilds. Although guilds had allowed women members, it was usual for women to gain membership only through marriage to a skilled craftsman; if she were left a widow she would then be able to continue in her husband's trade (Tilly & Scott, 1987; Oakley, 1985). There were some guilds which were entirely female but they did not survive into industrial capitalism; these were in trades such as millinery (Tilly & Scott, 1987). Thus, skilled work was largely monopolised by men who were organised into craft unions. They were able to obtain relatively high wages because they had a monopoly on skills which capitalists needed for their industrial production. They could therefore demand and receive a high price for their labour power. This meant that the capitalist class had an interest in breaking this monopoly in order to reduce their wage bill. Mechanisation and the introduction of unskilled labour were the main tactics used and they were, of course, resisted. The main source of unskilled labour was women although unskilled male labour, often immigrants from Ireland, could also be used (Pinchbeck, 1981). This set up competition between skilled workers, on the one hand, and women and unskilled workers, on the other, and in order to protect their jobs men in skilled trades attempted to exclude women and unskilled men from their organisations and from their work. A detailed case study of this process in the printing trade in London is provided by Hunt (1986).

Thus three processes occurred: the maintenance of family authority relations within the workforce which involved men occupying supervisory positions (Osterud, 1986; Hall, 1982; Lown, 1983); attempts by employers to substitute female labour for more expensive male labour; and the organisation of skilled workers attempting to protect their jobs from competition from lower paid women and unskilled workers (Brenner & Ramas, 1984; Barrett, 1980; Tilly & Scott, 1987; Lewis, 1984; Humphries, 1977a, b). None of these processes involved men in general fighting for women in general to be excluded from the workforce (Humphries, 1981; Brenner & Ramas, 1984). But they can all be understood as arising from the development of capitalist production within pre-capitalist social forms; specifically the peasant and pre-industrial family unit of production and the medieval guild organisation of skilled work. And they all contributed to a more rigid and institutionalised gender division of labour than had existed prior to capitalist industrialisation.

Although explaining the change from a flexible to a more rigid gender division of labour within the capitalist production process, the legacy of pre-industrial social relations does not wholly explain the emergence of the demand for a family wage which came to dominate the trade union movement in the latter part of the nineteenth century. There clearly was a gender ideology in pre-industrial society. Women's and men's work was differentiated and there were cultural assumptions about what was appropriate for each gender (Tilly & Scott, 1987; Charles & Duffin, 1985). However, it did not involve women's non-participation in paid work. The emergence of this specific gender ideology is located in the nineteenth century with the emergence of the bourgeoisie as the economic and soon to be politically dominant class. Hall (1979) traces the origins of this ideology to the late eighteenth and early nineteenth centuries. It is associated with Evangelism and the anti-slavery movement. Women's role in society was to be the guardian of the nation's morals through providing an example within the family and by going out and doing good, charitable work (Hall, 1979). This gender ideology was very different from that held by the labouring classes. However, the philanthropists who backed the reforms of the Factory Acts were deeply imbued with it and judged women's paid work accordingly. Hence the highly moralistic tone of their concern over women working in the mines for instance (Humphries, 1981). This ideology took root within the trade union movement in the form of the demand for a family wage to be paid to men and demands for women to be excluded from the workforce altogether. These, however, were not successful though they contributed to the gender division of labour within the workforce (Barrett, 1980; Barrett & McIntosh, 1980; Burton, 1985). As Humphries comments, the miners had a 'family wage' foisted upon them by the legislation prohibiting women's underground work. This effectively prevented miners' wives from working at all as most mining communities were devoid of any employment opportunities apart from mining; miners were there-fore forced to demand a family wage in order to survive (Humphries, 1981). However, in areas of textile production where women had always worked in the industry a family wage was never the norm and the Victorian reformers were not successful in their attempts to relegate women to the home (Lewis, 1984). In fact, despite the rhetoric and the aspirations of trade unionists, both male and female, that a family wage should be paid to the male head of household, a family wage has never been established as the norm (Barrett & McIntosh, 1980; Lewis, 1984).

Thus, it can be seen that pre-capitalist gender ideologies together with the development of the capitalist production process shaped the initial gender division of labour during industrialisation. This laid the basis for competition between male and female workers and the acceptance of a bourgeois gender ideology by the working class during the nineteenth century. This ideology of course related to the material conditions of working-class life. It made sense of the difficulties faced by women in combining production and reproduction and provided a solution – they should devote themselves to reproduction (Humphries, 1977a, b; Brenner & Ramas, 1984). And it was echoed in the gender division of paid work which maintained male authority within the work place and set up competition between male and female workers. This ideology provided an 'imaginary' solution to women's problems of combining child care with paid work and of men's problems in facing competition from lower paid women workers; women could stay at home in the private sphere while men went out to earn the family wage. Of course, as we have seen, this never happened.

This historical analysis suggests that it is neither capitalism nor industrialisation of themselves which give rise to gender divisions, but the fact that capitalist industrialisation takes place in the context of gender ideologies and associated cultural forms. As we have seen, struggles are waged at this level which affect the form taken by gender divisions, but these struggles take place within the constraints of capitalist economic development. They have been conceptualised by some as gender struggles (Walby, 1986). This is not to suggest that capitalism is not implicated in the maintenance of gender divisions. On the contrary, it has been argued that the domestic division of labour ensures that a not insubstantial part of the daily and generational reproduction of the workforce takes place with minimal cost to capital while familial ideology, a specific form of gender ideology, is important to capitalism because it produces a working class divided along lines of gender (Barrett, 1980). Thus women's low wages and their weak union organisation, combined with an ideology which defines their primary role as being within the home, guarantee a supply of cheap, flexible labour. This means that women can be used by capitalists to undercut male wage rates and to facilitate processes of deskilling (Braverman, 1974; Barrett, 1980; Hunt, 1986). It is therefore in the interests of capitalism that gender divisions and familial ideology are retained. Thus, although women are not confined to the home they are defined in terms of their position within the family; as wives and mothers, not workers. Men are defined as workers, not husbands and fathers.

However, while capitalism has an interest in the maintenance of gender inequality it can also be argued that it creates the material and ideological conditions for its supercession. Tilly and Scott suggest that the wage paid to an individual, together with the collective organisation of wage-labourers within capitalism, creates an identity outside of and separate from the family household for men and young people. Individualism is a creation of capitalism. In the agrarian societies from which capitalism emerged, people are identified as members of a family unit and define themselves in these terms. Once wages are paid for an individual's labour power, the basis for the emergence of individual identity and interests in opposition to that of the family unit is created. This has happened with young people and it has happened with men. It could be argued that feminist demands for disaggregation in the tax and social security systems are signs that it is happening with women. It could also be argued that notions of individual rights and freedoms emerged only with bourgeois democracy and that this, together with the individual nature of the wage, paves the way for a notion of gender equality. However, notions of gender equality are in contradiction to familial ideology, as discussions of equal pay for women reveal (Lewis, 1984; Pollert, 1981; Charles, 1986). Thus capitalism is contradictory in relation to gender divisions. On the one hand, its interests are served by the perpetuation of familial ideology and its material basis, the gender division of labour, and on the other hand, it lays the economic and ideological basis for gender equality.

From this point of view gender equality is theoretically possible under capitalism: attempts to achieve it are explored in Chapter 8. However, Barrett argues that gender equality is unlikely to occur in capitalist societies because gender divisions are deeply embedded in capitalist relations of production; she sees revolutionary transformation as the likely precursor of the elimination of oppressive gender divisions (Barrett, 1980). The next two chapters will consider this problem in relation to societies in which socialist revolutions have occurred.

/ 4 /

GENDER DIVISIONS IN SOCIALIST SOCIETIES

Since the advent of capitalism in Western Europe, many variants of socialism have been put forward as a more just and egalitarian alternative to the injustices and inequalities of capitalism. Most of these involve an ideological commitment to gender equality and envisage a transformation of the family as fundamental to a future socialist society (Tomalin, 1974; Rowbotham, 1972; Mill, 1971).

Until the twentieth century socialist prescriptions for gender equality had been put into practice only on a very small scale within capitalist societies. With the Russian revolution of 1917, however, this changed. The Bolsheviks were committed to establishing socialism and part of their programme was the emancipation of women. Since 1917 there have been other socialist revolutions, all committed to women's emancipation, and they have all attempted to put into practice the measures which Marx and Engels suggested were necessary for ending the oppression of women. However, now that the socialist 'experiment' has come to an end in almost all these societies, it is clear that gender inequalities persisted under socialism. In this and the following chapter the nature of gender divisions within 'socialist' societies will be explored and various explanations for the continuance of women's subordination examined. Such an analysis may throw light on the factors which perpetuate unequal gender divisions. First, however, it is important to define what is meant by a socialist society.

The features which distinguish socialist from capitalist societies are a matter of some controversy (see, for example, White, 1983) but have been usefully summarised by Maxine Molyneux. Within marxism, socialism is conceptualised as a transitional stage

103

between capitalism and communism. Communism will be reached when the state has withered away, when there is no longer any private ownership of the means of production and when all forms of exploitation and oppression have ceased to exist. Socialist societies are, therefore, neither capitalist nor communist and, because of this, they combine 'elements of different relations of production' (Molyneux, 1984: 57). They may contain capitalist or feudal relations of production, while, at the same time, be attempting to construct new, collective, non-exploitative social relations. State policies are generally redistributive and private ownership of the means of production has been (or is in the process of being) replaced by state ownership and a planned economy (Molyneux, 1984: 57). It is precisely these aspects of socialism which are being dismantled in the former Soviet bloc and in China.

Socialist state policies towards women have been based on the classical marxist analysis which locates the problem of women's subordination in their economic dependence upon men. This analysis links the subordination of women historically with the emergence of private property and the institutionalisation of monogamy, for women, to ensure the inheritance of private property by men's legitimate heirs. Women's economic dependence on men arose from their withdrawal from the public world of work and their relegation to the private sphere of the family where they reared children and carried out the housework. As one of the main purposes of a socialist revolution was to eliminate private property, the *raison d'être* of women's subordination to men would no longer exist and relations between women and men would be a 'purely private affair' (Engels, 1973: 94). In addition, it was envisaged that children would be educated communally and the abolition of private property would destroy 'the two foundation stones of hitherto existing marriage – the dependence of the wife upon her husband and of the children upon the parents' (Engels, 1973: 94). A commitment to transforming the status of women is implicit in the Communist Manifesto where women's emancipation is linked to socialism but, as Sheila Rowbotham points out, in Marx and Engels' analysis women are not conceptualised as active agents of their own liberation; the implications of this were to emerge later (Marx and Engels, 1973: 124; Rowbotham, 1972; Bebel, 1975). This contrasts with the way in which the working class is quite clearly seen as the active agent in the overthrow of capitalism. To be sure, Marx's analysis of capitalist exploitation was far more detailed than his and Engels' analysis of women's subordination. However, the fact that it has provided the basis for policies adopted by socialist societies towards women renders this omission significant (Rowbotham, 1972: 61).

Engels' *The Origin of the Family, Private Property and the State* has been particularly important in the development of socialist state policy towards women (Davin, 1987; Lapidus, 1978; Meyer, 1978; Murray, 1979; Molyneux, 1985; Kruks, Rapp & Young, 1989). But, as we shall see, only some of Engels' prescriptions for women's emancipation have actually been put into practice and this has allowed a distorted interpretation of Engels to gain currency: that is, that all that is required for women's emancipation is their re-entry into public production. Engels' argument is, in fact, more complicated than this. He, along with Marx, argued that the development of industrial capitalism was leading to the dissolution of the family, particularly within the working class. This view was shared by philanthropists of the time and resulted in much legislation to exclude women from certain branches of production, such as mining, and the development of special measures to protect motherhood and to encourage women to stay at home as full-time housewives (Donzelot, 1979; Davin, 1978; Wilson, 1977). The 'dissolution' of the family, from a unit of production and consumption into a unit of consumption only, was one of the outcomes of capitalist industrialisation and was seen as an important precondition for women's emancipation, as was women's participation in paid employment. However, as well as participating in public production women also needed to be freed from 'domestic slavery' (Engels, 1972: 137). This entailed that private housekeeping should be transformed into a public industry and the care and education of children be undertaken publicly. The relations between women and men could then be based on equality. Women would no longer be forced into financial dependence on a man because they would be able to earn their own living; and men would no longer need to ensure their biological paternity in order to pass on private property.

Thus, from classical marxism there emerge several conditions which need to be met to achieve women's liberation. Firstly, women need to participate in social production, secondly, housework and child care need to be socialised and, thirdly, private property needs to be abolished. A fourth condition, that a women's movement needs to exist to ensure that women's issues are attended to in their own right, is also present within the marxist tradition though not in the works of Marx and Engels (Rowbotham, 1972). These measures would result in economic independence for women and the ending of inheritance and women's enforced monogamy. The family would no longer be a socio-economic unit.

This analysis was based on the assumption that socialism would develop from an industrialised capitalist society with a high level of development of the productive forces[1] such that it would be possible for all needs to be met given a rational economic system. Within capitalist societies the peasant family had already been transformed. Agriculture had been capitalised, the rural population had been decimated and had migrated to urban centres for work, and during this process of economic transformation from a feudal economy to a capitalist economy the family had lost its function as a unit of production. Production had been removed from the household to the factory and this separation of home and work meant that the family was largely a unit of consumption. Alongside this process, as we saw in Chapter 3, went a reconstruction of gender divisions such that women were excluded from certain branches of production and their paid employment was seen as secondary to their role as wives and mothers within the home.

The removal of production from the family, together with women, men and children going out to work, was what Marx and Engels were referring to when they talked of the 'dissolution' of the family. The logical next step in this 'dissolution' is the removal of housework and child care from the private realm of the family rather than their reinstatement and elaboration which is the process that took place in nineteenth century Britain and elsewhere (Donzelot, 1979; Wilson, 1977). Such measures would remove production *and* reproduction from the family, they would become a public rather than private concern. The family would then have no economic function and, to use Marx and Engels' terms, would wither away. In this historical context the social evolutionism of

Marx and Engels is clear. It is as if socialism is conceptualised as finishing a process which capitalism has already begun.

But the first socialist revolution did not take place in an advanced, capitalist economy. It took place in semi-feudal, autocratic Russia in 1917. Indeed, most socialist revolutions to date have taken place in semi-capitalist or non-capitalist societies where the productive forces are underdeveloped, where poverty is extensive and extreme and often where foreign domination has been an important factor. The corollary of this is that capitalist development has been limited, there has been only a small working class and the majority of the population has been rural (Deere, 1986: 97). Land or agrarian reform has therefore been crucial to all socialist revolutions in order to facilitate the development of agriculture; this has repercussions for women and for gender divisions.

The measures for women's emancipation suggested by Marx and Engels were based on an analysis of the family and the position of women in industrial, capitalist societies rather than in agrarian, peasant societies. In such societies the family is not the same family as exists in an urban, industrial context and measures which have been developed with the urban, nuclear family in mind may not be appropriate. However, no new analysis of the way to achieve women's liberation was developed and the regimes, committed to the construction of socialism and the emancipation of women, by and large attempted to use Marx and Engels' analysis as a blueprint (Davin, 1987; 1989; Molyneux, 1981; Croll, 1983). In what follows I briefly outline the way in which this blueprint has been operationalised, looking particularly at the effects of land and family reforms on women and gender divisions of labour. In this chapter I provide a brief historical account of changes in gender divisions of labour associated with socialist societies. I look first at the former USSR and Eastern Europe and then at China, Nicaragua and Cuba. The following chapter offers an evaluation of explanations of continuing inegalitarian gender divisions in socialist, or formerly socialist, societies.

THE USSR

Immediately after the Russian revolution, the new Soviet state attempted to put Marx and Engels' blueprint for women's emancipation into effect. The Family Code of 1918 gave women legal equality with men, legalised divorce, recognised civil marriage and gave all children equal rights whether born within marriage or not. Women retained control of their earnings and property after marriage, they were allowed to live apart from their husbands and abortion was legalised. The Land Code of 1922 abolished private ownership of land and granted women as well as men rights to land (Goldman, 1989). The Bolsheviks were also committed to establishing social facilities such as nurseries and public dining rooms in order to free women from their 'domestic slavery' and enable them to participate in social production (Lenin, 1965: 429). A separate women's organisation, the Zhenotdel, was set up in 1919 to work with and organise women throughout the Soviet Union (Buckley, 1989; Lapidus, 1978; Goldman, 1989).

These measures were implemented in a predominantly peasant society, where the peasant household was the main unit of production and where both women and men within these households made significant contributions to production (Evans Clements, 1982; Buckley, 1981: 81–2; Sacks, 1978: 196; Goldman, 1989). Figures for 1926 show that 87% of women in peasant households particpated in production compared with 40% of urban women (Buckley, 1981: 83). As members of peasant households women had an interest in maintaining it and its traditions. This is particularly true of older women with the status of mother-in-law who were able to enjoy the privileges which this entails (Wolf, 1987; Stacey, 1983; Evans Clements, 1982). Attempts to reform the family by giving women rights to land and property and the right to 'free choice' marriage and divorce threatened to undermine the peasant household and met with considerable opposition (Goldman, 1989). Indeed, in rural Muslim regions of the USSR, and in China where similar reforms were introduced, many women were murdered by male members of their families for attempting to exercise these rights (Buckley, 1989; Lapidus, 1978; Croll, 1980; Davin, 1987). It was not simply that women were being denied or granted rights *as women*. But the granting of such rights threatened the very existence of the peasant family as a unit of production. This was because control of the unit over the labour of all members and potential members (through arranged marriages for instance) was crucial to its continued economic viability (Stacey, 1983; Croll, 1980; Evans Clements, 1982; Farnsworth, 1978; Goldman, 1989).

Such reforms were potentially more acceptable to the small, industrial working class than they were to the rural population and were more likely to be of benefit to urban women (Evans Clements, 1982). Where child-care facilities were set up it was usually in urban areas and there was more employment for women there than in rural areas (Lapidus, 1978). For instance, at the time of the revolution a third of factory workers in Petrograd were women. However, unemployment amongst women remained high until the drive towards industrialisation under Stalin in 1928, and the fledgling Soviet state was unable to put its promises into practice as far as the provision of child care and other social facilities was concerned. This meant that women, urban and rural, very often opposed their new-found 'freedoms', seeing the right to divorce, for instance, as a licence for a man to abandon all responsibility for his children and to plunge the woman who bore them into poverty and destitution (Goldman, 1989).

During and immediately after 1917 Bolshevik commitment to abolishing the family as an economic unit, socialising housework and child care and encouraging women's participation in production was given backing by the Zhenotdel, the women's association of the Party. Within the Party there was, however, some opposition to a separate women's organisation for fear that it would foster bourgeois feminism and undermine support for the revolution (Lapidus, 1978; Goldman, 1989). Kollontai, a leading woman Bolshevik and a feminist, and Lenin both argued strongly for the existence of a separate women's organisation, but it had to be under the umbrella of the Party. Attempts by women to organise separately were not tolerated for fear that it would weaken the revolution (Evans Clements, 1982; Buckley, 1989; Lapidus, 1978). This did not mean, however, that issues of importance to women were not discussed. Leading women Bolsheviks made sure they remained on the agenda in the early years (Lapidus, 1978; Farnsworth, 1978, 1980). An important aspect of Bolshevik views on women, even those of Kollontai, was that motherhood was a vital part of women's existence and, indeed, that having children was at the same time a joy and a duty for women in socialist society. This pro-natalist strand became central to Soviet policy in later years (Lapidus, 1978: 89). At this early stage, however, it was not allowed to interfere with the legal right of all women to control their fertility through the legalisation of abortion.

By 1917 the country had already been at war for three years and the post-revolutionary civil war lasted until 1921. There was severe social and economic dislocation which left many disenchanted with the Bolsheviks' failure to bring them 'Bread, Peace and Freedom' – the demands which had precipitated the October revolution (Lapidus, 1978: 68; Evans Clements, 1982). These conditions of extreme hardship meant that there were no resources available to the Bolsheviks to implement their promises as regards the socialisation of housework and child care; they did not even have the resources to feed the population.

In 1921 the New Economic Policy was introduced in order to get the shattered economy back on its feet. This policy marked a partial return to capitalism and resulted in high unemployment for women (70% of the initial job losses were amongst women) and a reduction in the provision of child care. Demand for female labour remained low until the inauguration of the first Five Year Plan in 1928 and provided the context for the new marriage law which established the family as a basic unit of socialist society (Lapidus, 1978: 97–8; Farnsworth, 1978, 1980; Goldman, 1989).

The new marriage law was drafted in 1925 and was affected not only by the economic situation, but also by the opposition of the peasantry to radical changes in gender divisions within the peasant household and by the traditional views on the family which persisted within the Party and gained ground after the exile of Kollontai in 1922 and the death of Lenin in 1923. Women were still expected to participate in paid employment and, indeed, were guaranteed a right to work (Lapidus, 1978: 127). But the family, rather than disappearing as a basic unit of society, was reinstated as being of prime importance in guaranteeing security for women and as preserving, or re-establishing, social stability which had disappeared in the post-revolutionary situation (Lapidus, 1978; Farnsworth, 1978; Goldman, 1989). The pattern of Soviet policy towards the family and its associated gender division of labour was thereby set in the 1920s as a response to, firstly, the need to restore social cohesion and stability; secondly, the opposition of the peasantry to measures which threatened the family as a unit of production; thirdly, the growing number of women who were left by men without any means of support; and, fourthly, opposition to anything more radical from within the Party itself (Farnsworth, 1978: 163; Lapidus, 1978). This was a move away from the measures suggested by Marx and Engels as being necessary for women's liberation (Molyneux, 1981). The family that was to be supported and the gender division of labour which it entailed was established as a 'transitional' form, but a 'transitional' form which bore a striking resemblance to the nuclear family that had been established during the upheavals of capitalist industrialisation in Western Europe.

After the immediate post-revolutionary period the USSR, under Stalin, embarked on a path of rapid industrialisation and the forced collectivisation of agriculture inaugurated in the First Five Year plan of 1928. Heavy industry was prioritised and women, as well as men, were drafted into the labour force. Indeed, the development of the economy required a large and expanding labour force and the entry of women into production on an unprecedented scale was given ideological support by appealing to the need for women to participate in production to ensure equality between the sexes (Buckley, 1989 and 1989a). In order to facilitate women's entry into production social facilities were provided on an *ad hoc* basis but provision was uneven and was still more readily available in the towns than the countryside (Lapidus, 1978). Between 1928 and 1940 the number of women in the labour force increased from 3 million to 13 million and by 1945 women made up 56% of the workforce. During this period women were praised for their heroic deeds which were themselves seen as proof that women were equal to men and that the USSR was the only country in the world to have achieved sexual equality (Buckley, 1989: 113; Buckley, 1989a: 261).

In 1930 the Zhenotdel was abolished; there was no longer any need for it as women had, supposedly, achieved equality. In its place, women's sections, zhensektori, were set up in urban areas to ensure that women realised the importance of participating in the first Five Year Plan and to mobilise women to participate in elections. However, the zhensektori were abolished in 1934 and work amongst women was no longer seen as necessary. An exception was made of the Muslim republics of the Soviet Union where there was continuing opposition to women's participation in the workforce (Buckley, 1989a, 1990: 125).

Although women were expected to be full-time workers, this was to be achieved solely by the public provision of child-care facilities, dining-rooms, laundries and so on to relieve women of some of their domestic work; the transformation of gender relations within the home was not seen as necessary to the achievement of gender equality (Lapidus, 1978; Buckley, 1989 and 1989a). Women's responsibility for the care of the home and children was unquestioned and, furthermore, it was assumed that women and men's physiological differences meant that women required special protection in terms of Labour Law (McAuley, 1981). To this end generous maternity provision enabled women to return to their jobs after the birth of a child and limited facilities were provided, mainly in urban areas, for child care. At the same time women were prohibited from undertaking certain jobs such as coal mining and were, on paper at least, prevented from working night shifts (Pavlychko, 1992; Shapiro, 1992). Thus certain occupations were reserved for men (McAuley, 1981; Lapidus, 1978). This protective legislation was one of the measures aimed at making it possible for women to combine childbearing and rearing with full-time employment. However, it had negative effects in that enterprises, interested in efficiency and productivity, were inclined to employ men rather than women because women were more likely to have time off to attend to sick children and were seen as a drain on the resources of the enterprise in so far as the enterprise was required to fund their women employees' maternity leave (McAuley, 1981; Buckley, 1989; Lapidus, 1978). Thus women were regarded as less efficient workers than men.

These employment practices were based on the assumption that women must be enabled to work full time in paid employment but that they also have a duty to bear and rear future generations of workers. Women's dual role as producers and reproducers was to be supported. At different times the emphasis was on different aspects of this dual role but women's reproductive duties have always assumed great significance within Soviet social policy, particularly in the light of falling birth-rates and high demand for labour (Buckley, 1981; Lapidus, 1978). The fall in the birth-rate was highest in those areas which had been industrialised the longest and where women's levels of education and workforce participation were highest; that is, the European parts of the USSR particularly the Baltic States and Russia. Birth-rates were higher in rural areas, particularly Muslim parts of Soviet Central Asia, where women's educational levels and workforce participation were lower (Buckley, 1981, 1989, 1989a; Lapidus, 1978). Falling birth-rates were coupled with an extreme imbalance in population due to the huge population losses, particularly of men, sustained during the pre and post-revolutionary period and the Second World War (Sacks, 1978: 190). At the same time the demand for labour was constantly increasing. There was thus a tension between needing women to work full time and expecting them to bear and rear large numbers of children to replenish the labour force of the future. This tension marked Soviet policy towards women.

Prior to the break-up of the Soviet Union in 1991 women made up 51% of the workforce and 53% of the population (Buckley, 1981: 80; Bystydzienski, 1989: 669). As there was very little part-time employment in the USSR (around 1%) this meant that women really constituted over half the workforce (Shapiro, 1992). In addition, economic activity rates amongst women were high, with 90% of women between 18 and 60 years of age either in full-time employment or studying (Bystydzienski, 1989: 671–2; Shapiro, 1992). Although women were guaranteed the right to work and enjoyed equal pay for equal work, their wages were roughly two-thirds that of men. This is due to vertical and horizontal segregation of the workforce along lines of gender, the undervaluing of women's work compared with men's, and the concentration of women in low-paid, labour-intensive sectors of agriculture and industry (McAuley, 1981; Buckley, 1989; Shapiro, 1992; Lapidus, 1978: 184–5; Croll, 1981; Bridger, 1992).

Alongside women's participation in production went provision of child-care facilities and maternity provision. The importance of child-care facilities to women's emancipation was recognised in the USSR but, despite this, provision lagged behind need and was uneven. It was greater in urban than rural areas and varied between republics (Buckley, 1981: 91; McAuley, 1981: 179). In addition, child care was not free, children did not start school until the age of seven years and therefore needed pre-school provision for a considerable period of time, and the shortfall of places for the youngest children was much higher than for older children (Lapidus, 1978: 132–3). Consequently, women had to rely on kin for child care, particularly in the rural areas where facilities were scarce and were often available only on a seasonal basis (Lapidus, 1978: 132). The public provision of child care closely followed the demand for female labour and can therefore be seen as directly facilitating women's participation in the workforce rather than as a commitment, on the part of the state, to the communal rearing and education of children as envisaged by Marx, Engels and Kollontai (Lapidus, 1978: 130).

Generous maternity provision existed in the USSR. Women were entitled to a minimum of 56 days paid maternity leave, were entitled to return to their former job and were allowed periodic breaks from work to feed their babies (Engel, 1987: 790). From 1981 women were entitled to partially paid leave for up to a year to care for a child and were allowed to take further unpaid leave to look after a child until it was 18 months old (Buckley, 1985: 47). Women were also allowed extra days off work to look after children. These measures did not apply to men. This is significant because it means that child care was viewed as a purely female concern, women were viewed as less efficient and productive workers because of their entitlement to leave to cater for their child-care responsibilities, and, significantly, no challenge was made to the domestic gender division of labour. Policies were, therefore, geared to facilitating women's participation in the workforce while leaving intact the domestic division of labour. This left women with a double burden that disadvantaged them in relation to men, both within the workforce and within the political sphere. Indeed, women's representation in the political sphere was kept artificially high by quotas and has decreased dramatically in recent years (Buckley, 1992).

After the death of Stalin, debate on the 'Woman Question' and women's double burden resumed and Khrushchev resurrected the zhensoveti which were charged with working amongst women and encouraging them to become active politically. These organisations, by attending to women's practical needs such as organising the daily shopping, can be seen as reinforcing rather than challenging the gender division of labour (Buckley, 1990) although it has also been argued that they offer a space for feminist organisation (Browning, 1987). Discussion of women's double burden centred on the best way of ensuring that women could continue to participate in production while, at the same time, fulfilling their duties as Soviet mothers (Buckley, 1981, 1989a). Demographers and economists were concerned that the difficulties of combining full-time employment with child care was leading women to forgo having children altogether or to have only one child. In the 1980s the possibility of reducing women's commitment to full-time employment by providing part-time employment was mooted. This coincided with the provision of extended maternity leave. These measures would serve to reinforce women's domestic role at the expense of their participation in production. However, other solutions to women's double burden were also being suggested, such as greater participation by men in domestic labour and the production of more consumer goods (Buckley, 1990, 1989a, 1989, 1985, 1982: 90, 203; Lapidus, 1978). It is significant that despite the variety of alternatives discussed, policies aimed to ease women's double burden rather than transforming the domestic division of labour were pursued (Waters, 1989). Thus Soviet socialism had not problematised the gender division of labour within households and aimed to facilitate women's participation in social production through the provision of state facilities which took over some of their domestic duties.

With the advent of glasnost and perestroika, the move of the former Soviet republics towards a profit oriented, market economy and the rejection of marxism as official ideology, the commitment to full employment for women and men has been abandoned. Calls to strengthen the family have been made and there is no longer any need for an ideological commitment to women's participation in social production (Buckley, 1990). This opens the door to returning women to the home as their participation in production is no longer politically required. And with economic restructuring, which involves mechanisation and increased efficiency, the demand for labour is plummeting and unemployment is increasing. It appears that rates of redundancy are twice as high amongst women than men (Shapiro, 1992). Given this situation it is likely that women's reproductive role will be stressed, they will be encouraged to return to the home either full or part time, and state provision of child care and other social facilities will be withdrawn (Pearson, 1991). Women will become dependent on men rather than their own wage and the state and will shoulder more of the burden of reproducing labour power.

There are indications that women may not oppose these moves because they are a solution (albeit 'imaginary') to the exhausting double burden they carried under socialism (Buckley, 1990; Shapiro, 1992). It is, however, a solution which is likely to be restricted to those women with male partners who are able to support them, and one which carries serious implications for women's emancipation.

From this brief discussion of gender divisions in the former Soviet Union it is clear that, apart from during the immediate post-revolutionary period when attempts were made to transform the family and socialise the tasks of housework and child care and a strong women's organisation existed, the measures advocated by Marx and Engels as necessary for women's emancipation were never fully implemented. It is true that at the end of the 1980s women's participation in production was higher than in any capitalist industrial society and that pre-school provision was more readily available. But the domestic division of labour was never significantly challenged and the family remained as the basic social unit of Soviet society; indeed, in rural areas it was an important unit of production (Croll, 1983). Marriage was not, however, regarded as a means of economic support for women whereas access to paid employment was (Lapidus, 1978a: 136). The emphasis on heavy industry at the expense of consumer goods meant that domestic labour was physically more taxing than for women in advanced capitalist societies but, on the other hand, Soviet women expected and were entitled to employment and the self-respect and status that go along with it. In addition, the service sector (the largest employer of women in Western industrialised societies) was small in the USSR and more women were employed in the agricultural sector (Shapiro, 1992). Despite the importance of women in the workforce the occupational and political structures were marked by a gender division of labour which disadvantaged women in terms of pay, status and power (Browning, 1987). And throughout the period there was tension between a strong pro-natalist stance, provoked by labour shortages and falling birth-rates, and support for women's participation in employment which, according to Soviet interpretations of marxism, was a non-negotiable condition of their emancipation and an integral part of socialism.

Gender divisions in Eastern Europe showed, until the recent upheavals, similarities with those in the USSR. In particular, Eastern European societies experienced a chronic shortage of labour which greatly facilitated their ability to guarantee the right to work for both women and men. At the same time the labour shortage meant that policies were adopted to encourage women to have children which, in most societies apart from the former German Democratic Republic (GDR), restricted women's reproductive rights and identified their participation in production as preventing them from producing enough children (Kiss, 1991; Einhorn, 1991; Lampland, 1989; Friszara, 1991; Heinen, 1990). Throughout the Eastern bloc, there was an adoption of an ideological stance which stressed the equality of the sexes. This ideology, together with the need for a large and expanding work force to facilitate rapid industrialisation and reconstruction after the Second World War, meant that women entered the industrial workforce in all these societies. There are, however, significant differences between them which have affected the form taken by gender divisions of labour. These differences concern, firstly, the extent of industrialisation prior to the introduction of socialism and, secondly, gender ideologies and religion. Thus, eastern Germany and, to a lesser extent, Czechoslovakia were industrialised at the end of the Second World War while Hungary, Romania and Poland were largely peasant societies (Heitlinger, 1979; Rueschemeyer and Szelényi, 1989; Kiss, 1991; Heinen, 1990). It has been suggested that the major world religions, which often incorporate gender ideologies which are repressive towards women, draw their strength from those sectors of the population which are not fully integrated into urban, industrial economies (Chafetz, 1990: 66; Ahmed, 1986; Tohidi, 1991; el Saadawi, 1980; Siddiqui, 1991: 81; Kandiyoti, 1989). In Eastern Europe large sectors of the population are neither urbanised nor integrated into a modern, industrial economy. Thus in Poland, a predominantly peasant society at the end of the Second World War, the Catholic church remains powerful and 95% of the population is Roman Catholic (Bystydzienski, 1989: 681; Friszara, 1991). Indeed it was the Catholic church that provided the space for opposition to Soviet domination which took a religious form. This situation compares with the Muslim, largely agricultural republics in Soviet Central Asia where opposition to the Bolsheviks and the Soviet state was long apparent. In these republics, cultural and religiously sanctioned practices which were opposed by the Soviet state, such as bride-price payments, the marriage of under-age girls and restrictions on women's activities outside the home, are still evident (Buckley, 1990). The GDR, by contrast, was industrialised at its inception and the dominant religion was one which, it has been argued, was less repressive towards women (Lane, 1983: 450; Lovenduski, 1986; Heinen, 1990).

These differences are reflected in women's participation in the workforce and in attitudes towards paid employment. Before reunification the economic activity rate of women in the GDR was high (figures vary from 80% to 87%) and women constituted 50% of the workforce (Lane, 1983: 451; Einhorn, 1989). As in the USSR, women in the GDR attached great importance to their employment and regarded it as being as important to them as their families (Lane, 1983: 451). A West German feminist has commented that East German women walk with more self-confidence than their West German counterparts and she attributes this to their unquestioned (pre-unification) right to work and the status they gained from this (Haug, 1991). In Czechoslovakia women made up almost 50% of the workforce, but there is evidence from attitudinal surveys that the view persisted that a woman's prime role is that of wife and mother. Having said that, it is also clear that women valued employment because of the independence it gave them as well as needing the money that they earned (Heitlinger, 1979: 162–3, 165). By contrast, in Poland and Hungary women made up around 44% of the workforce and economic activity rates among women were lower than they were in the GDR and USSR (Bystydzienski, 1989: 671; Rueschemeyer & Szelényi, 1989: 86, 94; Corrin, 1990). In these two societies women's full-time commitment to the work-force did not appear to be so high and their source of identity was more focused on their familial roles (Bystydzienski, 1989).

In common with the USSR, most of Eastern Europe experienced falling birth-rates and acute labour shortages and the response was to introduce policies aimed at halting the fall in the birth-rate. The GDR had very generous state maternity and child-care provision, which enabled women to combine full-time employment and motherhood, and abortion and contraception were freely available (Einhorn, 1989, 1991; Dolling, 1991; Haug, 1991; Heinen, 1990). The other countries of Eastern Europe introduced policies which discouraged women's full-time participation in the workforce and provided incentives, in the form of maternity allowances, for them to stay at home to look after children and to have more than one child (Heitlinger, 1979). They also placed restrictions on women's access to fertility control principally through limiting access to abortion (Kiss, 1991; Lampland, 1989; Friszara, 1991; Heinen, 1990). In these societies, the balance between women's productive and reproductive roles was being solved by encouraging women's partial withdrawal from production rather than encouraging men to participate in reproduction.

What is clear from this brief excursion into Eastern Europe is that the form taken by gender divisions varied even under socialism. Although relatively high rates of participation of women in the labour force characterised such societies different provisions were made to enable women to reconcile their productive and reproductive activities. These differences appear to be linked to two related factors: the level of industrial development of the societies or, to put it another way, the extent of peasant production, albeit in a collectivised form; and the strength of religion with its prescriptions about family life and reproduction and, particularly, the role of women. It seems that the society which reduced gender inequalities to a greater extent than any other was the one which was most industrialised and where the culture was less dominated by religion when it became socialist. There is a third factor which was shared by all Eastern European societies. Socialism was imposed upon them rather than being the outcome of an internal revolutionary transformation and in none of them was there a women's movement, autonomous or not, representing women's interests (again the GDR in the immediate post-war years provides an exception (Einhorn, 1989)). Indeed, the GDR and, to a lesser extent, Czechoslovakia, were the only ones to have their own tradition of revolutionary socialism and feminism (Heinen, 1990). Popular opposition to socialism and to Soviet domination may therefore partly explain the persistence of traditional attitudes towards women and the family and the adherence to religion characterising much of Eastern Europe (Bystydzienski, 1989). In these societies, therefore, the working class was not an active agent in the socialist transformation, and neither were women in the transformation of gender divisions. And, with the exception of the GDR, although women were drawn into the workforce and their participation rates were high throughout Eastern Europe, this happened within the context of conflicting gender ideologies. On the one hand, there was official state ideology which defined women as the equals of men in terms of employment and citizenship and as having a particular role to play in reproduction which entitled them to certain privileges and, on the other hand, there was a familial ideology which found expression in religion and in popular attitudes and values and which defined women primarily as wives and mothers.

The persistence of these 'traditional' views may have facilitated the maintenance of the contradictions in state gender ideology and policies towards women. On the one hand, the state encouraged women's full and equal participation in the workforce and in society at large and, on the other, it maintained a domestic division of labour which overburdened women and made such participation difficult if not impossible. These contradictions were manifest in all the Eastern bloc countries but the favoured solutions differed.

CHINA

The conditions faced by women in China prior to liberation in 1949 were extremely oppressive. China was a feudal society dominated by Confucian ideology which defined the family as the basic social unit. This family was patriarchal, patrilineal and patrilocal and within it sex, age and generation defined a person's rights and duties. Within this system men dominated women, the old dominated the young and the needs of individual family members were subordinated to the interests of the group. Marriages were arranged by families, were ideally contracted at an early age and brides moved to their husband's village. Young women had little autonomy in either their work or their personal lives; all decisions were made by the male head of household or, if they were married, their mother-in-law (Stacey, 1983: 30–34). In peasant families daughters were not valued. Any expenditure on them was regarded as wasted because they would move to their husband's home on marriage. On the other hand, sons were valued because they were themselves a source of labour and would bring new sources of labour (their wives) and potential labour (their children) into the household. Female infanticide was common and girl children were often sold into marriage in infancy. Foot-binding was still practised. This involved crushing the bones in young girls' feet in order to ensure that they could take only tiny steps which were considered feminine. Ideally women were not expected to work or even to be seen outside the home and deference to male authority characterised a woman's life. Obedience was due, first, to a girl's father and brothers. When she married she had to obey her husband and when widowed it was her eldest sons whose authority she had to accept (Wolf, 1987). As in many peasant societies a woman's status improved with age and she held most authority when her son married and she became his wife's mother-in-law (Wolf, 1987). The extended peasant family headed by the patriarch with his sons and their wives and children residing under the same roof was the basic economic unit of society where production and consumption took place. This, of course, meant that although peasant women were subject to male authority, there were significant areas of China, particularly the rice-producing regions of the south, where their participation in agricultural work was crucial (Davin, 1989: 355).

In the immediate post-liberation period the two major reforms affecting women were the Marriage Law and Land Reform (Stacey, 1983; Davin, 1987) and a national women's organisation, the All-China Democratic Women's Federation, was set up (Croll, 1980). The Marriage Law of 1950 abolished the feudal marriage system and introduced marriage based on free choice of partners, monogamy and equal rights for women. It prohibited 'bigamy, concubinage, child betrothal, interference with the remarriage of widows and the exchange of money or gifts in connection with marriage' (Croll, 1980: 231). Divorce was to be available if both partners agreed. As in the USSR, opposition to the new rights granted to women was considerable and attempts to exercise them, in combination with the right to land which had been granted women under the land reform, often provoked extreme reaction from men and older women and some tens of thousands of women were murdered as a result (Davin, 1987: 154; 1991a: 40).

Collectivisation of agriculture in China was a relatively gradual process starting with the organisation of peasant households into cooperatives in the early 1950s and culminating with the Great Leap Forward and the establishment of communes in the early 1960s. During the period of cooperatives, although women's participation in production was encouraged, by 1956 they were earning only 25% of the work points in the cooperatives (Stacey, 1983: 207). In addition, the peasant household remained the basic unit of accounting and all household members' work points were paid to the household head (Croll, 1980; Stacey, 1983). The household division of labour meant that women not only carried the burden of domestic tasks but also worked on the private household plots. This work was therefore 'invisible' and was not rewarded by work points. Pre-revolutionary lineage structures, which were normally village-based, were used to facilitate the formation of cooperatives and it has been argued that this actually strengthened male kin networks (Stacey, 1983: 210–11).

In 1958 the Great Leap Forward was launched which heralded the setting up of communes and a concerted attempt to collectivise domestic work and child care. In the towns and countryside public dining-rooms, sewing centres, crèches and so on were set up in order to remove these tasks from the family and to allow women to participate fully in production. In the towns women were encouraged to set up neighbourhood cooperatives where they made products, worked collectively and earned an income, albeit one that was lower than was earned by workers (mainly men) in the more industrially advanced state sector (Croll, 1980; Broyelle, 1977; Stacey, 1983; Wolf, 1987). In the countryside peasants were encouraged to set up small industrial enterprises in the communes.

During this period women's participation in public production increased enormously; estimates suggest that 90% of women who were able were drawn into public production (Croll, 1981a). However, the introduction of equal pay for women, payment to individuals rather than to the head of household and women's wholesale move out of the household into production threatened to undermine the peasant household. These moves met with opposition, not only from male heads of household whose authority was being undermined, but from women who had attained the status of mother-in-law or grandmother (Stacey, 1983: 215). And the socialisation of domestic labour was costly. For instance, public dining-rooms were expensive and meant that households could no longer be heated efficiently. This was because the stove in peasant households was used for cooking and heating and once cooking was removed from the household either the stove was not lit and the house remained cold or it was lit but used only for heating, which was perceived as an inefficient use of resources (Croll, 1980: 284). Additionally, domestic labour carried out by women in the household was not paid but the same labour performed in the public sphere was paid. This meant that the costs to the public authorities of socialising domestic labour were great and had to be met by contributions from individual households. This also aroused opposition because costs which had been invisible and internal to households now became a visible drain on household resources (Croll, 1980).

Although the Great Leap Forward was hailed as a huge advance in the emancipation of women, peasant opposition combined with a series of natural disasters and the withdrawal of Soviet aid led to a retreat from socialist policies in 1962. Much of the collective provision was abandoned and communes were reduced in size. Private plots were retained by households and the household regained its threatened status as a unit of production and consumption. Although the socialisation of domestic labour and the large-scale entry of women into production had been seen as a threat to patriarchal authority, an unequal gender division of labour had been maintained. Women were generally to be found in the least skilled and lowest paid sectors of both the urban and rural work force (Croll, 1980: 285). In rural areas women constituted around 40% of the collective workforce and 80% of peasant women worked in collective production (Croll, 1983: 23). They had access to the use of collectively owned means of production, their labour was allocated by the collective and was rewarded by work points. Thus the work done by women for the collective was remunerated, public and visible. Women also worked on the private plots allocated to individual households and in the domestic sphere (Davin, 1991a, 1991b).

During the Cultural Revolution, which began in 1965, the Women's Federation was temporarily disbanded and women were exhorted to become involved in every level of economic and political life. Teams of women, the Iron Girls, undertook previously 'men's' work to show that they were as able as men and to break long-held gender stereotypes (Young, 1989). During the 1970s a campaign, known as the anti-Confucius-anti-Lin Piao campaign, was initiated to counter 'feudal and patriarchal' ideology including repressive gender ideology (Kelkar, 1988: 143). The Chinese Communist Party (CCP) located the problem of continuing gender inequalities at the ideological level.

Although the Chinese Communist Party remains committed to women's emancipation and has given women formal, legal rights and equality, since 1962 attempts to transform the family have been noticeable by their absence. In 1978, after the Cultural Revolution and Mao's death in 1976, the family was reaffirmed as the basic unit of socialist society. Current economic policies, which have de-collectivised agriculture, returned collectively owned means of production to individual peasant households and recognised private property and its inheritance, have reinforced further the importance of the household as the unit of production in the countryside (Davin 1991a, 1991b). This has had important consequences for gender divisions.

The introduction of the new policies in 1978 has not removed women from agricultural work but most of this work is now on land which is allocated to the household. All family labour, including women's, is controlled by the head of household (usually male), access to the means of production is through the family, which for women means through a relationship with a man, and women work on family land with little contact with members of other households. Their work on family enterprises attracts neither work points nor wages and is therefore invisible (Davin, 1991a, 1991b).

In rural areas women predominate in non-mechanised agricultural work but this is not the only form of economic activity available. There are more lucrative activities such as employment in rural industry and household-based production of goods and services for the market (petty commodity production) (Hussain *et al.*, 1991; Judd, 1990; Davin, 1991a, 1991b). Rural industries have grown dramatically during the 1980s and policies have encouraged petty commodity production (Hussain *et al.*, 1991: 23; Croll, 1989; Judd, 1990). There are equal numbers of women and men working in rural industries but men occupy positions of authority and, as with agriculture, women are in the less mechanised and more labour-intensive jobs (Croll, 1980, 1981a, 1983; Davin, 1987, 1991a, 1991b; Stacey, 1983; Judd, 1990).

In urban areas the situation is different: the family is no longer a unit of production, there are more facilities available for child care, patrilocal marriage is no longer the preferred option and free-choice marriage is more common (Stacey, 1983; Davin, 1991a). The gender division of the urban workforce shows similarities with capitalist industrialised societies although economic activity rates among women are higher (90% in 1979) (Croll, 1983: 43). In the privileged state sector fewer than half the workers are women whereas in the cooperative and service sectors the vast majority of workers are women (Croll, 1983: 44–5). As in other socialist societies women suffer discrimination in selection for training for professional occupations, and enterprises are reluctant to employ them because of their entitlement to special dispensations for maternity and child care. Discrimination against women in employment has become more obvious since 1978 and women have been removed from the more 'masculine' jobs which they took on during the Cultural Revolution (Davin, 1991b). Unemployment is a fairly recent phenomenon in Communist China and suggestions have been made that married women should leave their jobs in order to reduce the problem. Both the CCP and the Women's Federation have strongly opposed this (Croll, 1983; Kelkar, 1988; Davin, 1989, 1991b). There is some evidence that unemployment is affecting state sector employees, among whom men predominate, rather more than women (Fu *et al.*, 1992). On the other hand, there is pressure on women to take longer maternity leave and early retirement (Young, 1989: 240). Many women, as in rural areas, work in small family enterprises which were encouraged during the 1980s, but this mode of income generation is far more precarious than employment in state enterprises (Davin, 1991b). Women workers generally receive less pay and fewer benefits than do men and are concentrated in the less prestigious areas of the workforce; these are, however, the areas in which innovation is being encouraged with the reform programme (Fu *et al.*, 1992).

Other policies may also enhance women's employment. For instance, the CCP is concerned to lighten the burden of women's domestic labour and to this end is expanding the production of household appliances. This expansion has the effect of providing more jobs for women as they predominate in light industry. There is also a renewed effort to collectivise child care and household tasks. It is estimated that about 25% of Chinese children have access to pre-school provision though this is higher in the urban than rural areas. In the countryside there are often no nursery facilities at all. Services also exist to undertake shopping, house-cleaning and so on, but again they are to be found in urban areas and the services are charged for. However, attempts to transform the domestic division of labour are half-hearted and the need for women and men to share housework was not mentioned in the new Marriage Law (Croll, 1983: 64). In fact Croll's research indicates that sharing of housework has decreased since the 1970s (Croll, 1983: 65–6). Grandparents, particularly grandmothers, are an important source of assistance with household tasks and child care and this is facilitated by the widespread co-residence of extended families, even in urban areas (Stacey, 1983). The ideology that women as 'model workers' are expected to put production first and the needs of their families second, which was prevalent before the economic reforms, has been replaced by an emphasis on women's employment needing to be appropriately 'feminine' and fitting in with their responsibility for the domestic sphere (Davin, 1991b; Young, 1989). There is evidence that this view may be shared by Chinese women (Croll, 1983: 71).

Unlike the former USSR and Eastern European societies where, with the exception of the GDR, abortion was the main means of fertility control, China has made contraception as well as abortion widely available to the population. Late marriage has also been encouraged as a way of reducing fertility levels (Broyelle, 1977; Davin, 1987a; Chen, 1985). These policies have been justi-fied on two counts: one, that women's emancipation is facilitated by fewer children and, two, that China's population was set to multiply at an alarming rate and, despite higher productivity in the countryside and more equitable mechanisms of distribution, would rapidly outstrip its food supply. There has been an intensive family planning programme which, since 1979, has taken the form of the single-child family policy. In the decade prior to 1979 policies were aimed at encouraging a reduction in family size to two or three children and, before that, contraception and family planning advice had been widely available to enable people to space the births of their children and to limit the number of children they chose to have (Croll, 1985). Since 1969 these population policies have successfully reduced fertility levels and, it is argued, they have had an effect independent of the effect that is expected with modernisation and industrialisation (Chen, 1985: 135).

In China the contradiction between women's productive and reproductive roles takes a different form from that in the USSR and the Eastern bloc. There, women's high labour force participation and levels of education were associated with low birth-rates and state policies aimed to increase the birth-rate by reducing women's access to the means of fertility control and/or partially withdrawing them from social production. In China, particularly in rural areas, women's inclinations are to have *more* children than the state deems appropriate and women's participation in the workforce is not as high as the CCP would like (two not unrelated factors). The one-child family policy has been developed in order to reduce levels of fertility and increase women's participation in the labour force. However, it appears to be having adverse effects on women, particularly in rural areas where children are an important source of labour to peasant families and where boys are a more valuable resource than girls. Female infanticide has re-emerged in some parts of China and women who become pregnant when they already have a child have been forced to have abortions against their will (Wolf, 1987; Hong, 1987; Mandle, 1987; Davin, 1987a). In addition, couples who have only one child are given a variety of material incentives, including privileged access to welfare services, while those who have more than one are penalised (Croll, 1983; Hillier, 1988).

It is not a peculiarity of socialist states to have an interest in fertility (Jenson, 1987; Petchesky, 1986). In France, for instance, there are various incentives to encourage women to have children in the face of very low levels of fertility. International aid is often tied to reductions in levels of fertility which, in some Third World countries, has resulted in forced sterilisation programmes. The difference is, however, that socialist regimes are ideologically committed to gender equality but their pro-natalist population policies are often in contradiction with these aims. A notable exception was provided by the GDR. This is obviously a complex issue involving a balance, not only between the needs of society and the interests of women, but also between individual freedom of choice and the needs of the collective. Historically, in China, the needs of the collective, in the form of the family and the lineage, have overridden individual freedom of choice. However, part of the effect of industrialisation and the emergence of wage-labour is to assert individual needs and this is almost bound to exacerbate any potential conflict of interests. In addition, although China's one-child family policy may be perceived as lightening women's domestic burdens, most women in China reside in the countryside in peasant households and many share the interests of the household as a productive unit. As we have already seen, these interests dictate the birth of more than one child and particular importance is attached to male children (Croll, 1983).

Despite the commitment of the CCP to Marx and Engels' prescriptions for women's emancipation and the recognition of the importance of a separate, but not totally autonomous, women's movement to protect and further women's interests, gender divisions which subordinate women persisted in China even before the economic reforms introduced in 1978. China remains a largely peasant society, 80% of its population is rural, and it has been argued that the policies of the CCP have preserved the patriarchal peasant family which provides a material basis for the reproduction of gender divisions (Stacey, 1983; Croll, 1983). The participation of women in production appears to be far higher, particularly in the urban areas, than in pre-liberation days but it has not reached the levels achieved in the former USSR and GDR. There is a commitment to provide child-care facilities and women have access to contraception and abortion, but, since the reassertion of the importance of the family as the basic socio-economic unit of society and the decollectivisation of agriculture, there has been more of an emphasis on the importance of women as mothers and socialisers of the next generation than on the overriding importance of women's full economic and political participation in society (Croll, 1983; Young, 1989). Similarly, discussions of a more egalitarian sharing of domestic tasks are less frequent. The CCP, therefore, emphasises women's participation in production but, at the same time, has retreated from a restructuring of child care, domestic labour and marriage.

CUBA AND NICARAGUA

Similar processes can be observed in Cuba and Nicaragua, two Third World societies which have been committed to women's liberation and socialism. Both societies, prior to their revolutions, were dominated by United States capital and were reliant on the production of one or two cash crops, sugar and tobacco in Cuba and coffee and cotton in Nicaragua. As in the USSR and China, land reform was a priority in order to eliminate land hunger and to increase productivity in agriculture (Deere, 1987a; Luz Padilla *et al.*, 1987; Stubbs & Alvarez, 1987).

At the time of the Cuban revolution in 1959 the rural workforce, apart from seasonal work, was virtually 100% male (Croll, 1981a: 386) and, although Castro publicly committed the state to women's emancipation and their full participation in production, in the face of high levels of male un- and underemployment, the first priority was to provide full male employment (Nazzari, 1983: 253–4; 1989: 115). The land reform introduced at this time distributed land to household units and as men were seen as household heads they were the ones who became involved with the state organisation which was providing credit and developing services (Deere, 1986: 199). This situation changed, however, due to the regime's ideological commitment to women's liberation and to the expansion of the sugar cane industry in the late 1960s. This latter increased the demand for temporary, female labour in the countryside which was, at first, organised by the Cuban Women's Federation on a voluntary basis as part of a policy aimed at integrating women into the agricultural labour force (Deere, 1987a: 176). By the mid 1970s this labour was paid, women had equal pay with male agricultural workers and were working not only as seasonal but also as permanent workers. In the 1970s all members of households became entitled to membership of cooperatives, rather than membership being open only to heads of households, and women now have access to training and credit in the same way as do men (Deere, 1986a). Land reform has resulted in a rural economy composed of a mixture of state farms, which were previously the enormous privately owned plantations, and small, peasant farmers organised into cooperatives or farming their own land. Men predominate in the permanent labour force in the collectivised state sector while women are mobilised seasonally for the harvest but work predominantly in the cooperative and small farming sectors. Thus, a gender division of labour continues to operate, and in the cooperative and small farming sectors women's labour is allocated by the head of household and women are not paid independently (Croll, 1981a: 387–8; Deere, 1987a; Luz Padilla, *et al.*, 1987). Women's participation in cooperatives as full members is low and women agricultural workers continue to be disadvantaged relative to men (Deere, 1987a: 185; Stubbs, 1989: 44).

Industrial expansion after 1959 resulted in full male employment and led to calls for women to enter the workforce. But the social facilities which would have made this possible were not provided, not because they were not seen as necessary but because material resources were scarce and such facilities were not given priority (Nazzari, 1983: 254–5). These problems provoked widespread discussion of the heavy burden of domestic labour carried by women and resulted in the Family Code of 1975. This code stipulated that women and men had equal rights and responsibilities within the family; it therefore advocated an egalitarian division of domestic labour if both partners were in employment (Nazzari, 1983: 255; Croll, 1981a: 391; Murray, 1979: 101–2). Cuba is alone in the world in writing an egalitarian domestic division of labour into law which is an enormous achievement in itself. However, it is often a very large step from giving women rights in law and creating real changes in women's and men's practices. Thus far the impact of this law seems not to have been very great and Nazzari suggests that women who are dependent on their husband's wage are unlikely to press them to perform their share of domestic labour (Nazzari, 1983; Croll, 1983). Women are fairly likely to be in a position of financial dependence as their pay is generally lower than men's and employment is guaranteed for all men but only for women who are household heads. Despite this, women's participation in employment has increased from 23% of the workforce in 1974 to 38% of the workforce in 1988 (Nazzari, 1989: 121; Stubbs, 1989: vi). In Cuba women have access to fertility control including abortion, fertility levels are decreasing and health care is widely available (Chinchilla, 1990; Turner, 1989: 110).

In Nicaragua the Sandinista National Liberation Front (FSLN) held power for eleven years, from 1979 to 1990, with a commitment to implementing the classic socialist guidelines for women's emancipation and influenced by the women's organisation, Amanda Luisa Espinosa Association of Nicaraguan Women (AMNLAE) (Randall, 1981; Deighton *et al.*, 1983). Women's interests were incorporated into the land reform programme from its inception, allowing women to be beneficiaries of land reform in their own right (Luz Padilla *et al.*, 1987: 128). Despite this paper commitment, a gender division of labour pertains in Nicaraguan agriculture which is similar to that in Cuba, that is, women predominate in temporary, seasonal work while men constitute the permanent workforce and women are often not paid in their own right (Collinson *et al.*, 1990: 42; Luz Padilla *et al.*, 1987; Deere, 1987a). This is despite a decree passed in 1982 implementing the law that wages should be paid to individuals in the rural sector rather than to the male head of household (Molyneux, 1985a: 153). And, as in Cuba, women's participation in farming cooperatives is low; only 6% of full members of cooperatives are women and only half the cooperatives contain female members although women make up the majority of the workforce in many of them (Collinson *et al.*, 1990: 51). Women's participation in production increased during the 1980s when they replaced the men who were away fighting the Contras. In the mid 1980s women constituted 42% of the economically active population in urban areas, they formed the majority of petty traders in the informal sector of the economy and in rural areas they made up around 35% of the workforce (Stead, 1991: 69; Collinson *et al.*, 1990; Ruchwarger, 1989: 78). In industry women are paid less than men, even in textile production where they predominate, and they are generally to be found in the less skilled sectors of the workforce. Domestic service continues to be an important source of income generation for women but the number in domestic service has decreased since 1979 as other opportunities for women's employment have emerged (Collinson *et al.*, 1990). Women continue to carry the burden of domestic labour (Ruchwarger, 1989; Collinson *et al.*, 1990). As I discuss in Chapter 7, the employment patterns of women in Nicaragua show a great similarity with those of other developing societies.

Other measures were aimed at altering gender inequalities within the domestic sphere. Soon after the FSLN came to power they stipulated that domestic tasks were to be shared, and laws were passed which regulated family life and attempted to reduce male desertion of women by making them liable for maintenance payments for any children (Molyneux, 1985a: 154, 158). The family retains its importance in Nicaragua and in the 1987 constitution is referred to as the 'fundamental nucleus of society'. However, it is significant that this fundamental nucleus is not defined. This was a response to women's protests at its definition in earlier drafts as consisting of a heterosexual couple plus their children and reflects the reality that almost half of household heads in Nicaragua are women (Collinson *et al.*, 1990; Ruchwarger, 1989: 75). During the 1980s issues of violence against women and, to a lesser extent, sexuality began to be discussed and the 1987 Constitution also included a commitment to fight male violence against women (Collinson *et al.*, 1990: 17).

The influence of the Catholic church is strong in Nicaragua and, as a result, the FSLN was unable to legalise abortion or to make contraception widely available (Chinchilla, 1990). This means that abortions continue to be carried out illegally, endangering women's health (Molyneux, 1985a: 159; 1988). During the latter part of the 1980s this situation was publicly debated and AMNLAE began campaigning for the decriminalisation of abortion (Collinson *et al.*, 1990: 120). The image of women as mothers, however, remains strong. This particular stereotype was not challenged by AMNLAE and the birth-rate remains high (Collinson *et al.*, 1990; Molyneux, 1985a: 159). Religious prohibitions on fertility control are reinforced by the notorious Latin machismo which regards fathering children as proof of masculinity and the use of contraception as a slight on a man's virility. The FSLN was committed to the provision of child care which steadily increased in the years after 1979, though still fell far short of demand. By the mid 1980s this expansion was cut back because of the financial stringencies necessitated by the Contra war (Stead, 1991: 54).

In both Cuba and Nicaragua strong women's organisations existed. In Cuba the Women's Federation is not autonomous from the Cuban Communist Party but in Nicaragua, although in the early years the role of AMNLAE was to mobilise women in support of the revolution and it had a very close relationship to the FSLN, in the mid 1980s this changed (Chinchilla, 1990). AMNLAE became much more independent, ensuring that issues of direct relevance to women, such as violence against women, fertility control and sexuality, were put on the political agenda (Molyneux, 1984a; Stead, 1991; Chinchilla, 1990).

Cuba and Nicaragua have now taken different paths. While Nicaragua, even before the 1990 elections which the FSLN lost, was committted to a mixed economy, Cuba is more firmly committed to the type of planned economy previously characterising most socialist societies. In the late 1980s openings for private enterprise were being closed, a trend in direct contradiction to that taking place in the rest of the formerly socialist world. At the time of writing, Cuba remains committed to communism and a planned economy. Its isolation has, however, meant a reduction in state spending on social facilities and a prioritising of goods for production rather than consumption with all that this means for women. And it is still largely women who are responsible for domestic labour in Cuba. Recent figures show that 82% of women in Havana, Cuba's capital city, and 96% of women in the countryside are responsible for domestic labour (Momsen, 1991: 38). In Nicaragua the FSLN has been replaced by a government committed to the 'restoration of the traditional Nicaraguan family'. It has recently criminalised homosexuality and is trying to reverse many of the measures taken during Nicaragua's brief socialist experience (Stead, 1991; Chinchilla, 1990; Nicaragua Solidarity Campaign, 1992).

In this chapter I have briefly sketched the main characteristics of gender divisions in societies which are, or have been, attempting to construct socialism and the measures introduced in an attempt to end women's subordination. In most of these societies only one of the conditions laid down by classical marxism as necessary for women's emancipation has been met, and that is the full participation of women in public production and, in some, even this has not been achieved. The other measures, in particular the socialisation of child care and domestic labour, have not been put into practice for various reasons. However, in some of the societies major changes in gender divisions of labour have occurred. These appear to relate to the extent and nature of industrialisation. Thus, those societies which are most industrialised are characterised by a gender division of labour which is not dissimilar to that in capitalist, industrial societies. Fertility levels are low and there are high levels of female education and labour force participation;

indeed women's labour force participation tends to be higher than in industrial, capitalist societies and state provision of social facilites is more widespread. Those which are least industrialised and where a large proportion of the population is engaged in agricultural production show different patterns of gender divisions. This is particularly apparent in the persistence of household-based peasant production and the control exercised by heads of household over female labour. Levels of fertility also tend to be higher. In all the societies discussed, women have been granted individual rights and formal equality and certain forms of male control over women's labour have been challenged. It seems, however, that industrialisation and a high demand for labour have been crucial in transforming gender divisions of labour and enabling women to exercise their rights. Additionally, in those societies where women's participation in the workforce has been highest, the state has taken over many of the tasks associated with social reproduction. But although gender divisions have been changed, in none of these societies have gender divisions which subordinate women been eliminated. Moreover, the gains made by women under socialism have been easily reversed in the transition from planned economies with maximum state intervention to market economies with minimum state intervention. Possible reasons for this are explored in the following chapter.

NOTES

1. The term productive forces refers to the means of production (raw material, tools, machinery, factories, technology) and labour power (the ability to work).

EXPLAINING GENDER DIVISIONS
IN SOCIALIST SOCIETIES

Socialism, as an ideology that emerged as a critique of capitalist society, promised an end to women's subordination. Socialist regimes have consistently written women's emancipation into their programmes and given women equal legal rights with men. They have also attempted to transform the material barriers which prevent women from exercising their rights. All these interventions have been aimed at reducing the disadvantages suffered by women due to their biological and social role in reproduction in order to enable them to participate in society as do men. Men's participation in production and politics has been taken as the norm to which women can and should aspire. Thus, definitions of womanhood and femininity have been transformed in order to encompass their roles as workers, political activists and mothers while it has not been thought necessary to make any changes to definitions of manhood and masculinity. However, what the discussion in the previous chapter indicates is that this is an essential part of overcoming women's subordination for, without it, women will continue to carry the burden of reproduction which limits their participation in production and in political life. A recognition that this may be so was apparent in discussions of women's roles and the domestic division of labour in the former USSR and China, in the Marriage Law of Cuba and in the rights of fathers and grandmothers to parental leave in the former GDR. However, even before the events of 1989, progress on this front was hampered by socialist regimes' support for the family with its highly inegalitarian gender division of labour, as the basic unit of socialist society.

Because of the continuing existence of gender divisions in

socialist societies and the dearth of women at the top of the occupational and political hierarchies, many feminists have concluded that socialism has nothing to offer women, that changes in the economic structure have no significant impact on gender divisions and that women are in fact subordinated by a system of patriarchy which exists regardless of whether societies are feudal, capitalist or socialist (Hartmann, 1986; Stacey, 1983; Wolf, 1985). They argue against a marxist position, which links changes in the form of the family and gender divisions to changes in the mode of production, and conclude that women, as women, have no interest in socialism and that class exploitation bears no relation, either theoretically or practically, to gender oppression although the two can and do coexist (Brownmiller, 1986; Walby, 1986). These arguments are often put forward without undertaking a comparative analysis which might throw some light on these issues. In addition, when gender divisions in socialist societies are being discussed they are usually compared with those in advanced capitalist societies, by those who wish to defend the achievements of socialism as well as by those who do not (Lane, 1983; Heitlinger, 1979) and often very little distinction is made between socialist societies (Jancar, 1978; Molyneux, 1984, 1985). It seems to me that this approach is misleading as it does not take account of the dynamics of social and economic development and, instead of comparing societies with similar levels of development, very different types of society are compared without acknowledging that this may of itself have an impact on the form taken by gender divisions. Thus a society like China, which has only recently begun to emerge from feudalism,[1] is compared unproblematically with the United States, where it never existed, or with Britain which has had four hundred years of post-feudal development. This criticism, of course, rests on the assumption that social development can be periodised and that different historical epochs are distinguished by differences in the relations of production which characterise them. In the discussion which follows I hope to show that this way of understanding social development and change helps to throw light on the way in which gender divisions are transformed and the reasons why gender equality was not achieved in socialist societies. In the process I shall explore and evaluate the main explanations for the continued subordination of women in socialist societies.

These explanations can be grouped under three main headings. First, there are those which link women's continued subordination to the way in which modernisation and industrialisation have occurred in socialist societies; second, there are those who argue that it is patriarchy which explains women's subordination in socialist as in capitalist societies; and, third, there are those who argue that women's subordination arises from the nature of socialism as a transitional stage in which non-socialist relations of production continue to exist and provide a material basis for the continued reproduction of gender inequalities. For all three types of explanation the support of socialist societies for the family is defined as one of the major obstacles to women's liberation, albeit the way that the family is conceptualised varies. I look first at the type of explanation that conceptualises women's subordination as an inevitable part of the process of socialist development.

MODERNISATION

This explanation conceptualises the process of transformation put in train by socialist revolutions as a process of modernisation and industrialisation. Modernisation theory argues that modern, industrial societies have developed from traditional, rural-based economies and that this development is linear and progresses through a series of stages evolving from a less developed to a more developed stage. The most developed modern societies adopt Western values which are appropriate to an industrial economy and this form of society is the aim of economic development (for a useful discussion, see Foster-Carter, 1985: 102–6). As we have already noted, most socialist revolutions (with the exception of those in Africa which I discuss in Chapter 7) have occurred in societies which are semi-feudal and/or dominated by foreign capital which often maintains feudal forms of land ownership. One of the major challenges facing socialist regimes has been to transform these largely rural economies into modern, industrial, urban economies. Under these conditions one of the main tasks of the revolution is seen as breaking up pre-capitalist forms of production thereby freeing the population to take part in wage-labour in the growing industrial sector. In many of the societies which have experienced a socialist revolution the rural, peasant family has been the unit of production in which the majority of the population was located. And linked with this is the strong hold of religions or ideologies with their high valuation of tradition, women's subordination and reverence for authority. Regimes wishing to transform this type of economy have attempted to undermine the peasant family and break the hold of religion and pre-existing ideologies over the rural population (Lapidus, 1978; Molyneux, 1984; Croll, 1983). This is where the emancipation of women has a part to play.

It is argued that a major way of undermining the family as a unit of production and weakening the conservative hold of religious authority is by giving women rights which will encourage them to challenge male authority within the family and enable them to assert their independence through earning a wage. Thus, in the Muslim areas of the USSR and in China the new marriage laws gave women the right to free-choice marriage and divorce which were an immediate challenge to the family and to the organisation of production in those societies. And, as we have seen, opposition to these changes was violent resulting in the death of hundreds of thousands of women. This reaction cannot simply be understood as men opposing women's liberation but as women becoming the focus of opposition to a fundamental transformation in the family as a unit of production. This is because women's rights to land and property threatened the viability of the peasant household as an economic and productive unit (Goldman, 1989). A transformation of women's status could therefore contribute to the transformation of the peasant family and, as such, the emancipation of women coincided with the modernising intentions of the revolutionary regimes. The first stage of modernisation, then, is conceptualised as the break-up of social relations which stand in the way of industrialisation. Once these relations begin to be undermined people have to seek alternative ways of subsisting. They are therefore available to provide the labour power necessary for the industrialisation process.

The transformation of the peasant family and the granting of rights to women enables women as well as men to become part of the industrial workforce, a prerequisite for women's economic independence and, eventual, emancipation. The modernisation explanation argues that it is not only essential for women's emancipation, but it is also essential for the process of industrialisation which, in economies which are poor in everything but their human resources, is a highly labour-intensive process in its early stages. Thus, rapid industrialisation sets up a demand for labour which makes it essential that women as well as men participate fully in the workforce. As we have seen, this high demand for labour was a feature of the USSR and Eastern European socialist societies; and in China, during the Great Leap Forward when the process of industrialisation was being intensified, women's participation in the workforce increased dramatically (Heitlinger, 1979; Lapidus, 1978; Croll, 1980, 1981; Molyneux, 1981, 1984, 1985).

Once women have entered the workforce, it is argued, there is a tendency for socialist states to announce that gender equality has been achieved (Buckley, 1989) or to appear less enthusiastic about implementing the other measures which Marx and Engels, never mind modern feminists, considered necessary for women's emancipation. The support of socialist regimes for a nuclear family which retains economic responsibility for the rearing of children and in which women carry the main burden of domestic responsibility is explained in terms of economic necessity and the level of development reached by such societies. Ideally socialist regimes are committed to the universal provision of child care and the collectivisation of housework. In reality this sort of provision is costly and it is cheaper to rely on women performing unpaid labour than to direct scarce resources to fund the collectivisation of domestic work (Nazzari, 1983; Molyneux, 1985; Croll, 1983; Kruks, Rapp & Young, 1989). Thus, socialist regimes prioritise rapid industrialisation and capital accumulation over the provision of social facilities and consumer goods (Lapidus, 1978; Molyneux, 1981, 1984, 1985). It is argued that this means that modernisation takes place at women's expense and that the goals of women's emancipation are subverted to the goals of rapid industrialisation. Women retain responsibility for the reproduction of labour despite the fact that some of this burden is shared by the state through provision of social facilities. This, however, is costly and is therefore not prioritised. This emphasis is given ideological support by the rhetoric of building socialism and defending the gains of the revolution which are prioritised over and above any sectoral interests. And it takes organisational form in the control that is exercised by the party or modernising regime over the women's organisations. Socialist modernisation, therefore, prioritises economic development over women's emancipation.

The issue of socialist regimes' support for the nuclear family is important. This support, which exists alongside their support for women's full participation in production and political life, is in contradiction to the classical marxist prescription for women's emancipation but is seen as functional for a rapidly industrialising society. However, it fails to resolve the contradiction which is apparent, particularly in the most industrialised socialist societies, between women's productive and reproductive roles (Molyneux, 1985; Lapidus, 1978). This contradiction became acute in the USSR and Eastern Europe with the declining birth-rate and continuing labour shortages; there were worries that there would not be enough workers in the next generation because women were not having enough children. In some of these societies the response was to curtail women's right to control their own fertility and in others there were signs of a move away from the commitment to women's full participation in production. One way of solving the contradiction is to enable the withdrawal, partial or total, of women from the workforce. Before the events of 1989 there were signs that this was on the agenda in the USSR and in most of Eastern Europe (Lapidus, 1978; Heitlinger, 1979; Buckley, 1989). Now it is being put into practice through phenomenally high levels of unemployment and the withdrawal of state subsidies from child-care provision and other social facilities which partially relieved women of the burden of reproductive tasks. This forced, but perhaps not unwelcome, withdrawal of women from the workforce will enable them to combine child rearing and housework with part-time employment or with intermittent participation in the workforce. Thus women's responsibility for reproduction is maintained rather than being redistributed either to men within domestic units or to the state.

There is a parallel here with the capitalist industrialisation process. After the initial period of rapid industrialisation concern was voiced over the survival of future generations and the reproduction of the workforce. The solution was sought in state intervention in the economy in order to regulate the employment of women and children and to support a specific family form in which men were the primary wage earners and women were defined as economically dependent on them (Marx, 1974; Wilson,

1977; McIntosh, 1978). This last point reveals an important difference between capitalist societies and socialist societies. In the former, marriage is defined as a means of providing economic support to women; in the latter, it was not, although this does not, of course, mean that this was always reflected in reality (Nazzari, 1983).

This way of resolving the contradiction – that is, by reducing women's participation in the workforce – is not the only possible solution. Another way of resolving it which would have been in the interest of greater gender equality would have been to encourage male participation in the domestic sphere and to introduce shorter and more flexible working hours for women and men. Although this option was discussed in many socialist societies, and, in some, men's participation in the domestic sphere was encouraged, most socialist societies never seriously challenged the domestic division of labour. On the contrary, women were expected to become social men and domestic work was to be taken over by the state; men were taken as the model to which women should aspire. The only society which was able to afford very high levels of social provision and which facilitated some sharing of domestic tasks was the GDR, a society which was industrialised prior to the advent of socialism. However, even here measures reinforced the gender division of labour by giving *women* with children, rather than women *or* men, rights to a shorter working week and a 'housework day' each month (Einhorn, 1989, 1991). Union with the Federal Republic of Germany initially gave rise to a strong defence of these provisions but, despite this, most of them are vanishing with the removal of state subsidies (Dolling, 1991; Einhorn, 1991; Haug, 1991; Behrend, 1992). Indeed, a comparison of the two Germanys is interesting as it reveals that in terms of social facilities and reproductive rights, women in the East were far better off than their sisters in the West, while the shortage of consumer goods made their household chores more burdensome and time-consuming (*Guardian* letter, August 1990; Einhorn, 1989; Dolling, 1991).

Explanations which attribute women's continuing subordination under socialism to the demands of socialist development suggest that in the early stages of socialist construction women's emancipation is supported because it serves the aims of modernisation. However, once industrialisation is under way there is a conflict of interests between women's emancipation and the demands of modernisation because of a lack of resources. Thus, the family and motherhood are supported because this is the cheapest way of ensuring the reproduction of the workforce and women's interests are subordinated to those of modernisation.

It is appropriate at this point to look briefly at the experience of nationalist movements in the Third World and their relation to women's emancipation and gender divisions. This is particularly important as many of the socialist revolutions I have discussed have taken place in the context of national liberation movements. It also points up the close links between women's emancipation and modernisation.

Women's emancipation is part of the ideology of many independence and nationalist movements. For instance, the burgeoning national independence movement of eighteenth-century China debated women's rights and education for women and that of nineteenth-century India supported women's emancipation. This century there have been independence movements and liberation movements to end imperial and colonial domination in many Third World countries and the mobilisation of women has been important to them also. Such movements arise not only in opposition to foreign, imperialist powers but also as part of a reaction against national oligarchies, feudal structures, exploitative local rulers and traditional patriarchal and religious structures (Jayawardena, 1986). They are a response to the poverty and exploitation associated with dependence. It has been suggested that there are two main reasons for support being given to women's emancipation by modernising nationalist movements, both of which arise from their commitment to rapid industrialisation. Firstly, the process of industrialisation in its early stages is generally labour-intensive and is likely to require women's as well as men's participation in the workforce. Secondly, in order that women may be available for production and that, as mothers, they will socialise their children into the values appropriate to a modernising, industrial society, it is necessary to reform gender relations within the family and challenge restrictive gender ideologies. To this end, traditions which restrict women's mobility and enforce their seclusion are attacked, as are practices such as widow-burning, veiling, polygamy, concubinage and so on. Eliminating such practices and transforming gender relations within the family is seen as a way of freeing women to become a source of cheap labour for industry, on plantations and in agriculture and establishing the modern, nuclear family in place of previous family forms (Jayawardena, 1986). This process can be viewed as a transformation of pre-capitalist family forms and social practices such that a family form appropriate to industrialisation is established which 'allows' women to participate in paid employment. This process of modernisation is accompanied by the institutionalisation of new forms of gender divisions which, although still subordinating women, in many ways give them more freedom than before.

There are, however, nationalist movements in the Third World which are opposed both to modernisation and women's emancipation. These movements can also be seen as responses to foreign domination and the poverty and social dislocation resulting from dependent 'development'. But the class character of these movements differ as do their prescriptions for women. Thus, modernising liberation movements are likely to be led by sectors of the middle class or the middle class in alliance with the proletariat, while anti-modernisation movements may be led by sectors of the landed classes and the clergy. Support can be gained from other social groups for whom a foreign-dominated development process has negative consequences, such as the rural and urban poor, the urban lower middle class, artisan classes and women (Kandiyoti, 1989). Women may support such movements, even though their ideologies opppose women's emancipation, because they appear to represent stability in the face of rapid social change and because they often place a high value on the family and motherhood (Afshar, 1989: 117; Kandiyoti, 1989; Jabbra, 1989; Fagen *et al.*, 1986).

It is important to remember that for all nationalist movements and ideologies, women's role as reproducer of the nation through the reproduction and socialisation of children is crucial although the balance between women's productive and reproductive roles is defined differently (Yuval-Davis & Anthias, 1989), Thus, modernising nationalist movements emphasise a public role for women in production as well as attaching importance to their reproductive role whereas other types of nationalist movement emphasise women's reproductive role to the exclusion of any role outside the domestic sphere. Both types of movement may create dilemmas for women who consider themselves nationalist *and* feminist: one because nationalist ideology restricts women's participation in public life, emphasising the importance of motherhood and the family; the other because, despite the rhetoric, there may be a conflict between the goal of modernisation and women's emancipation (Patel, 1991; Siddiqui, 1991; Kumar, 1989; El-Wathig Kamier *et al.*, 1984; Ghoussoub, 1987; Barrios de Chungara, 1978, 1983; Kimble & Unterhalter, 1982; Beall *et al.*, 1989). This conflict, as far as modernising regimes are concerned, has usually been resolved in favour of the needs of a modernising economy.

It is argued that socialist liberation movements also pursue women's emancipation because of its contribution to the goals of modernisation. Women's emancipation extends the base of support for the modernising government, increases the size and/or the quality of the labour force and helps to harness the family more securely to the process of socialist reproduction (Molyneux, 1984a). Women's support for the construction of socialism is seen as crucial because their position in the family enables them to challenge traditional customs and privileges and to influence the values and attitudes of their children. However, there are important differences between socialist and capitalist modernisation as far as women are concerned. For instance, socialist modernisation improves women's health and welfare and opens up new opportunities for them in terms of work and political participation (Molyneux, 1984a, 1985; Ruchwarger, 1989; Collinson *et al.*, 1990). And enabling women to participate in wage-labour involves a certain educational level and creates the possibility of women's escaping economic dependence on a male relative. Other benefits which accrue to women are an increase in literacy rates and levels of education (Lapidus, 1978a, 1978: 64; Molyneux, 1985a; Collinson *et al.*, 1990). These improvements occur because the consolidation of support for socialist modernisation is achieved by the political organisation of women as workers and peasants, their mobilisation into trade unions, neighbourhood associations and women's organisations; this enables them to organise to further their interests.

It is significant that women's movements or organisations are associated with most socialist modernising regimes. The type of explanation discussed here suggests that these movements represent women's interests in so far as they are compatible with the goals of modernisation and ensure that women are mobilised to support these goals. They can therefore be seen as representing women's practical gender interests rather than their strategic gender interests. This distinction has been made by Molyneux (1984a) who argues that a movement can be defined as feminist if it has strategic objectives aimed at overcoming women's subordination. Practical gender interests, on the other hand, 'arise out of women's immediate perceived needs and experiences' (Safa, 1990: 363) and may not challenge their subordinate role in the gender division of labour (Safa, 1990; Schirmer, 1989). It is argued that most women's movements in socialist societies represent women's practical gender interests, and that if they represent women's strategic gender interests, as in Nicaragua in the 1980s, the economic policies pursued by modernising regimes make their goal of ending women's subordination difficult if not impossible to achieve. This is because economic policies absorb women into production without relieving them of the burden of child care and domestic labour and a lack of resources for such facilities sets a limit on the possibilities for women's liberation.

Explanations which link women's continuing subordination under socialism to the needs of a modernising economy do not conceptualise the difference between capitalist and socialist modernisation. Indeed, giving explanatory power to concepts such as modernisation or industrialisation makes such a distinction impossible. There is also a tension within this type of explanation. On the one hand, it is argued that there is a neat fit between the requirements of industrialisation and women's unpaid labour within the family household and that women's emancipation is limited by the requirements of industrial production and social reproduction. On the other hand, it is argued that these societies offer the possibility of further movement towards women's liberation and, in this, they differ from capitalism in some way that is analytically undefined (Croll, 1983; Molyneux, 1984, 1984a, 1985). The two positions are mutually incompatible. Thirdly, underlying these arguments is the assumption that industrialisation, whether socialist or capitalist, has an interest in women's subordination because a gender division of labour which assigns to women the main responsibility for reproductive activities within the domestic sphere allows for maximum accumulation of capital and minimum expenditure on social reproduction. The gender division of labour within the domestic sphere is therefore functional to industrialising societies and this explains its persistence.

This analysis shares much with the explanations looked at in Chapter 3, particularly those arguing that women's domestic labour is functional for capital because it keeps down the value of labour power and ensures its daily and generational reproduction. And, in common with early variants of explanations relying on notions of social reproduction, there is little explanatory power given to concepts of class or gender struggle.

RELATIONS OF PRODUCTION

The second type of explanation locates women's subordination in the continued existence of non-socialist forms or relations of production within socialist societies. These include household-based peasant production (Croll, 1980, 1983; White, 1988: 167, 171; Davin, 1991a, 1991b), the continued existence of the wage as a major form of distribution (Nazzari, 1983) or an insufficiently transformed domestic division of labour which maintains women's responsibility for reproduction (Lane, 1983). Croll, for instance, argues that state policies which emphasise capital accumulation and industrial production rather than production for consumption, together with the structure and function of the peasant household in the rural economy, result in a gender division of labour in which women are subordinate (Croll, 1983).

Croll's analysis is based on China, where 80% of the population is rural and the structure of the peasant household affects the majority of the population. But it has relevance to the situation in other socialist societies where large sectors of the population are rural and peasant production remains important. This is true even of the former USSR where a third of the population is rural, a high proportion for a developed society (Bridger, 1992; Davin, 1978: 184). It is therefore useful to look at her argument in some detail.

The peasant household, since the dissolution of the communes in China, has been reinforced as the basic unit of production in the countryside, although even before this it remained significant in terms of production as well as consumption. Under the commune system the rural economy consisted of three sectors, the collective, income-earning sector, the private sector and the domestic sector.

Women's labour was crucial in all three whereas men's labour was most significant in the income-earning sector. Thus, women and men worked on commune land, projects and industry but it was women who were responsible for the sideline activities of the private sector, growing food and raising animals for domestic consumption, and domestic labour, which included grinding corn, preserving vegetables, cooking, sewing and child care. Women working in the collective sector earned wages which made their labour visible but in the private and domestic sectors their labour was unpaid and therefore invisible. Thus women's labour was of crucial significance to the welfare of the peasant household and access to female labour was necessary for a peasant household to be viable.

In China the private hiring of labour had been prohibited in order to prevent the development of exploitative class relations. But at the same time the wealth and welfare of peasant households depended upon access to and control over labour. This meant that the recruitment of labour had to take place by means other than hiring, such as marriage and the birth of children. Given the long tradition of patrilocal marriage, one way of recruiting labour into the household is to give birth to sons who can be married young and whose wives provide labour themselves and also ensure a future supply of labour by having children. In such a system daughters are considered inferior to sons because they eventually move away from their natal home. They are temporary whereas sons are permanent members of the household and can contribute to its maintenance throughout their lives. Croll argues that with the prohibition of hiring of labour the acquisition of daughters-in-law through marriage became the most important way of increasing the household's labour resources. So women continued to be exchanged between households and their subordination was an integral part of the structure of the peasant household. The betrothal gift is still widespread in the countryside, despite the CCP's attempts to abolish it, because it is seen as compensation to the bride's family for meeting the cost of her upbringing.

The reforms initiated in 1978 have reinforced the peasant household as the basic unit of production in the countryside. Commune land has been distributed to individual households and the, usually male, head of household allocates family labour. As we saw in the previous chapter, this change means that women are now working on family land under the control of the head of household rather than working on collective land. And they do not receive remuneration in the form of work points for this. They only have access to independent remuneration if they work for wages in rural industry or are in charge of a 'specialised household' (Judd, 1990; Davin, 1991a, 1991b). Women are still likely to marry out of their villages and they then lose their jobs in village-based industry (Davin, 1991a, 1991b). Women's subordination, even more than under the commune system, is integral to the economy of the peasant household, although some argue that with specialised households and rural industry new opportunities for autonomy and independence are available to women (Judd, 1990).

The importance of children, particularly male children, in augmenting the labour to which a peasant household has access throws light on rural opposition to the one-child family policy. In the peasant household there is strong pressure to have as many children as possible and as early as possible to augment the labour supply and to ensure security in old age. Additionally, within peasant households it is the older generation which manages the household budget. Such families are three generation families and it is very difficult for younger women, or men, to achieve independence as their wages are all pooled and, more often than not, paid directly to the head of household. These practices continue despite attempts by the CCP to legislate them out of existence.

Thus the patrilocal peasant household circumscribes the role and independence of peasant women and the interests of the household are directly opposed to many of the policies aimed at redefining women's roles. Indeed, the peasant household is predicated upon a gender division of labour in which women are subordinate and in which this subordination is crucial to the successful maintenance and reproduction of the household. Thus it provides a material basis for the reproduction of gender divisions.

The existence of patrilocal marriage and patrilineal kinship groups means, also, that groups of male kin are co-resident in villages while women are separated from their agnatic kin. This coincidence of patrilineal kinship groups with villages means that collective decisions about training young people to become, for instance, barefoot doctors, often discriminate against women. This is because investing in training a young woman is regarded as a waste of resources as she will leave the natal village on marriage. This facilitates the monopoly of skilled work by men and creates a gender division of labour coinciding with the skilled/unskilled distinction (Croll, 1983; Sidel & Sidel, 1982).

Thus Croll argues that, although ideology is an important factor in maintaining women's subordination, it is not the most significant cause of continuing gender divisions. These divisions are in fact reproduced by the relations of production in the countryside which reproduce the subordination of women as a necessary part of the process of production of the rural economy based on the patrilocal peasant household. The CCP identifies ideology, rather than material conditions of production, as the cause of women's subordination and, since the failure of the Great Leap Forward, has been reluctant to enforce its policies on women in the face of opposition from the peasantry (Croll, 1983; Stacey, 1983). This has to be seen in the context of the importance of ensuring that food continues to be produced in the countryside to supply not only the needs of the rural population but also of those who live in urban areas. Any attack on the basis of the peasant family may jeopardise these food supplies and necessitate a violent and costly programme of forced collectivisation as occurred in the USSR. The maintenance and increase of food supplies is obviously crucial in China, with such a huge and growing population, and experience elsewhere shows that peasants can easily withdraw their products from the market if they are not gaining anything by participating in it. This can quite rapidly lead to a situation of famine (Roesch, 1988; Rudebeck, 1988). There are thus very real material barriers in the way of eliminating women's subordination and they clearly relate to the continued existence of the peasant household as the basic unit of production in the countryside (Croll, 1983).

Croll also argues that the CCP and the Women's Federation have assumed that if policies benefited the development of China then they would also benefit women and that little attempt to evaluate the impact of policies on gender divisions has been made. Current policies provide an obvious example. The programme of modernisation which was set in motion after the death of Mao involves more emphasis being placed on the rural household as a unit of production. The implications of this for gender divisions have not been discussed by policy makers but as we have already seen it has reinforced male control over female labour within peasant households and ensured that women's access to the means of production is through her relationship with a man. This reorganisation makes women's agricultural labour less visible because they are working on family rather than collective land and their work no longer attracts work points. The policies have also seen a rise in unemployment which has prompted suggestions that married women should give up paid work and, in urban areas, outwork is becoming common. This means that women are working at home for cooperatives and are not entitled to any benefits (Croll, 1983). In other words, there is evidence that the impact of these reforms on gender divisions will have negative repercussions for women (Bettelheim, 1988: 28). However, alongside these developments emphasis is still being put on the socialisation and modernisation of domestic labour and the socialisation of child care. Provision of all these facilities is higher in the urban than rural areas and, indeed, it is possible to argue that the urban family is moving closer in form to the nuclear family than to the extended peasant family from which it originates (Stacey, 1983; Croll, 1983). China therefore exhibits the rural–urban divide characteristic of many Third World countries despite its strenuous efforts to minimise this problem. And it can be argued that gender divisions in the countryside take a different form from those in urban areas because the policies of the CCP have, so far, failed to eliminate the peasant family's control over female labour which arises from its continued existence as the major unit of production in the countryside.

Insufficient transformation of capitalist or pre-capitalist social relations is also invoked by Nazzari as an explanation for women's continued subordination in Cuba. She argues that it is the persistence of women's dependence on a man's wage that maintains their subordination in Cuban society. She argues that Cuba's system of distribution now largely relies on the wage whereas, in the first years after 1959, many resources were provided by the state and access to them was not therefore dependent on access to a wage. This was an attempt to implement the communist dictum, 'from each according to their ability, to each according to their need'. This goal, was, however, abandoned in the face of the need for hard work and increased productivity to

ensure economic development. Material incentives were introduced and enterprises required to show a profit. This meant that
distribution relied more heavily on the wage and, as Nazzari
points out, the wage, material incentives and production for
exchange are features of capitalist relations of production (Nazzari, 1983: 453). Employment amongst married women in Cuba is
low (18%) and she argues that it is access to a husband's wage
that allows them to remain outside the workforce (Nazzari, 1983:
457). In addition, the Family Code states that children must be
supported by parents not by the state, as Castro had declared in
the early days of the revolution. Children's reliance on parental
support as well as low female participation in production compel
women to secure access to a male wage. Thus, in Cuba,
distribution through the wage together with lack of employment
for women reproduces women's dependence on men and an
unequal gender division of labour, despite the provisions of the
Family Code that housework should be shared (Nazzari, 1983).

This argument, again, points to an insufficient transformation in
economic relations which continue to provide the material basis
for the reproduction of women's subordination. It also suggests
that it is the exigencies of economic development and lack of
resources that have led to this retreat from the principles of
communist distribution which would have enabled women to
survive without access to a male wage. Thus the argument is that
inegalitarian gender divisions remain because the transition to
socialism has not gone far enough, and that one of the reasons that
it has not gone far enough is the underdeveloped nature of the
economy and resulting lack of resources (Kruks, Rapp & Young,
1989). Another way of conceptualising this, which is more in
keeping with the definition of socialism as a transitional period
between capitalism and communism, is that, because of the nature
of socialism, non-communist relations of production remain
throughout the transitional period and it is these that give rise to
contradictions and unevenness in the implementation of policies
aimed at eliminating inegalitarian gender divisions of labour.
Capitalist or semi-feudal relations of production continue to exist
during this transitional period of socialism and give rise to non-
socialist or, more accurately, non-communist forms of social
relations (Croll, 1983; Nazzari, 1983; Stacey, 1983: 261n).

None of the explanations looked at so far invokes patriarchy to explain the persistence of inegalitarian gender divisions under socialism. However, it has been argued that in China the CCP has democratised patriarchy and constructed a patriarchal socialism (Stacey, 1983). Other analysts have argued that the continued existence of patriarchy, particularly a patriarchal state, explains women's continued subordination in socialist societies (Wolf, 1985; Dolling, 1991; Einhorn, 1991). Stacey argues that gender divisions which subordinate women persist in China because the revolution was based on the patriarchal peasant family and the CCP, despite various attempts, has baulked at challenging it. She argues further that the patriarchal family has been strengthened by the socialist transformation of the Chinese countryside and stabilised as the basic unit of production. She draws on the evidence presented earlier in this chapter and in the previous one to support her view that the CCP has retreated from its aims of women's emancipation in the face of opposition from the peasantry.

Her analysis is based on the notion that the sex-gender system is relatively autonomous from the economic system. She argues that the sex-gender system has been rendered less oppressive to women by the socialist revolution but that it remains patriarchal despite the transformation in the mode of production. For her the sex-gender system and the mode of production together form the material basis of society. This is a similar approach to that adopted by Walby (Walby, 1986; Stacey, 1983). This process is not conceptualised as a male conspiracy. Rather it is conceptualised as an inability or unwillingness to implement unpopular policies in the countryside. This is partly explained by the long history of the close relations between the CCP and the peasantry and the characterisation of the revolution as a peasant revolution.

Her analysis is not, however, totally convincing as she points out that policies such as the one-child family policy and, possibly, the four modernisations, come into direct conflict with the interests of the peasant household. And there is no sign that the CCP is about to backtrack either on the need to limit population growth or on the efforts to modernise agriculture and raise productivity. As she herself points out:

To raise agricultural productivity, China will have to expand its rural labour force, and women are an obvious source. Likewise, women must reduce their childbearing if China's population is to stop growing (Stacey, 1983: 270).

Her own analysis suggests that the interests of the patriarchal peasant family may conflict with the demands of modernisation. This indicates that perhaps the sex-gender system that she defines as patriarchal is not so autonomous from the mode of production as she would have us believe. She is undoubtedly right to point to the continued existence of the patriarchal peasant family as an important brake on women's emancipation, but whether this indicates the existence of a system of patriarchy throughout society is less clear. Indeed, she does not attempt to demonstrate that this is so; nor does she argue that the CCP is itself patriarchal and, therefore, inevitably defends patriarchal systems while at the same time declaring itself to be opposed to patriarchy. It seems to me that invoking the concept of patriarchy does not actually explain why CCP policies aimed at women's emancipation have so far failed to achieve their aims. If the whole system is patriarchal and thus causes women's continued subordination, as she seems to be arguing, then it appears perverse in the extreme for the Chinese leadership to persist in professing their avowed commitment to women's emancipation, and even more extraordinary that they should attempt to implement policies which put this commitment into practice. On the other hand, if she is arguing that, despite attempts to transform the peasant family, which, seemingly, are still continuing, it still remains a site for the reproduction of gender divisions, then her argument has much in common with Croll's.

CONCLUSIONS

From the material presented here and in Chapter 4 it seems clear that actual socialist development has not followed Marx and Engels' prescriptions concerning women. Most socialist societies have enabled women's full participation in wage-labour and facilitated their economic independence, and most have attempted to provide child-care facilities to allow women to participate full time in the workforce. However, after a longer or shorter initial period of attempts to eliminate the family as the basic unit of society, all socialist regimes have affirmed their support for it as the most efficient means of reproducing the workforce (Molyneux, 1985). This has been explained by the underdevelopment of the economies in which socialist revolutions have taken place and the resulting lack of resources to socialise the tasks carried out by women within the domestic sphere (Croll, 1983; Molyneux, 1981, 1984, 1985; Nazzari, 1983; Lane, 1983; Leahy, 1986). In such societies rapid economic development and modernisation become a priority and, in certain respects, a prerequisite for women's emancipation. And it has also been explained by the continuing existence of economic relations which are predicated upon inegalitarian gender divisions of labour.

This evidence suggests that changes in the mode of production produce changes in gender divisions of labour. For instance, the gender division of labour which characterises a feudal peasant household is different from that which characterises an urban, nuclear family in an industrialised socialist (or capitalist) society; and, in some socialist societies, both forms of the gender division of labour continue to exist. One of the major differences between these two family forms is that in the peasant family women's labour is controlled by the head of household and the interests of the collective take precedence over individual rights. In contrast, the family within industrialised socialist societies encompasses the notion of individual rights for both women and men, and for both women and men these rights are civil, political, social and economic. The socialist transformation of a society, therefore, does transform gender divisions, although whether this is a result of socialism or modernisation is a moot point.

The other significant point to emerge from the material presented here and in Chapters 3 and 4 is that a high demand for labour greatly facilitates women's entry into production. There is a danger that once this stage of industrialisation is over and it becomes less labour-intensive, women's withdrawal from the labour force and their 'return' to the family will be seen as the most sensible (and cheapest) way of reducing levels of unemployment and relieving women of the heavy double burden they carry in most socialist societies. This is particularly likely to be seen as the solution to the contradiction between women's productive and reproductive roles, unless the domestic division of labour has been transformed. As we have seen, this did not happen in most socialist societies. To be successful such a transformation would involve changes in definitions of masculinity and femininity and a restructuring of work patterns. This would mean that men, as well as women, were 'disadvantaged' in production by domestic responsibilities, and that the special dispensations currently available only to women and operating to their disadvantage in the occupational structure would be made available to men.

A third factor of importance in explaining the persistence of inegalitarian gender divisions is the continuing strength of religions and ideologies with their prescriptions for family life and their emphasis on women's role within the family. These religions and ideologies give far more support to male dominance than is found in more secular societies. And it is no coincidence that they are strongest in those areas where peasant production predominates, or did until recently; where modernisation and industrialisation have failed to incorporate large sectors of the population; and where patriarchal authority is a functional part of the basic economic unit of society, the peasant household. These ideologies are, of course, linked to agrarian economies and provide an ideological legitimation for divisions of labour (including those of gender) that constitute the relations of production in such societies.

In conclusion, it can be said that gender divisions of labour in socialist and capitalist societies share many similarities. In both types of society women are to be found in the lowest paid and least skilled jobs and the occupational structure is stratified according to gender. In addition, very few women are active in the field of national politics. And in both types of society women's role in reproduction prevents them from participating fully in public life. However, there are important differences which relate to women's right to work and their independence from men. And in the industrialised socialist societies state provision of social facilities to take over the tasks of child care and housework were far more widespread than in capitalist societies, even Sweden which is often held up as a model. It is not possible to conclude, therefore, that industrialisation *per se* produces a specific gender division of labour and requires a specific family form, which is the argument of those who explain the continued existence of women's subordination under socialism in terms of the needs of a modernising economy. It seems, rather, that concepts of class and gender struggle are necessary in order to be able to explain such differences. This is because class and gender struggles influence the nature and extent of state involvement in social reproduction which, in turn, has a significant impact on gender divisions of labour (see Chapter 3, and Chapter 8 below). Nor does the evidence suggest that changes in gender divisions are totally independent of changes in the economic organisation of society. The evidence points, tentatively, in the direction of support for the argument that changes in the gender division of labour and the form taken by the family are linked to changes in the mode of production. It also suggests that gender ideologies are closely related to the form taken by gender divisions. This thesis will be explored further in the following chapters which focus on gender divisions in developing societies.

NOTES

1. I describe pre-liberation China as feudal following the analysis of Mao Tsetung. Although I am aware that considerable disagreement exists on the accuracy of this term to describe agrarian societies in many parts of Asia, it is not appropriate to enter into this debate here.

/ 6 /

Gender Divisions in the Third World

In the preceding chapters changes in gender divisions of labour have been linked to transformations in social relations of production and to the associated processes of modernisation or industrialisation which have taken place in capitalist and socialist societies. The next two chapters explore the changes in gender divisions of labour which are consequent upon colonial expansion and the incorporation of pre-capitalist or non-capitalist societies into a capitalist world economic order. Although most attention is focused on the effects of the development of capitalism on gender divisions, gender divisions in societies which are attempting to pursue a socialist path to development are also discussed.

THEORETICAL ISSUES

In the past two decades the attention of agencies concerned with economic development has turned towards women in the Third World. This has been prompted by increasing problems of poverty and hunger which threaten to erupt into social unrest. Women have increasingly been seen as vital to solving these problems, first, because in many societies they are the main producers of food and, second, because their education and participation in wage work is seen as the key to reducing population growth (Blumberg, 1981; Youssuf, 1974; Tinker, 1990; Kandiyoti, 1990). The importance of women's economic contribution to society was brought to public attention during the United Nation's decade for women, 1976–1985. During this period international conferences were

157

held and development agencies were encouraged to 'integrate' women into the development process. Third World governments were encouraged to set up women's departments in order to aid this integration and money was set aside for women's development projects (Brydon & Chant, 1989; Rogers, 1980). Substantial discussion and research emerged during this decade and attempts have been made to 'include' women in development projects (Wallace with March, 1991). However, much development work aimed specifically at women remains welfare and home economics-oriented and men continue to be targeted in attempts to improve agricultural productivity (Rogers, 1980; Heyzer, 1986; Feldman, 1984; Elson, 1991; Akeroyd, 1991: 153). This is particularly ironic given the importance of women in food production in many parts of the Third World, and lays development planners and agencies open to charges of male bias and deliberately attempting to 'domesticate' women in the interests of men or of capitalism – or both (Rogers, 1980; Mies, 1986; Jayawardena, 1986; Lewis, 1981; Elson, 1991).

Much of this debate was sparked off by Ester Boserup's book *Woman's Role in Economic Development* which was first published in 1970. Since then, there has been a proliferation of material analysing the situation of women in the Third World and the impact of colonial rule and 'development' on gender divisions of labour. Much of the literature is feminist inspired but can be distinguished theoretically in terms of the way in which development is conceptualised. Thus, Boserup adopts a modernisation perspective which distinguishes between a 'modern' and a 'traditional' sector and argues that the goal of the development process is a fully-fledged industrial society of the West European or North American type. Others, particularly marxists writing within the Latin American context, conceptualise the development process as taking place within the framework of structural dependency (Cardoso, 1982) and distinguish peripheral capitalism from the capitalism of the core countries (Alavi, 1982). This approach does not conceptualise the development process in the periphery as inevitably repeating the stages of capitalist development experienced in Western Europe (Hettne, 1990). A third approach can be identified which conceptualises development as a process of development of different forms of patriarchy and regards the development of capitalism as the stage of patriarchy which turns women the world over into housewives (Mies, 1986; Mies *et al.*, 1988).

The first and third approaches tend to regard women as relatively undifferentiated by class, caste or 'race'; women are all disadvantaged relative to men by development (Rogers, 1980; Mies, 1986). The second approach, however, recognises the diversity of situations in which women and men find themselves as a result of development and situates gender divisions in their wider social and economic context (Navarro, 1979: 115). Those adopting a modernisation approach argue that women are disadvantaged because they are 'left out' of the development process; they therefore need to be integrated into it (Boserup, 1989; Rogers, 1980). Those adopting a marxist or marxist-feminist approach argue that the problem is not that women are 'left out' but that they are integrated into a transformed gender division of labour which rests on their continued subordination (Elson & Pearson, 1984; Benería & Sen, 1981; Elson, 1991).

As we have already noted, modernisation theory distinguishes between the modern, industrial sector and the traditional, subsistence sector. Marxist approaches, on the other hand, talk of peripheral or dependent capitalism and pre-capitalist or non-capitalist social forms or modes of production (Meillassoux, 1972; Wolpe, 1972; Stamp, 1986; Henn, 1988). Marxist approaches argue that capitalist production depends on the subsistence sector or non-capitalist modes of production for a supply of cheap labour. This means that the capitalist sector does not have to meet the full costs of social reproduction – that is, the reproduction of the workforce on a daily and generational basis and the maintenance of the non-working population – because reproduction takes place in the non-capitalist sector. During the 1970s there was considerable debate as to whether non-capitalist modes of production continued to exist alongside the capitalist mode of production or whether non-capitalist forms of organisation continued to exist when the relations of production had in fact been transformed (for a useful summary of this debate, see Alavi, 1982: 174–5). Whichever way it is conceptualised, the significance it holds for understanding gender divisions is that women are the ones who undertake the bulk of activities in the non-capitalist or subsistence sector. Women's labour is therefore crucial in keeping down the costs to capital of social reproduction and the tasks in which women are engaged are conceptualised as reproductive activities. There is an obvious parallel with the marxist-feminist analysis of domestic labour under capitalism and the contribution it makes to the reproduction of labour power (Stichter & Parpart, 1988) and with explanations of inequitable gender relations in socialist societies. There is also a parallel with modernisation theory. In marxist-feminist terms it is women's responsibility for reproductive tasks that ensures the reproduction of gender divisions which disadvantage women, whereas in the terms of modernisation theory it is women's confinement to subsistence activities that ensures the 'exclusion' of women from the development process.

Before discussing these different approaches further, it is useful to consider some basic statistical information concerning the main regions to which I refer in this and the following chapter.

In sub-Saharan Africa there is a history of colonialism which lasted from 1880 to 1960 approximately. Colonisation and government by Europeans meant 'increasingly widespread penetration of capitalism and capitalist relations of production, an increasing monetisation of local economies and the beginnings of commoditisation of productive resources such as land' (Brydon & Chant, 1989: 33). The region is characterised by female farming with women being responsible for between 60% and 80% of agricultural production (Brydon & Chant, 1989; Boserup, 1989; Leacock, 1981). The extent of urbanisation is lower than in other regions of the Third World although it varies considerably between different societies. For instance in Zambia 38% of the population lives in urban areas whereas in Mozambique the corresponding figure is 9%. Similarly, women's participation in the workforce varies between societies, being lowest in those areas where Islam is an influence. A comparison of male and female economic activity rates can be seen in Table 6.1. These figures should be treated with some caution, however, as the International Labour Organisation from whom they come warns that:

The activity rates for females are frequently not comparable internationally, since in many countries relatively large numbers of women assist on farms or in other family enterprises without pay, and there are differences from one country to another in the criteria adopted for determining the extent to which such workers are to be counted among the economically active. (ILO, 1991: 3)

Table 6.1 Official economic activity rates of men and women and women as percentage of economically active population in selected countries*

| | Economic activity rates | | Women as percentage of economically active population |
	Men	Women	
Sub-Saharan Africa			
Nigeria (1986)**	40.7%	19.7%	32.2%
Tanzania (1978)	44.4%	45.2%	n/a
Mozambique (1970)	53.4%	18.7%	n/a
Zimbabwe (1982)	41.4%	25.4%	47.8% (1986–7)
South Africa (1989)	46.8%	24.5%	32.3%
Latin America			
Brazil (1988)	57.1%	29.7%	27.4% (1980)
Colombia (1990)	53.9%	33.2%	40.7%
Chile (1990)	51.6%	22.3%	31.0%
Mexico (1988)	51.2%	22.8%	33.2% (1988)
Peru (1989)	51.2%	33.1%	24.7% (1981)
Bolivia (1990)	48.1%	14.6%	44.0% (1989)
El Salvador (1990)	50.7%	34.7%	44.7%
Puerto Rico (1980)	35.0%	19.6%	36.8%
Cuba (1988)	55.4%	31.7%	31.3% (1981)
Nicaragua (1990)	47.1%	22.4%	21.2% (1980)
South and South-east Asia			
Bangladesh (1985–6)	53.6%	6.5%	10.4%
Pakistan (1990–1)	49.4%	6.8%	3.7% (1984–5)
India (1981)	55.2%	21.9%	30.0% (1981)
Indonesia (1989)	51.2%	34.0%	39.9%
Malaysia (1987)	56.5%	31.1%	35.4%
Singapore (1989)	59.6%	37.8%	39.3%
Hong Kong (1990)	61.6%	36.8%	36.4%
China (1982)	57.3%	47.0%	43.7%
Industrialised societies			
UK (1988)	58.4%	41.2%	42.8%
USA (1989)	56.1%	44.0%	44.9% (1990)
USSR(1989)	55.0%	45.8%	48.3%

* Economic activity is defined as 'all production and processing of primary products, whether for the market, for barter or for own consumption, the production of all other goods and services for the market, and in the case of households which produce such goods and services for the market, the corresponding production for own consumption'. The economically active population is defined as 'all persons of either sex who furnish the supply of labour for purposes of economic goods and services'. (ILO, 1991: 3)

** Date of national censuses from which the figures are taken

Source: ILO *Yearbook of Labour Statistics*, 1991: 17–126, 1982, 1988, 1990; ILO *Yearbook of Labour Statistics*: Retrospective edition on population censuses, 1945–89, 1990.

In South Asia, which includes India, Nepal, Pakistan, Bangladesh and Sri Lanka, two-thirds of the population depends upon agriculture for survival. The official economic activity rates for women in India, Nepal and Sri Lanka are lower than for sub-Saharan Africa. South-east Asia, which includes Indonesia, Malaysia, Singapore, Thailand, Laos, Kampuchea, Vietnam, Burma and the Philippines, has a varied colonial history. This region includes the Newly Industrialised Countries of Malaysia and Singapore, and there is a high number of so-called world market factories which are particularly important when considering women's employment. Around 30% of the population is urbanised and the rates of female employment are amongst the highest in the Third World. This is true of rural and urban areas where women constitute 26% of the labour force.

Latin America is the most urbanised region of the Third World with 42.5% of the population residing in settlements of 100,000 or more people. Around a third of the labour force is employed in industry and between 26% and 45% of women over fifteen years of age are in paid employment; they constitute between 16% and 35% of the workforce. This part of the world experienced colonial expansion in the sixteenth century, and has a longer post-colonial history than the countries of sub-Saharan Africa.

These figures indicate that the majority of the population of the Third World is rural and although most peoples are integrated into the capitalist cash economy this integration is uneven and, to a greater or lesser extent, partial. Thus, in the same region there may be people living as foragers, horticulturalists, small peasant producers, petty commodity producers and industrial wage workers. This has implications for gender divisions for, as we shall see, particular forms of social and economic organisation seem to be linked to specific forms of the family or household, specific fertility levels and specific gender divisions of labour. In this and the following chapter I explore the impact of colonisation, the development of capitalism and industrialisation on gender divisions in the Third World.

BOSERUP REVISITED

Boserup is one of those who argue that women are 'left out' of the development process remaining in the 'traditional, subsistence' sector while men move into the 'modern' sector (Boserup, 1989). This she sees as detrimental, not only to women but also to economic development, because potentially productive human beings are rendered unproductive and a society's overall productivity and growth are affected negatively. Her analysis has been extremely influential (Tinker, 1990; Acosta-Belén, 1990) and many studies have been conducted subsequently in order to refine and test the validity of her conclusions (see, for example, Deere, 1987; Stoler, 1977; Kandiyoti, 1977). It is, therefore, appropriate to take as the starting point of this chapter her discussion of the ways in which development, or, perhaps more appropriately, underdevelopment, affects gender divisions of labour.

Boserup's main contribution to our understanding of the relationship between economic development and changes in the gender division of labour has been to point out women's significant, and largely ignored, contribution to subsistence production, particularly subsistence agricultural production. She distinguishes two main types of agricultural production. The first, largely undertaken by women, is based on the hoe and associated with shifting agriculture. The second, largely undertaken by men, is based on the plough and associated with more intensive, settled agriculture and private ownership of land (Boserup, 1989: 25). The regions of the Third World where 'female agriculture' predominates are Africa and parts of India. In female agricultural systems women put considerably greater amounts of time into agricultural production than do men (Boserup, 1989: 20). High female participation in agriculture is also associated with regions where wet rice is grown such as South-east Asia. Wet-rice cultivation is labour intensive requiring the mobilisation of all sources of labour.

Boserup observes that agricultural production in Africa and South-east Asia is marked by high female participation rates while the agricultural labour force in the rest of Asia is predominantly male as is that of the Arab countries and Latin America. She offers a partial explanation for the lower rates of female participation in these areas, linking it to the existence of private property in land and a class of rural wage labourers. In situations where agricultural wage-labour is available, and where farming households have adequate resources, wage-labour is hired enabling women to retire from field production (Boserup, 1989: 31). This, she argues, makes it possible for agrarian societies to practise female seclusion which, indeed, predominates in precisely those regions of the Third World with these types of farming practice (Huber, 1991).

She argues that increases in population density brought about a change from shifting agriculture to settled agriculture (Boserup, 1990). This necessitates more intensive agricultural production and precipitates the change in technology which makes this possible; that is, the change from hoe to plough. It is not clear, however, why it should be men who take over agricultural production as a result of this technological change. It is also problematic to argue that intensification of agriculture is a *result* of increases in population; the relationship may, in fact, be the opposite way round (Ember, 1983). The association of men with more advanced technology is, however, a pattern that can be observed throughout the development process and is in need of explanation.

Boserup argues that women's status declines with the change from shifting cultivation of land which is not privately owned to permanent cultivation of land which is privately owned, a process which has been precipitated by colonial expansion in many regions of the Third World (Boserup, 1989: 57). In her view the process of colonisation has taken advantage of previously existing gender divisions of labour. In regions of shifting agriculture the colonists perceived men as 'idle' leaving the women to do all the work. They therefore put the men to work in plantations, mines and so on. Subsistence agricultural production could be left safely in the hands of women because men's contribution is generally limited to preparing the ground on which the women will grow crops and they are not required to be constantly present for subsistence agricultural production to continue. Wages paid to men did not have to cover the cost of upkeep of their families; women's agricultural activities could be relied upon to feed themselves and their children. In Asia, however, the process of agricultural production required both women and men; women would therefore be unable to continue subsistence production if men were recruited for plantation work. In this situation the cheapest option for plantation owners was to recruit women, men and children thus getting several labourers for the price that they might otherwise have had to pay for one (Boserup, 1989: 76–7). Boserup regards both these forms of employment – on the one hand, only men and, on the other, whole families – as a means whereby labour costs can be kept to a minimum at women's expense. More recent research shows that in South-east Asian rubber plantations men were employed initially and it was only later that women and children joined the workforce. This was seen as a way of ensuring a future supply of plantation workers as well as keeping down the costs of labour (Heyzer, 1986).

Boserup also points out that women predominate in trade in many parts of the Third World, particularly Africa, South-east Asia and Latin America, and suggests that this is linked to women's involvement in agriculture. Women are also found in home industries or petty commodity production, engaged in, for instance, carpet weaving as happens in Iran, lacemaking as in parts of India, making mats and baskets in Southern Iraq and so on (Afshar, 1985; Mies, 1982; Boserup, 1989: 108). She observes that this is likely to be an option taken by women who are in seclusion and therefore cannot work outside the domestic sphere. Additionally women work in urban areas in what Boserup calls the 'bazaar and service' sector. This is more commonly referred to as the 'informal' sector and includes activities such as domestic service, petty commodity production, trading and prostitution. Boserup regards this sector of the economy as an intermediate stage between 'traditional' and 'modern' occupations. And although many men are also to be found in this sector they predominate in the 'modern' sector.

Boserup paints a picture of men being forced out of subsistence production into the 'modern' sector of developing countries' economies, whether this be in cash cropping in rural areas or industrial employment in urban areas, leaving women behind in subsistence activities mainly in the rural areas. For her, female participation in the 'modern' sector is a measure of a society's economic development (Boserup, 1989: 180). Thus, she ranks the regions of the Third World in these terms, judging Latin America to be the most developed region followed by South-east Asia where urban as well as rural employment is high for women. In the Arab countries female participation in the 'modern' sector is low, (5%), although, as she observes, seclusion may actually increase the demand for professionally trained women to teach and offer health care to the secluded female population. And in Africa, except for South Africa, female participation in the 'modern' sector is almost non-existent. Youssuf, in a comparison of Latin America and the Middle East, suggests that women's participation in the workforce is not an indication of a society's level of development and that women's economic activity rates are not solely determined by economic factors. She suggests that cultural factors are extremely powerful and, in societies where female seclusion is practised, this has a far greater effect on women's participation rates than the level of economic development. Boserup disagrees, arguing that seclusion is ignored in situations where women's labour is needed. Indeed, Youssuf herself suggests that where poverty is such that men are no longer able to fulfil their obligation under Islamic law to support their wife or wives, women are likely to take up work outside the home. However, petty commodity production within the domestic sphere or domestic service, by definition within the domestic sphere, may be the preferred options in these situations (Youssuf, 1974).

As I have already indicated, Boserup regards women's low levels of participation in the 'modern' economic sector as being 'bad' for development as well as 'bad' for women themselves. This is because economic development in areas such as India and Africa, which are characterised by high female participation in the agricultural workforce and low participation rates in the urban workforce, is leading to a reduction in the proportion of the population active in the workforce. In these circumstances families which migrate to the towns are likely to experience a decrease in their levels of economic activity and a decline in their level of living because women will cease to be economically active. This, she argues, has implications for attainable levels of growth and she suggests that the provision of jobs for women in urban areas would aid economic development, provided that measures were taken at the same time to limit rural–urban migration. This could be done by adopting more labour intensive methods in agriculture, thus providing work for a greater number of people and stemming the need to migrate in search of a job. Providing jobs for urban women would help to prevent male migration to towns because there would be fewer jobs available and rural men, in particular, would not be tempted to migrate in search of work. This would ensure a greater supply of labour in rural areas for the labour intensive agriculture which would, thereby, improve the food supply to both rural and urban areas.

Feminists working within the marxist tradition have criticised Boserup for her theoretical approach, for failing to distinguish between capitalist and socialist development, for not giving proper consideration to the social processes which underlie the technical changes affecting gender divisions of labour and for tending to regard 'woman' as a unitary category for whom development, as currently occurring, is negative (B/nería & Sen, 1981; Deere, 1987; Stoler, 1977). Benería and Sen, for instance, argue that capitalist development affects women in different ways depending on pre-existing gender divisions of labour and the socio-economic relations pertaining in particular societies. Thus, in Africa, women's agricultural work may be increased and intensified by capitalist development; in South-east Asia, young migrant women may be recruited into 'world market' factories; in some areas of Latin America, women may be marginalised from agricultural production while, in others, male migration may loosen patri-archal control over women who thereby gain in autonomy (Benería & Sen, 1981: 288–9). The differing ways in which capitalist development affects gender divisions of labour are important and form the bulk of my discussion. First, however, I wish to discuss the other criticisms that have been levelled at Boserup's analysis.

Benería and Sen take Boserup to task for not having a 'clearly defined theoretical framework' (Benería & Sen, 1981: 282) although they suggest the implicit theoretical framework is that of neoclassical economics. They point out that the model of develop-ment she discusses is capitalist, although she does not specify the capitalist nature of the processes she is analysing, and, finally, and most damningly in their eyes, she focuses on women's role in production ignoring their crucial role in reproduction (Benería & Sen, 1981: 282).

Benería and Sen are most critical of Boserup's disregard for women's work within the household. They suggest that 'women's participation in paid production is conditioned by their work in and around the household' (Benería & Sen, 1981: 294) and that women's prior engagement in reproductive or domestic activities conditions their involvement in productive or public activities. This position is similar to those we looked at in Chapter 2 which relate women's subordination to their association with the domestic sphere and explain women's subordinate position in the occupational structures of industrial societies in terms of their prime role as housewives or domestic labourers (Secombe, 1974, 1975; Delphy, 1984; Mies, 1986).

Benería and Sen's advocacy of a focus on women's reproductive work within households raises important issues relating to the status of the concepts of household and reproduction. It is, of course, important to explore gender divisions within domestic units, from both a theoretical and a practical point of view. Theoretically it is important because it is necessary to problematise the relationship between gender divisions at the level of the domestic unit or household and those within the rest of society. It is not possible to assert unproblematically that women's 'productive' activities (whatever they may be) are determined by their 'reproductive' activities. Indeed, many feminists have posited the obverse relationship (Sacks, 1979; Blumberg, 1981; Coontz & Henderson, 1986; Huber, 1991: 39). Much recent feminist analysis has focused on this issue, producing a wealth of empirical data but conflicting evidence on the relation between women's productive and reproductive activities (see, for example, Stichter & Parpart, 1990; Blumberg, 1991; Dwyer & Bruce, 1988). It is important practically because economists and policy-makers have hitherto regarded the household as an entity within which resources are pooled and whose members share common interests (Guyer, 1981; Blumberg, 1991; Dwyer & Bruce, 1988; Jenkins, 1991). Feminists have analysed gender divisions within households and shown that income is not necessarily pooled, interests are not necessarily shared and that intra-household relations may be marked by conflict as often as cooperation and by relations of power which are usually disadvantageous to women and younger household members. Despite such analysis much official policy, in both the Third World and in advanced capitalist societies, assumes a unitary household. Indeed, the assumption of an unproblematic 'household' also finds its way into some feminist analyses (see, for example, Jacobs, 1991; Dennis, 1991). Additionally, it has been pointed out that, although an analysis of gender relations at the domestic level is crucial to understanding women's subordination and to formulating effective development policies, it is questionable whether the concept of 'household' is applicable to all types of society (Guyer, 1981; Guyer & Peters, 1987; Vaughan, 1985; Caplan, 1984; Harris, 1984; Guyer, 1986; Folbre, 1991). This is particularly problematic in the African context when, for instance, polygamy is practised and a man may have more than one wife, each of whom has her own dwelling and cooks for herself and her children and, regularly but not always, for her husband, or in a situation where social groups live in long-houses within which smaller domestic groups cook separately such as occurs in parts of Latin America and South-east Asia (Buenaventura-Posso & Brown, 1980; Heyzer, 1986; Guyer, 1981; Guyer & Peters, 1987).

Reproduction is similarly problematic, not least because there is considerable confusion about what is to be defined as reproductive work or reproduction (Edholm *et al.*, 1977; Harris & Young, 1981). It is often seen as synonymous with domestic labour but it is difficult to see how the domestic labour of women in different societies can be meaningfully compared. The domestic labour of an African woman, for instance, may involve tending to crops and livestock, fetching water and fuel as well as processing food crops, participating in handicraft production, preparing and cooking food, keeping the home clean and looking after children (Etienne, 1980). In parts of India caring for cattle is considered a household activity (Charlton, 1984: 66). The domestic labour of a woman in an advanced industrial society is of a totally different order. It has been suggested that part of the problem with the distinction between reproductive and productive economic activity arises from the development of these concepts to describe the separation of productive and reproductive work within capitalist societies. Productive work is conceptualised as taking place in the public sector for a wage, while reproductive work takes place in the domestic sphere and is unwaged. As Harris and Young argue, reproduction or the work that maintains labourers is not socialised under capitalism. It is therefore not part of social production and is analytically separable from productive work. However, it is problematic to apply these concepts to societies where social production and reproduction may not be separated as is the case in many Third World societies. Thus, although in most societies it is women who are responsible for cooking, providing shelter, servicing and caring for labourers, the social significance of this work may vary considerably. In pre-industrial Europe, for instance, women's involvement in domestic work did not preclude them from other sorts of production which were carried out within the same unit, and this is the case in many Third World societies today. Indeed, it is highly problematic to assume that all the work carried out by women within the domestic sphere is reproductive because it obscures women's crucial contribution to productive activity such as food production or petty commodity production, both of which are vitally important to the economies of Third World societies (Harris & Young, 1981). Moreover, the use of the concept in this way tends to reinforce the association of men with production and women with reproduction and may result in a misleading description of women's economic activities. Finally, there is a definitional problem. Many definitions seem to rest on an equation of reproduction with production of use values rather than exchange values, or simply as subsistence production; that is, work which takes place outside the capital-wage labour relation (Benería, 1982: 129, cited in Chaney, 1987: 195). However, as we have already seen, neither social reproduction nor the reproduction of labour power can simply be equated with the production of use-values, whether this be a result of domestic labour or other subsistence activities. Indeed, much of the work done by men contributes to the reproduction of labour power and does not necessarily take place in the domestic sphere (Mackintosh, 1984; Babb, 1986).

The most cogent criticism of Boserup made by Benería and Sen is not, however, her neglect of the household and women's reproductive labour but her technological determinism and the insufficient attention she pays to the varying social and economic circumstances in which women find themselves and which mediate the effect of capitalist development on women. In addition, a point which they do not make but which is important, Boserup attributes much of the negative impact of development on women to the attitudes of colonial regimes and employers in developing countries. She, thus, infers that gender divisions which disadvantage women were imposed from without and that their origin can be traced back to the advent of colonisation.

GENDER DIVISIONS IN NON-CAPITALIST SOCIETIES

The technological determinism of Boserup's analysis is most apparent when she discusses the impact of the change from farming systems using the hoe to more intensive farming systems using the plough (Benería & Sen, 1981). Boserup observes that these systems are associated with different gender divisions of labour, but she does not offer a satisfactory explanation of why such associations occur. A more detailed discussion of this association, rather than seeing a change in the gender division of labour as emerging from the adoption of new, supposedly heavier, technology, links both changing gender divisions and technological change to changes in the production process.

It is possible to classify non-industrial societies into those based on foraging – that is, hunter-gatherer societies, horticultural societies where shifting cultivation is practised – and those where agriculture is permanent – that is, agrarian societies. Although such a classification is loose and there is considerable variation in social arrangements within each category, ethnographic evidence confirms that there are significant differences in gender divisions of labour and levels of fertility between these different types of society. In foraging societies, examples of which we looked at in Chapter 1, the gender division of labour assigns to women and men different roles in production which are more or less independent of each other. Thus in !Kung society, for instance, men hunt and women gather, women being the primary producers. Women therefore have a great deal of autonomy and control over the means of production and the labour process in which they are engaged and these societies are generally egalitarian. In this sort of society productive activities are not household based and women's labour is not, potentially or actually, controlled by anyone other than themselves (Pine, 1982). Fertility levels are low and births are spaced, the average interval between births being four years, and women normally have two children. These societies are characterised by a considerable amount of leisure, approximately twenty hours a week are spent working, and women's productive activities are compatible with their child-care responsibilities (Blumberg, 1981: 79).

In horticultural societies the separation between male and female spheres of activity is largely maintained, although, as ethnographies show, the production of food and handicrafts may entail a certain reciprocal division of labour between women and men (Etienne, 1980). Women's and men's responsibilities and obligations are, however, clearly defined with women having responsibility for feeding specified kin and having access to land on which to grow food crops. This access may be through patrilocal marriage where a woman has use rights to a plot of land by virtue of having moved to reside with her husband, or it may be that she has ownership rights in land by virtue of her membership of a matrilineal kin group (Coontz & Henderson, 1986; Whitehead, 1985). Women are the dominant labour force in four-fifths of contemporary horticultural societies (Blumberg, 1981: 79). In such societies, as Blumberg points out, women's control over the means of production is highly variable and depends on rules of residence and patterns of inheritance (see Coontz & Henderson, 1986). For instance, in matrilineal matrilocal societies, such as the Iroquois of North America, women retained economic control, whereas in patrilineal patrilocal groups, male kin groups often controlled the economic base while women carried out a large amount of the agricultural production (Albers, 1989; Blumberg, 1981: 80). Fertility levels associated with this type of society are higher than those associated with foraging societies, the birth interval decreases to approximately three years, and the accumulation of a surplus is made possible. Hence, the development in parts of Africa and Latin America of extensive state organisation in hierarchically structured federations of societies which, nevertheless, retained considerable female autonomy and/or rights of inheritance, particularly for women in the higher strata of these societies (Afonja, 1986; Silverblatt, 1980; Okeyo, 1980; Sacks, 1979). Such societies could be defined as emergent agrarian societies but their development was cut short by the advent of colonial expansion (Nash, 1980).

Agrarian societies are characterised by a greater population density than horticultural or foraging societies, greater surplus accumulation, higher levels of fertility and they are based on the plough. They are also stratified and women's status is generally low. Women's role in agricultural production continues to be important but, with the exception of areas dominated by wet-rice production such as South-east Asia, the tasks they undertake are carried out in and around the domestic sphere. Men become responsible for agricultural production and women come to be viewed in terms of their reproductive rather than productive potential. Indeed, women's productive activity becomes invisible because it does not take place in the public sphere. Blumberg notes that although plough cultivation is less labour intensive than hoe cultivation, because a greater area is under cultivation the demand for labour is high. There is, therefore, pressure to have large numbers of children to supply this labour. In agrarian societies fertility levels are higher with birth intervals decreasing to an average of two years.

Agrarian societies are highly stratified. Blumberg suggests that this may be the key to understanding women's low status but does not adequately explore the way in which this relationship operates. Stratification arises from unequal distribution of the main means of production, land. This results in the formation of a class of surplus labour made up of peasants with no access to land. Production is generally household based and the production process is controlled by men, but the resources available to households are highly variable and depend upon their place in the class hierarchy. Blumberg observes that women in the households of élite men are most disadvantaged relative to men of their social class and less likely than other women to be involved in productive activity. It is amongst these classes that practices such as veiling, purdah, foot-binding and suttee (widow-burning) are, or were, most widely observed (Blumberg, 1981: 81; Huber, 1991). The only role open to these women is that of reproducer of heirs whereas in poorer households women's role in production remains important. It has been suggested that female seclusion (and by implication equivalent practices) has a practical significance in wealthier households because it ensures that property is not dispersed, particularly in societies where women are able to inherit. The confinement of women to the household ensures that they will not develop an interest in managing and controlling any property they may have and will have no other option but to hand control of it over to the males of the household (Sharma, 1989).

Religions which support male authority over women are associated with the emergence of agrarian societies. Thus, Islam emerged at a time when nomadic peoples were adopting settled agricultural production, Catholicism retains its strongest hold in societies where patriarchal peasant production predominates, and Confucianism is associated with Chinese feudal society and retains its roots in the peasant household of contemporary China (Croll, 1983; Ahmed, 1986). In regions of wet-rice cultivation, such as South-east Asia, women's participation in agricultural production is important and visible and gender ideologies tend to stress the complementarity of the genders (Errington, 1990; Ong, 1989). Specific types of gender ideology appear to be associated with specific gender divisions of labour and forms of economic organisation.

Agrarian societies differ from horticultural and foraging societies in the control that can be exercised by men over women's labour. Useful here is the distinction between sex-segregated and sex-sequential labour processes. In the former the labour process requires the input of only one gender whereas in the latter women and men are involved at different stages of the same labour process; that is, inputs from both genders are required for the labour process to be completed (Whitehead, 1985). In hunter-gatherer societies the labour process is sex-segregated. In societies which have become sedentary there is a variety of forms moving from almost entirely sex-segregated to labour processes which are sex-sequential. For instance, the Kusasi of North-east Ghana grow millet as their staple crop. Both male and female labour is required for its production although it is men's land on which the millet is grown. Women and men also farm their own plots and control the produce, but it is men who control the produce from the collective or household plots (Whitehead, 1984: 102–4; Trenchard, 1987). All the labour processes, whether carried out on collective or individual plots, require the input of male and female labour and are therefore sex-sequential. The Kusasi follow patrilineal inheritance rules and patrilocal marriage but similar patterns can be observed amongst matrilineal-matrilocal societies. Thus, amongst the Manganja of Southern Malawi the agricultural labour process was sex-sequential but non-agricultural production was sex-segregated, with the men hunting and trading cloth and iron, and women producing and exchanging salt and pottery (Vaughan, 1985: 38). As Whitehead points out, where the labour process is sex-sequential, there is a greater possibility for the emergence of control by one gender of the labour of the other. As we have already seen, this is likely to be male control of female labour in societies which are patrilineal and patrilocal (see Chapter 1). However, because of the mixture of sex-segregated and sex-sequential labour processes which can be observed in horticultural societies, the potential for such control varies and women often enjoy a great deal of independence and autonomy.

In agrarian societies where production is based on the peasant household the agricultural labour process is sex-sequential and under male control. All family members, men, women and children, participate in production although, as we have seen, women's participation may be 'invisible' in that it takes place in the domestic sphere. This was the system of agricultural production pertaining in China and in most other parts of Asia, in feudal Europe and in post-colonial Hispanic America. Women's participation at certain stages of the agricultural production process is required, but it is under male control and men are the ones who prepare the ground for planting using ploughs. Women, in this type of society, have neither control over the labour process nor autonomy, although the work that they do remains essential to the survival of their households and the society in general.

Although Blumberg's observations are important, the precise mechanisms which lead to the transition from horticultural to agrarian society are not adequately analysed. This transition and the accompanying changes in gender divisions of labour are analysed by Carol Ember (1983). She locates the explanation for the changing gender division of labour in changes in the production process. She suggests that the changing nature of the production process increases women's workload in the domestic sphere. This means that they are less available for agricultural tasks which fall increasingly to men. Hence men's monopoly of the more advanced technology is explained by changes in the nature of the labour process attendant upon intensification of crop production.

There are various factors of importance here. The first relates to the nature of the crop grown. In areas of intensive agriculture more time is needed to process crops and prepare food. This is because crops are more likely to be cereal crops and they need far more processing than, for instance, vegetable and root crops and this, in turn, requires more time spent in water and fuel collection (Ember, 1983: 288). In addition these crops require storing and there is likely to be a greater volume of crops to prepare for storage.

Higher fertility levels also mean that women will spend more time in child care. Higher fertility levels may be related to improved diet associated with the nature of the crops grown in areas of settled agriculture, a desire for children to help with agricultural tasks and an associated decrease in post-partum sex taboos (Ember, 1983: 295–6). These conditions seem to pertain in agrarian societies. Ember also argues that men are more available for agricultural work in stratified agrarian societies than in horticultural societies because the social division of labour and increased specialisation mean that tasks such as warfare and trading are undertaken by specialised groups of men rather than all men. Conversely, in horticultural societies women are more available than are men to carry on the basic tasks of agricultural production. Thus Ember links women's apparent decline in status in agrarian societies to the changing nature of the labour process and women's participation in it being located in and around the home. She argues that in societies where women are visible outside the home they are more likely to be able to achieve leadership roles and their status will be higher (Ember, 1983: 300–1).

The change from hoe-based female farming to plough-based male farming thus involves complex changes in the labour process which in turn lead to a gender division of labour in which men have effective control over the labour of women and children. These changes result in men's greater involvement in agricultural production and the use of the plough. The change in technology and changing gender divisions are both related to changes in the relations of production and the labour process. Population growth is associated with these changes but is not causal as is suggested by Boserup. It should be stressed that in agrarian societies women's work does not decrease in any absolute sense, on the contrary, it may increase. It decreases relative to the increased agricultural work of men (Ember, 1983; Boserup, 1989).

With the emergence of highly stratified agrarian societies it is obviously no longer possible to make statements about the gender division of labour which hold true for all strata, although prescriptive gender ideologies may exist which define a 'normal' gender division of labour. Neither is it possible to generalise about the effects of development on women as if women formed a unitary category and shared interests on the basis of their gender. Gender and age are no longer the only categories defining an individual's access to resources; such access is also related to their position in the class structure or system of stratification. And as we have seen, access to and control over resources, particularly productive resources, affect the form taken by gender divisions of labour. It is therefore reasonable to suppose that gender divisions vary between different strata or classes. Similarly, because access to and control over resources are determined by class as well as gender and age, disadvantages of gender or age may be neutralised by advantages of class, or vice versa (Savané, 1986).

Capitalist development, if it takes place in a highly stratified agrarian society, is therefore likely to affect women from different strata in different ways. Thus Stoler argues that, in Java, women from the strata which had access to resources, particularly land, prior to development have been able to benefit from development whereas women, and men, from the poorer strata have seen their access to resources reduced and both have been further disadvantaged by development (Stoler, 1977: 88–9, 1988).

Boserup is not unaware of the variation of gender divisions within stratified societies. Citing a study by S.C. Dubé she describes four social groups in a village in Andhra Pradesh, Southeast India. In the highest status group women observed purdah and the men's work consisted of supervision of those they employed to undertake agricultural work. In the next group was the local 'cultivator caste' where women were occupied in domestic work and men ploughed their own fields. In the third group women assisted men in the fields and also traded in the market; they usually worked as family labour not hiring themselves out unless it was a period of peak demand. In contrast, in the lowest group women and men had to become wage labourers in order to support themselves and their families (Boserup, 1989: 70). However, she does not consider the way in which such variation may mediate the impact of development upon women.

A further point of interest is that Boserup relates these varying gender divisions of labour to the varying cultural traditions within India. This explanation is problematic, both in relation to her own position that economic necessity overrides prescriptive gender ideologies and because similar variations in the gender division of labour can be observed in all class societies, even those such as Morocco where cultural tradition prescribes strict observance of female seclusion (Mernissi, 1975; Maher, 1984). A more plausible explanation relates variations in gender divisions, within a specific culture, to variation in access to resources such as land, labour and other means of production. This access influences the type of work done by women and men and, hence, the gender division of labour. Indeed, recent studies have highlighted the significant effect of class on gender divisions. For instance, in India, Peru and Colombia women's participation in agricultural field production is strongly associated with poverty. Women in better-off rural households are more likely to confine their work to farm-based production or associated domestic activities (Deere, 1987; Deere & León de Leal, 1982; León de Leal & Deere, 1979; Sen, 1982). And, as we have already seen, practices which are restrictive for women are more widely observed in the higher strata of agrarian societies (Blumberg, 1981). Gender divisions therefore vary not only between different societies but within societies and are crucially affected by access to productive resources.

COLONISATION AND THE DEVELOPMENT OF CAPITALISM

Existing advanced industrial societies (socialist and capitalist) emerged from agrarian societies in most of which patriarchal peasant production based on the household prevailed; women's labour was controlled by men; large landowning strata or classes extracted a surplus from the peasantry; and gender ideologies defining women's role as purely reproductive predominated. However, nowhere has this transition taken place without a greater or lesser degree of coercion (Moore, 1967). In sixteenth-century England the landowning classes saw the commercial opportunities presented by the wool trade and enclosures deprived the peasantry of their livelihood, forcing them off the land and into the ranks of the agricultural workforce. This process was termed primitive accumulation by Marx (Marx, 1974). The peasantry, now no longer a peasantry in the strict sense of the term, had to work for wages in order to buy the food that they had previously been able to grow themselves and, in this way, a home market was created, a market for goods produced in capitalist agriculture and industry. In the Third World it was colonial expansion which paved the way for subsequent capitalist development. This is occurring not only in agrarian societies but in those based on shifting agriculture and foraging where women enjoy a relatively high degree of autonomy in the labour process, have independent access to productive resources, and production may be neither household based nor controlled by a male head of household.

Nash has defined the process of development in the Third World as 'a process that displaces rural populations from a given subsistence mode of production (and) that fails to reintegrate people into new forms of employment' (Nash, 1986: 6). In other words it precipitates the simultaneous destruction of pre-capitalist or non-capitalist modes of production and the integration of societies into the capitalist economy. The basic change that occurs is that, instead of production being geared to the production of use-values (production for consumption) with some production of commodities for exchange, commodity production becomes generalised. Thus, instead of people's being able to produce enough food and other subsistence articles to meet their own needs through limited exchange, they are forced to meet their subsistence needs through the cash economy. These processes were set in train by colonial expansion.

From the point of view of the colonising power, the colonies were regarded as both a source of raw materials and a potential market for manufactured goods. The labour force for the extraction of the raw materials or the cultivation of crops for export was to be provided by the indigenous population. To encourage their participation they were required to pay taxes which served as a means both of raising revenue and of forcing their participation in the cash economy. To pay taxes people had to have access to cash, either through selling their labour power or through selling their products. They could not continue to produce and trade in the ways to which they were accustomed.

There are certain measures which the colonial powers adopted in order to obtain control over the indigenous population and which had significant repercussions for gender divisions. These measures were, firstly, the imposition of taxes normally payable by adult men. It was assumed by the colonial powers that men were heads of households and women were dependent upon them; this is why men were taxed rather than women. Secondly, private property in land was introduced. This very often involved giving title to men regardless of the systems of inheritance and patterns of land use which actually obtained. These measures meant that men had to obtain cash to pay taxes either through working for a wage or growing a crop which could be sold; that is, a cash crop which could be exported. Manufactured goods from the colonising power became available, undermining the handicraft production of the indigenous population. The disruption of the indigenous mode of production entailed in these processes gave rise to male control of female labour in societies where it had previously been only latent or non-existent, and to new forms of male control over female labour in societies in which it had previously existed. In this way non-capitalist societies were absorbed into the cash economy and the process of the formal subsumption of labour under capital was set in train (Alavi, 1982: 186). This process did not necessarily imply the destruction of non-capitalist forms of social organisation but simply that these forms were being transformed from within by capitalist production relations. With land reform, which has occurred in many Third World countries, the penetration of agriculture by capital becomes more rapid. It is no longer impeded by forms of land ownership and tenancy that are non-capitalist in nature, and the differentiation of the peasantry and the proletarianisation and pauperisation of a large proportion of the rural population proceeds apace. This process has been accelerated by the introduction of modern technology into agriculture, the most well-known example being the green revolution technology in India and other parts of Asia. This marks the real subsumption of labour under capital (Alavi, 1982: 186).

For Boserup, the process of colonisation and the attitudes of the colonisers are held responsible for women's loss of status in the Third World. The discussion which follows explores the complexity of this process and suggests that an analysis of the social relations and gender divisions of labour which predated colonisation is important in understanding the subsequent transformations in gender divisions and women's status. The rest of this chapter focuses on the effects of colonisation and the resulting absorption of non-capitalist societies into the cash economy. I draw examples mainly from sub-Saharan Africa, as colonial expansion in this region is relatively recent (late nineteenth century) and ethnographic data demonstrate the ways in which colonisation disrupted indigenous gender divisions of labour.

In sub-Saharan Africa the process of colonisation involved the introduction of taxes, the takeover of agriculturally rich land and the associated concentration of the indigenous population into less productive land, the use of migrant male labour to work in mines and plantations, the introduction of cash-crop farming and the introduction of private property in land (Etienne, 1980; Okeyo,

1980; Whitehead, 1984; Afonja, 1981; Vaughan, 1985; Crehan, 1984; Feldman, 1984; Staudt & Col, 1991; Hansen & Ashbaugh, 1991; Awe & Ezumah, 1991). These processes did not all occur in the same places and at the same time. Thus in eastern and southern Africa Europeans confined the indigenous population to reserves and appropriated the most fertile land. Here cash crops were grown on European-owned farms and minerals extracted from European-owned mines by means of male migrant labour. They were paid extremely low wages, a practice which was made possible by women's ability to maintain themselves and their dependants through subsistence activities (Trenchard, 1987: 156; Boserup, 1989; Folbre, 1991). In West Africa, however, particularly the coastal regions, cash-crop production by the indigenous population on their own land was encouraged by the imposition of taxes and labour laws (Trenchard, 1987: 156).

Prior to colonisation land tenure in most African societies was vested in the lineage, and rights to allocate or use land depended on membership of a lineage or kinship group. There was no private property in land. In patrilineal societies it is generally male lineage elders who control the allocation of land amongst members of the patrilineal descent group and women have use rights in land by virtue of marrying into their husband's patrilineage (Trenchard, 1987: 157). In matrilineal societies, on the other hand, men often have to prove themselves worthy of land by working on land belonging to their wives' descent group before any land is allocated to them (Vaughan, 1985). In most societies rights to land use and inheritance were very clearly defined and this affected the gender division of labour and control over the crops grown. For instance, in a patrilineal society such as the Kusasi men and their wife or wives grow millet on a 'collective household plot'. The crop belongs to the male 'household head' and it is his duty to supply this staple to his wives and children (Whitehead, 1984; Trenchard, 1987). Kusasi women have to provide other foods and have their own plots on which they can cultivate crops over which they retain control (Whitehead, 1984). Marriage does not involve a pooling of resources. In matrilineal societies such as the Kaonde in north-western Zambia, although men clear the fields for their wives or other matrikin, the produce belongs to the women who have grown the crop and they control access to it (Crehan, 1984). In both cases the rights and duties of women and men who are married to each other are clearly defined and gender divisions are not shaped by notions of female dependency.

The process of colonisation and capitalist development has transformed the gender division of labour in such societies, undermining the material basis of women's autonomy. Afonja explores this process as it affected the Yoruba of Nigeria, a society often cited as one in which women did, and still do, enjoy a great deal of autonomy and self-determination (Dennis, 1984; Leacock, 1981: 489–50; Johnson, 1986; Afonja, 1990). Pre-colonial Yoruba society was patrilineal, highly stratified, slavery was practised, and the Yoruba were involved in long-distance trade. Agricultural production was marked by a gender division of labour such that men cleared the bush while women and children undertook the tasks of planting and weeding, and were responsible for harvesting, processing and marketing (Afonja, 1981). Although Yoruba society was patrilineal, women were able to achieve positions of political power, and their marketing and trading activities enabled them to form guilds and control market-places. Afonja notes that the increasing involvement of Yoruba society in long-distance trade created opportunities for women's wider participation in trade and the political process which tended to undermine their secondary roles (Afonja, 1986: 152–4). This 'egalitarian trend towards increasing political authority', however, existed within the framework of male control over land and over women's access to land. Colonisation reinforced this control rather than the 'egalitarian trend'.

Afonja argues that the impact of colonialism, despite the strengthening of male domination in general, cannot be seen as entirely negative for Yoruba women. This is because of the stratification of pre-colonial Yoruba societies and the possibilities for female inheritance (Afonja, 1986a). Colonisation and subsequent capitalist development have resulted in some Yoruba women's owning cocoa farms and hiring labour. Women's ownership of land is a result of colonial imposition of individual property rights and has occurred in areas where women were able to inherit prior to colonisation (Afonja, 1981: 310; 1990). Most cocoa production, however, is dominated by men who have an advantage over women cocoa producers in that they are able to mobilise family labour during periods of peak demand as well as relying on hired labour. Thus, women may be involved in cash-crop production both as owners of land and as family labour on their husband's land. At the same time, most women are involved in subsistence farming and trading activities (Afonja, 1981: 309; Spiro, 1987). Their farming activities take place on their husband's farm, if they are married, and if this work is in cash-crop production they are usually remunerated. If this remuneration is in cash they invest it in trade. Wives of cash-crop farmers are therefore at an advantage over wives of subsistence farmers in their ability to engage in successful trading (Afonja, 1981: 310).

Afonja points out that despite the fame of West African women traders men dominate the more lucrative long-distance trade while women trade in items such as food, cloth, pots and so on – items that are produced within the subsistence economy. This gender division means that most women trade items to meet family needs rather than for profit and they continue to dominate the market-place while larger retail establishments are owned by men. Yoruba women's participation in wage-labour, in common with that of most sub-Saharan African women, is lower than that of men (Bujra, 1986: 121). Thus, women continue to fulfil the tasks of feeding and nurturing their families and their participation in productive activities does not differ markedly from the activities they undertook in pre-colonial society, apart from their (usually subordinate) participation in cash-crop production (Afonja, 1981: 313).

In contrast to Boserup, Afonja argues that Yoruba men developed the cash cropping of cocoa and took advantage of the opportunities for increased trade presented to them by colonisation. It was not forced on them by a colonial administration (Afonja, 1981: 310). She argues that women's subordination cannot, therefore, be explained by the imposition of an external and alien ideology as it already existed within Yoruba society, albeit in a different form.

Another example of the way in which colonisation has affected gender divisions is provided by Mona Etienne's analysis of the Baule of the Ivory Coast. This society was characterised by cognatic descent and matrilineal inheritance patterns. Group membership was indeterminate and often depended on women's preferences. Relations between elders and juniors and between women and men were not marked by domination and subordination and there were no mechanisms to ensure male appropriation of women's surplus production. Production was based on a gender division of labour such that the production of some subsistence items was the responsibility of women, some the responsibility of men and others were produced by both women and men. In the former case the producer 'owned' the product and in the latter it was the initiator of the process of production who 'owned' the product but each participant was entitled to a share in the product (Etienne, 1980: 219–20). Land was available to all. Etienne concentrates her analysis on the production of yams and cloth. Yam production was initiated by men and cloth production by women. To a greater extent than yams, cloth was important in ritual and prestige and in long-distance trade. Etienne comments that it served as a 'form of currency and/or commodity' (221). She also comments that the fact that the distribution of this valuable product was allocated to women gave them power and autonomy, both in relation to their husbands and more generally. They were also involved in long-distance trade and there is no reason to suppose that colonisation would automatically have disadvantaged them. However, in the production process itself there 'were possibilities for the man to minimise the woman's control of the product' (222) and these internal contradictions eventually led to women losing control over the production of cloth.

In pre-colonial Baule society a man would prepare the ground on which yams were to be grown, usually for his wife or wives. This meant that the 'yam crop was to feed her and her children, as well as the man, for whom she cooked', that she would do the female tasks on the plot and that she could intercrop between the yam mounds and once the yams were harvested (222). Women always grew cotton as an intercrop as well as condiments, corn, cassava and rice. Cotton production was therefore initiated by the woman but, unlike the other crops which she processed herself, cotton required men to weave and sew it into the finished article. Thus, the woman cleaned, carded and spun the cotton into thread and then passed it over to her husband who wove according to her instructions. He gave her the whole product, part of which she returned to him as the reward for his labour. Etienne posits this reciprocal and interdependent gender division of labour as the norm from which there was a possibility of deviation. This could happen if a woman did not produce enough cotton for her husband to weave or produced too much. If she did not produce enough a man who was a good weaver could obtain supplies of cotton from women to whom they were not married. This placed a man in a position which he could use to his advantage because women with surplus cotton or without a man to weave for them needed him to obtain their cloth. And the fact that it was men who produced the finished product could also be used to their advantage. Women could also benefit from this imbalance but the position of men in the process of production gave them an edge over women (224).

The opportunity for male advancement came with the changes brought about by colonialism and enabled capitalist production relations to penetrate the pre-colonial mode of production. This happened because manufactured goods became available and enabled male weavers to purchase factory-made thread. This freed them from dependence on their wives and made women seem redundant to the production of cloth. Secondly, cotton became a cash crop produced by the Baule who were forced to do so by the colonial administration. Cash-crop cotton was grown the year after yams on the same plot, a right which had previously been granted to women. However, male preparation of the ground created ambiguities about who 'owned' the product, and this, coupled with colonial assumptions about men being the head of household and the farmer and therefore responsible for paying taxes and for adopting new agricultural techniques, led to the cash crop becoming a man's crop. Additionally, forced labour had been used by the colonists to produce cotton on 'collective fields'. So cash became necessary for men to pay taxes and they obtained it through cotton production. This, in turn, enabled them to buy thread from the nearby factory.

Other crops also became 'male' cash crops and because women need men's cash income they continue to fulfil their 'conjugal obligation to assist a spouse'. They, therefore, work on their husband's fields and receive, in turn, a share of the profits. This is because the principle of remuneration for their labour still operates (228). However, women are dependent upon men for their reward and this dependence is a new aspect of the gender division of labour. Women continue to grow subsistence crops and may also produce a surplus of 'women's' crops which can be traded. But their workload has been increased because as well as continuing with subsistence activities they also work in the cash-crop sector where their labour is controlled by men. And the relationship of interdependency between women and men in the marriage relationship has been replaced by one of dependency (Etienne, 1980: 232). The integration of Baule society into the cash economy has transformed the nature of the gender division of labour and has eroded women's control over the products of their labour while enhancing the control of men, not only over the products of their own labour but also over the products of their wives' labour and even the *labour* of their wives.

These examples indicate that contradictions internal to pre-colonial societies were exploited by the external forces of colonialism and that transformations in gender divisions of labour were not simply the result of the attitudes and assumptions of male colonialists. They also suggest that an important effect of colonisation was to increase or introduce the possibility of men's control over women's labour. Such control is likely to result in the subordination of women. Similar processes occurred during colonisation in North and South America (Silverblatt, 1980; Nash, 1980; Albers, 1989: 144).

It is hazardous to generalise about the numerous and diverse societies which existed in pre-colonial sub-Saharan Africa. However, in most societies there seems to have been a strict allocation of responsibilities between marriage partners, such that women's obligations were to feed their children and husbands and men's were to clear land on which their wives could grow food crops. Nowadays, men are also expected to contribute towards clothing and educating their children. There was no obligation that men should provide food for their children; this was clearly a woman's responsibility (Trenchard, 1987; Whitehead, 1984, 1985; Guyer, 1986; Robertson, 1987; Crehan, 1984; Ventura-Dias, 1985; Jacobs, 1991). The introduction of a cash economy and men's participation in it, either through growing cash crops or through wage-labour, often involving migration, gave men access to cash but, because of the separate responsibility of husband and wife, this did not mean that it would be shared with their wives or used to feed their children. Feeding children has remained the responsibility of women who have to meet their needs with access to fewer resources than previously and with limited access to cash. Their decreased access to resources is largely due to insufficient land, many women have lost their use rights in land as a result of the introduction of individual private property in land. This was introduced by the colonists and usually vested land ownership in the male 'head of household' (Okeyo, 1980). This meant that land could be bought and sold and the most productive land was turned over to cash-crop production. Subsistence production was often confined to poorer land which resulted in lower productivity. Land shortage also became a problem, particularly in areas where the indigenous population was confined to reserves and soil has become exhausted. The reserves of South Africa and parts of Zimbabwe are cases in point.

In order to obtain access to cash women have to trade their products and, in some cases, work for their husbands. This latter option is very unreliable as women are often under-remunerated by their husbands and many women either do not have husbands or have husbands who are not cash-crop farmers (Guyer, 1988). Thus, while men's access to cash is mainly through cash cropping and/or wage-labour, women's access to cash is mainly through trading. In many parts of Africa women's trading activities have increased with the transformations brought about by capitalist development because subsistence needs can no longer be met without access to cash. In addition, tasks such as fetching water and fuel have become more onerous for women as they can no longer rely on the assistance of their children who are now expected to be in school. These changes have led many to argue that women's workload has intensified with the development of capitalist relations within agriculture (Agarwal, 1985; Boserup, 1989).

The development of capitalism in agriculture in sub-Saharan Africa is creating an impoverished mass of subsistence producers on the one hand, amongst whom women are overrepresented, and peasant farmers on the other who, by producing cash crops as well as subsistence crops and relying on family labour, are managing to survive. There are, of course, also the capitalist farmers, often descendants of European settlers as in Zimbabwe (Jacobs, 1984, 1991). The effects of capitalist development on the indigenous population has not been uniform. Thus, in South Africa the male African population supplied labour for the mines and other industrial enterprises while African women, children and older people were confined to the reserves supposedly to farm. The population density in the reserves was too high for the land to support them and African women have also been forced to seek employment in the urban areas. This has resulted in many of them taking up domestic service in white households. Few African women are employed in industry (Gaitzkell *et al.*, 1984).

In other parts of sub-Saharan Africa colonialism and capitalist penetration have permitted sectors of the indigenous population to take advantage of opportunities presented to them by the increase in trade. This clearly happened amongst the Yoruba where cash cropping and private ownership of land have enabled some women and men (albeit far more men than women) to prosper. Thus one effect of capitalist penetration of agriculture in Africa is that stratification within the rural population has developed and/or become more marked and a relative surplus population has been created. The resultant impoverishment and loss of land has led to migration to urban areas. Male migration occurred during the colonial period and is still more extensive than female migration. This has resulted in a situation where between a quarter and a third of rural 'households' are headed by women (Folbre, 1991: 105). There are few jobs for women in the so-called formal sector and if they move to urban areas they generally continue in trading activities or petty commodity production within their homes. They may also be able to find employment as domestic servants, although this is often difficult for women who have children as they often have to live in, or they may resort to prostitution. Men are also to be found in the 'informal' sector in petty commodity production and trading, but they are more likely than women to be able to find employment in the 'formal' sector (Pine, 1982; Dennis, 1984, 1991, 1991a).

Thus the effect of colonialism and the subsequent penetration of capitalism on gender divisions and women's status can be summarised as follows. In pre-colonial societies women and men gained access to land, the most important means of production, through marriage or by virtue of being a son or daughter of a particular kin group. Even in patrilineal societies women were guaranteed access to this crucial means of production which was held in common by the lineage although such access was through men. With the imposition of individual ownership of land, women have often lost their rights to land. Most frequently individual men now own land, although some women also do (Caplan, 1984; Afonja, 1981), and to survive women and men have to enter into capitalist relations of production either through petty commodity production and trading or through cash-crop production and wage-labour. Previously for production to be possible, the lineage was required to distribute land, and women and men, through marriage and other kinship relations, co-operated to produce what was necessary for survival and for social reproduction. Now the lineage is no longer significant. Land can be bought and sold and, in order to survive, women and men have to participate in the cash economy. Thus, although forms of kinship and the gender division of labour may appear to have survived and similar labour processes might be undertaken – that is, men may still prepare land on which women or women and men will grow the staple crop – the social relations which govern these processes have changed.

Pre-existing gender divisions of labour have been transformed even in areas where societies were matrilineal and/or matrilocal. Women and men may still perform similar activities in the labour process but, as we have seen, women are now dependent upon men in ways that they were not previously. This is because men have access to women's labour in ways that women do not have access to men's labour (Roberts, 1988). Men's ability to control women's labour has emerged from the contradictions inherent in the nature of reciprocal obligations between women and men under previous modes of production, together with the imposition of taxes and forced labour on male 'heads of household' by the colonial powers. Thus, women's work on their husband's land may *appear* to be the same as previously but it is now part of the capitalist sector and women are providing under or unpaid labour which, rather than ensuring that she and her children have access to the staple crop and have adequate food, ensures that her husband has access to cash which may not benefit her and her children at all. Thus, the pre-existing gender division of labour ensures that women and men enter the capitalist sector in different ways. As we have seen, men are more likely than women to be wage labourers or to produce cash crops while women are more likely than men to work in the cash-crop sector as unpaid or badly paid labourers or to derive a small income from trading and/or petty commodity production. In addition to this they continue to farm their plots, the produce of which can be traded or exchanged for items of subsistence or consumed directly by themselves and their children. It is significant that where Muslim marriage is practised many women are said to prefer it to traditional marriage. The former obliges men to support their wives and children while the latter assumes that women will support themselves. With the undermining of pre-capitalist modes of production this much-vaunted autonomy and self-reliance has meant a radically increased workload for women. In this context, it is easy to see how a guaranteed source of support from a man, even with its attendant loss of independence, may not be unwelcome (Longhurst, 1982).

From the evidence presented here it seems clear that colonial pressure and assumptions about male heads of households cannot be held entirely to blame for the way in which gender divisions have changed. Clearly, many African societies were strongly patrilineal and women were regarded, in terms of gender ideology, as in the charge of men before the advent of colonialism (Robertson, 1987). In others, men's potential or actual control over female labour in non-capitalist modes of production gave them an advantage once capitalist penetration of agriculture occurred, an advantage which was often accentuated and accelerated by the introduction of individual male ownership of land and taxes to be paid by male 'heads of households' (Etienne, 1980). In societies which were matrilineal and/or matrilocal external pressures were often more significant but also the process of transformation in relations between the genders often took a considerable length of time (Vaughan, 1985). In both cases the development of capitalism is undermining the material basis of women's autonomy by destroying the non-capitalist modes of production of which it was part. Boserup is right, therefore, to point to colonialism as having deleterious effects upon women. It does this specifically by disrupting pre-existing modes of production. This disruption enables men to gain control over female labour and introduces female dependency upon men, thus reducing women's independent access to productive resources and, hence, their autonomy.

/ 7 /

ECONOMIC DEVELOPMENT AND
WOMEN'S SUBORDINATION

In the previous chapter I argued that in order to understand fully
the effects of colonisation and the resulting transformations in
gender divisions it is important to take into account the type of
society which existed prior to the colonial period. Sub-Saharan
Africa was typified by horticultural societies in which female
farming predominated. Colonisation and capitalist penetration of
such societies has deleterious effects on the majority of women,
reducing their autonomy and increasing their workload. In this
chapter I wish to focus on the effects that the development of
capitalist agriculture and industrialisation have on gender divisions. In particular I shall focus on the question of whether
economic development reinforces or undermines male authority
over women. In the case of sub-Saharan Africa it seems clear that
it reinforces and even creates it. In other societies where colonisation occurred much earlier, as in Latin America, or which were
highly stratified and agrarian prior to capitalist penetration, the
effects of capitalist development on gender divisions may not be so
clear cut.

THE DEVELOPMENT OF CAPITALISM IN AGRICULTURE

Latin America is characterised by Boserup as a region of 'male
farming' although more recent research suggests that it would be
more accurate to refer to it as a region of family farming (Deere &
León, 1987: 3). During the sixteenth and seventeenth centuries,
indigenous modes of production were disrupted and various

191

relations of production (ranging from slave to semi-feudal semi-capitalist) were forcibly imposed on the indigenous population.

The effect of the colonial period was to create a rural social structure which had a great deal in common with European feudalism, where large landowners extracted surplus from a peasantry (which was either bonded or free) and where the unit of production and consumption amongst the peasantry was the household. Indigenous forms of production persisted for considerable lengths of time in more inaccessible areas (Buenaventura-Posso & Brown, 1980).

Capitalisation of agriculture and industrialisation have a much longer history in Latin America than in Africa and they have affected women differently and differentially. In rural areas the penetration of capitalist relations has resulted in the differentiation of the peasantry and, for poor peasants, the undermining of household production and the impoverishment and proletarianisation of large sections of the rural population. This has had a contradictory impact on gender divisions of labour, depending upon the position of individuals and households in the class structure. In order to explore this I discuss various studies which show, firstly, that gender divisions of labour vary with class and, secondly, that the continual undermining of subsistence production is leading not only to male migration, as in sub-Saharan Africa, but also to the migration of women (Young, 1982; Deere & León de Leal, 1982; Deere, 1987; de los Angeles Crummett, 1987). I shall also assess the extent to which capitalist development in agriculture reinforces or undermines male control over female labour.

Boserup asserts that women do very little agricultural field work in Latin America, particularly when compared with women in sub-Saharan Africa. However, Deere has shown that the amount of work contributed by women to agricultural production, particularly in the non-wage sector, is consistently and considerably underenumerated in Latin American censuses. For instance, Peruvian census data show that the proportion of women economically active in agricultural production has declined from 19% in 1940 to 7.3% in 1961 to 3.8% in 1972 (Deere, 1987: 200). Deere points out that the questions asked in each census differed – in the 1940 census people were asked to describe the various 'income-generating activities' in which they were engaged whereas in the latter two they were asked their 'principal occupation'. Consequently most rural women are listed as housewives (Deere, 1987: 200). Deere also points out that in the 1961 and 1972 censuses time limits entered into the classification of occupation. Thus the 1961 census required that to be considered economically active a person had to have engaged in their occupation for at least one third of a 'normal working day' during the week before the census and in the 1972 census this qualification became fifteen hours (Deere, 1987: 201). These time limits were applied to the category unpaid farm worker, a category which includes a very large number of women. Women's agricultural work is often seasonal and they, or their husbands, are often likely to describe their main occupation as housewife, they will therefore be classified as economically inactive when in fact they are not (Deere, 1987; Deere & León de Leal, 1982).

This underenumeration of women's economic activity is not confined to rural production nor to Latin America but is a problem which is widespread throughout the Third World and is officially recognised (Benería, 1982; Rogers, 1980; ILO, 1991). It particularly affects women because they are more likely than men to be working within the domestic sphere either in agricultural work or in handicraft production, or in the informal sector where their trading activities, for instance, may be sporadic. The categories developed for census taking are those appropriate to formal industrial employment and lead to systematic underestimation of women's productive activities. For instance, it is argued that censuses underenumerated women's productive activities during the nineteenth century in Britain and, due to the way in which economic activity is defined, currently exclude much of the work undertaken by domestic labourers in the home (Benería, 1982; de Lattes & Wainerman, 1986). Thus, drawing conclusions about women's economic activity rates from official statistics often produces unreliable data with a consistent underestimation of women's productive activity.

In Peru, Deere found, in opposition to data derived from the 1972 census, that in the department of Cajamarca, even when using a 'restricted definition' of agricultural field work, women contributed '21 percent of the total number of agricultural labour days employed on peasant agricultural units' (Deere, 1987: 202). This compares with the 1972 census figure of 3.8%. However, she goes on to argue that women's participation in agricultural field work varies with the rural class structure.

In Cajamarca 71.3% of the landholdings are insufficient to support a family, 18.5% can be regarded as middle peasant holdings and 2.6% are large landholdings. Thus there is a very unequal access to the main means of production – land. Clearly in peasant households whose landholdings are insufficient to support a family it is likely that one or more members of the household will have to enter the labour market in order to meet subsistence needs. Also the use of family labour is more likely to characterise the poorer peasant households while the richer ones will be able to hire labour (Deere, 1987: 204). The ability to hire labour enables women in better-off households to withdraw from agricultural field work (Deere, 1987: 212).

The gender division of labour is most clearly demarcated in the middle peasant and rich peasant households where it 'is not considered proper for women to participate in a good number of agricultural tasks', particularly those defined as male, whereas women from poor peasant households both make a greater contribution to family labour *and* perform a greater variety of agricultural tasks than do other rural women (Deere, 1987: 206). Deere relates this to rural poverty and to male participation in wage-labour. In poor peasant households men are likely to hire themselves out as wage-labour leaving women to take over the farm work for which men are no longer available. She also argues that, as far as decision-making is concerned, male dominance marks middle and rich peasant households, whereas in poor peasant households women's participation is higher. This suggests that male authority and control over women may be less in such households. However, as Deere points out, in poor peasant and landless households agricultural work, much of which is done by women, is likely to be far less important as an income-generating activity than in middle and rich peasant households; wage work, either in urban areas or for middle and rich peasants and usually performed by men, becomes more significant.

In another study Deere and León de Leal compare gender divisions of labour in three areas characterised by different levels of capitalist penetration of agriculture. In all areas proletarianisation is taking place but its extent varies. Thus, in El Espinal (Colombia) it is most widespread, with 90% of peasant households containing one or more labour market participants while in Garcia Rovira (Colombia) only 20% of peasant households are in this situation (Deere & León de Leal, 1982: 66). They characterise Garcia Rovira as 'non-capitalist' despite its participation in the cash economy through the production of tobacco as the main crop. This is because the majority of peasant households are independent producers and sharecropping (a feudal form of rent) is common. El Espinal is characterised by large capitalist farms and a peasantry concentrated on the least productive land therefore forced to sell their labour power. The third area, Cajamarca (Peru) is characterised by a modern dairy sector and a smallholding sector.

They find that in the least capitalist region women's participation in field work and marketing is low but in the other agricultural activities, processing crops, agricultural servicing and caring for animals, their participation is high. In the most capitalist region women are engaged in a wider range of agricultural activities but to a much lesser extent, and in the 'predominantly' capitalist region they are employed in all agricultural tasks including field work and marketing (Deere & León de Leal, 1982: 70–1). They conclude that increased capitalist development tends to break down rigid gender divisions which traditionally confined women to processing activities within the domestic sphere and left field work and marketing, both public activities, to men.

Their data also show that women's participation in agricultural field work increases with capitalist penetration of agriculture but that they are significant as family labourers rather than as hired labour. This is related to the differentiation of the peasantry and, as in the previous study, women are more likely to participate in field work if they are in poor peasant households. Thus they conclude that capitalist development in agriculture, because it impoverishes households, forcing their male members to seek employment in the capitalist sector and their female members to take over 'male' tasks, undermines the gender division of labour and male authority over women. Indeed, men's and women's participation in wage-labour is highest amongst the poor and landless sectors of the peasantry although men are more likely to participate in wage labour than women. The type of employment they find also differs, with men working in the local industries and as permanent agricultural labourers while women, although they are employed in the textile industry, are more likely to be found working as domestic servants, cooks, laundry workers, etc. and their pay is lower than that of men (Deere & León de Leal, 1982).

This study shows how the gender division of labour in peasant households is affected by developing capitalist relations of production. In the better-off peasant households capitalist development does not affect the gender division of labour, women remain subordinate to their husbands, carrying out their agricultural work within the domestic sphere. It is only in households which experience proletarianisation that the gender division of labour changes, giving women a wider range of agricultural tasks to perform and transforming some of them into wage labourers as well. Their husbands move into wage-labour and therefore perform less agricultural work. In addition women's position in wage work is subordinate to that of men in terms of wages and, as we shall see, in terms of the types of jobs in which they are employed. Thus a transformed gender division of labour is created by capitalism because it undermines the material basis of the poor peasant household and removes women, by enabling their participation in wage work, from labour processes which are controlled by their husbands.

Kate Young focuses on a similar process of proletarianisation or, as she puts it, the creation of a relative surplus population in the Mexican highlands near Oaxaca (Young, 1982). This region was relatively isolated and, until the mid 1930s, its economy was not monetised. This does not mean, however, that it had been totally unaffected by capitalist development in the region, for although money was not a medium of exchange, coffee, a regional cash crop, was bartered for manufactured goods, and coffee and pitchpine served as media of exchange (Young, 1978: 138). Penetration of capitalism into the regional economy was accelerated after the 1930s by the introduction of taxes which led villagers in the more isolated regions to begin producing coffee as a cash crop. Those whose land was not suitable for coffee had to sell their labour power. These changes resulted in stratification, with the development of a commercial class which hired labour. Sandwiched between the commercial class and the hired labourers were those households (a majority) who produced for subsistence and for exchange but neither hired labour nor worked regularly for wages. A slump in coffee prices in the mid 1950s coupled with the continued need for cash and the lack of opportunities for earning it led to outmigration, both seasonal and permanent. A man who was married with several children was the typical seasonal migrant whereas the typical permanent migrant was a young woman under twenty years of age.

The outmigration of young women occurred because they had, in effect, been made redundant by the penetration of their society by capitalist economic relations. Prior to the introduction of coffee into the region in the late nineteenth century, maize had been the staple crop and cotton had been produced by the peasant women (Young, 1978). This production was undermined by the introduction of manufactured cloth and cash cropping of coffee. The advent of manufactured goods reduced women's productive work in the household and, rather than engage in 'male' agricultural labour or in 'male' village administration, the option of outmigration was adopted. Young suggests that this happened because agricultural labour and village administration were 'defining features of maleness' and define a man's authority as head of household; and, secondly, because women did not have the necessary skills to participate in agricultural labour. Thus, men continued to carry the burden of subsistence production while women's productive activities were undermined by the availability of manufactured goods. There was thus pressure on young men to remain in the village to carry on agricultural production while young women had been made redundant and there were plenty of opportunities for their employment in towns as domestic servants. Young argues that this process occurred as a result of capitalist penetration of a rural, subsistence economy which broke the reproductive cycle and created a relative surplus population (Young, 1982: 171). Young women rather than older women with children or men can be spared from the household economy and therefore migrate to towns in search of employment. Kinship ties remain important and sending household members to earn money away from home, some of which they will contribute to the household, is often conceptualised as part of a household survival strategy. Similar strategies were employed by peasant households during the nineteenth century in Britain and France (Tilly & Scott, 1987).

It is important to beware of using uncritically the notion of 'household strategy' employed by Young (1982), Tilly and Scott

(1987) and many other writers. As we saw in Chapter 2, recent feminist research has shown that conceptualising the household as a unit with unitary interests is problematic. The notion of a household survival strategy has similar drawbacks because of its implicit assumption that members of households have shared goals (Dwyer & Bruce, 1988; Wolf, 1990, 1991; Sen, 1990; Blumberg, 1991). Households, it is argued, should rather be conceptualised as a collection of individuals involved in processes of negotiation and conflict, many of which centre on women's attempts to ensure that they have the means to feed their children. This may involve subsistence farming and trading, working on their husband's fields for remuneration (as in parts of Africa) or insisting on men's handing over their wage (Fapohunda, 1988; Roldán, 1988; Guyer, 1988; Folbre, 1988). Assuming that individual interests can be clearly demarcated within households is, however, also problematic and relies on 'another set of economic terms' (Wolf, 1990: 67; Sen, 1990: 131; Salaff, 1990: 131; Sharma, 1990: 242). It may be more accurate to acknowledge that groups of individuals within households pursue both individual and household strategies and that these may be in conflict with each other but equally may not. This type of approach is adopted by Papanek and Schwede in a study of Indonesian women and seems more fruitful than assuming either that household members share a strategy or that, as individuals pursuing individual strategies, they are always in conflict (Papanek & Schwede, 1988). Indeed, the assumption of a shared strategy begs the question of relations of power and domination within households (Wolf, 1990, 1991).

What these studies show is that although capitalist development in agriculture undermines pre-existing gender divisions of labour it does not necessarily undermine them in the same way. In one case, women participate in 'men's' agricultural work but in the other they do not; gender ideology and the separation of male and female tasks is not challenged because young women are sent into urban areas to do work which is regarded as 'feminine'. However, a move out of the patriarchal peasant household might provide an opportunity for the undermining of patriarchal familial authority, although if young women go into domestic service they are simply substituting the authority of one male household head for another. Thus, although capitalist development may change the *form* taken by the gender division of labour, Young's study illustrates that women's subordination is maintained. This contrasts with Deere and León de Leal who suggest that proletarianisation and poverty are likely to undermine male authority. Clearly the processes involved are complex and although capitalism 'loosens all ties' they seem to be reconstituted with remarkable rapidity in new contexts. Thus the setting free of the rural population, which marks the period of primitive accumulation, results in a movement of population to urban areas. A movement which in Latin America consists of more women than men although previously, as currently in Africa, migration was more common amongst men.

There are similar processes of differentiation of the peasantry: proletarianisation and pauperisation of poor peasants; displacement of agricultural workers through the development of capitalism and the introduction of new technology; and migration from rural to urban areas occurring in South and South-east Asia (Heyzer, 1982, 1986; Agarwal, 1985; Sen, 1982; Stoler, 1988). Two studies from India demonstrate this and describe the effects of capitalist development on women's subordination.

Much of Asia differs from Latin America because of the practice of female seclusion. This particular aspect of the gender division of labour is not necessarily undermined by capitalist development and may take on particularly exploitative forms. In India, for instance, it is customary for men to have a duty to support their wives and children. In some areas capitalist development in the countryside has resulted in male unemployment and women, prevented from going out of the home to work, have become the main source of household income. This has not led to any weakening of traditional male–female authority patterns, however, but has given men control over the income that their wives earn.

Maria Mies studied this process amongst the lacemakers of Narsapur in Andhra Pradesh, India. Women in this region were originally taught lacemaking by missionaries in the nineteenth century, but with the development of capitalist farming in the district and an increased demand for the lace in the 1970s the lacemaking industry expanded. The industry's importance to Andhra Pradesh is indicated by the fact that 95% of its foreign exchange earnings comes from the lace industry of Narsapur. The lace is exported. Most of the exporters were previously middle level or rich peasants who benefited from the green revolution and wished to invest their surplus in business. The lacemakers are women from landless or poor peasant households, usually belonging to the same caste as the exporters. Lacemaking is organised as a putting out system with girls and women making lace in their own homes. They are paid piecework rates by middlemen who also provide them with thread. The pay is very low, under one third of the official minimum wage for agricultural workers, but the women and the exporters regard the women as housewives rather than workers. This is despite the fact that many of them are actually the sole earners in the household. These women are also officially invisible as workers. Although between 150,000 and 200,000 of them are making lace in their homes they are not recorded in the census. Mies analyses the intricacies of caste, class and gender divisions which lead to a situation in which men in poor households of the Kapu caste trade the lace made by their wives and, hence, control the product of their wives' labour, while women of the Harijan or untouchable caste, *if* they have employment in agricultural labour, are earning far more than the lacemaking women who look down upon them (Mies, 1982). Mies' argument is that capitalist penetration of agriculture and of the lacemaking intensifies male control of women's labour and requires their domestication.

In contrast, Sen, in her study of the impact of land reform and the green revolution on female workers from poor peasant and landless labourer households in Haryana/Punjab and Thanjavur, argues that capitalist penetration of agriculture may modify or undermine patriarchal control (Sen, 1982).

Haryana/Punjab is a wheat growing area in North-west India with a high proportion of farmers owning their land as opposed to renting it. It is a region where women do little field work although in poorer households women's participation is higher. It should be remembered that although women do little field work, this does not mean they are not making considerable and essential contributions to agricultural production. The introduction of land reform and new technology has created a demand for agricultural labour. In the 'backward' regions this is filled by women and men from landless labour households, whereas in the more 'advanced' regions women from cultivator households undertake this work. This is explained by the fact that some cultivator households may need extra income in order to be able to afford new technology or to supplement an insufficient income from the farm. Women's employment in agricultural labour brings in extra income while the men remain working on their own farms.

In Thanjavur, characterised by large landowners plus a class of landless labourers and peasant smallholdings, women have traditionally worked in the fields both on family farms and as hired labour. Land reform and the introduction of green revolution technology has increased the number of landless labourers which creates greater competition for jobs and women are losing their jobs to men. Thus, in one area female participation in wage-labour has increased while in the other it has decreased. The overall effect is that female participation in wage-labour in the two regions has become similar, but the impoverishment in the area with a high labour surplus is greater (Sen, 1982). It is not clear how this development may undermine patriarchal gender divisions unless, as Deere argued for Peru and Colombia, the fact that in one region women are working outside the home whereas they were not before, and in the other men are taking over 'women's' jobs, indicates an increased flexibility in the gender division of labour. Sen's conclusions are tentative, suggesting that processes of proletarianisation *may* undermine patriarchal control rather than demonstrating that this is indeed what is happening.

CAPITALIST INDUSTRIALISATION

Thus far we have considered the effects on gender divisions of capitalist penetration of agriculture and it is now appropriate to turn our attention to capitalist industrialisation. As we have seen, one of the effects of the development of capitalism in agriculture is to displace large sectors of the rural population which then have to seek alternative ways of making a living. However, in most Third World societies, the development of the capitalist industrial sector has provided relatively few jobs because, until relatively recently, industrialisation strategies have been based on import substitution. This means that goods which had previously been imported from abroad, such as cars, began to be manufactured in Third World countries often under licence from foreign companies. These industries were usually capital intensive thus creating few jobs, and the jobs they did create were considered skilled and appropriate for men rather than women. Industrialisation strategies began to change in the 1950s and 1960s from import substitution to export-oriented industrialisation (Stichter, 1990; Pearson, 1992; Ríos, 1990). This involves labour-intensive assembly operations in the textile, garment and electronics industries and, more recently, data processing. These sorts of jobs are regarded as suitable for women because they are repetitive and require manual dexterity, an attribute that women 'naturally' have (for a critique of this view see Elson & Pearson, 1981) and this type of industry has therefore provided low-paid, unskilled jobs for women in the 'modern', manufacturing sector (Pearson, 1991, 1992).

Much attention has been focused on women's work in the export processing sector although only a minority of Third World women are involved. This disproportionate interest arises because women's involvement in factory production is, according to modernisation theory, a measure of their integration into the modernisation process; and, according to marxism, women's participation in social production, of which wage-labour is taken to be the archetype, is a precondition for their emancipation. The effect of Third World women's factory work on gender divisions has therefore been explored in greater depth than the effect of other forms of economic activity and to an extent which is out of proportion to its actual occurrence (Lim, 1990).

Women's official economic activity rates have increased over the last forty years in all regions of the Third World with the exception of Africa (Stichter, 1990; Chinery-Hesse, 1989: 36). This is due partly to the advent of export-led industrialisation but also to the expansion of the service sector which provides the type of jobs regarded as suitable for women. This is particularly marked in Latin America where 70% of the economically active female population works in the service sector (Chinery-Hesse, 1989: 38; Safa, 1981, 1986, 1990; Schminck, 1986; Nash, 1983, 1986; Scott, 1986; Arizpe & Aranda, 1981; Chinchilla, 1977; Nash & Fernandez-Kelly, 1983; Stichter, 1990; Ríos, 1990). This contrasts with 24% of economically active women in Asia and 20% in Africa (Chinery-Hesse, 1989: 38).

However, much of women's economic activity is officially invisible precisely because it takes place within the home and is often interspersed with domestic labour and household tasks (Feldman, 1991). Despite its official invisibility it is vital for the survival of women and their children and is often the only means of survival for many Third World households (Folbre, 1991). In Latin America and the Caribbean, for instance, high levels of male unemployment coupled with migration in search of work have led to large numbers of female-headed households in both rural and urban areas. The incidence of female-headed households varies within the region, being lower in South America than in Central America and the Caribbean (15% compared with 20%) (Agarwal, 1985). This has led to women forming households with other women rather than men, enabling them to share the burden of child care with others and to benefit from more than one income generator in a household (Safa, 1981; Bolles, 1986). Such households are overrepresented amongst low income households.

The nature of women's work and income-generating activities in the informal sector varies widely but, to a greater extent than men's, is unskilled, low paid and insecure (Scott, 1991). These activities include petty commodity production, trading, street-selling, domestic service and prostitution (Arizpe, 1977; Jelin, 1977; Nash, 1989: 238; Bunster & Chaney, 1989; Feldman, 1991). Informal economic activity also includes work that is part of the capitalist production process such as outwork, homework and various forms of subcontracting from capitalist enterprises to small, often family-based, enterprises (Feldman, 1991; Pearson, 1992). This informalisation of capitalist production processes in, for example, the garment industry, and reliance on subcontracting to small, unregulated enterprises often relying on female family labour, is part of a global economic restructuring and affects labour markets in advanced capitalist countries as well as in the Third World (Redclift & Mingione, 1985; Phizacklea, 1990). It is the labour-intensive parts of the production process that are 'informalised' thus reducing labour costs and overheads for the capitalist enterprise.

Studies of women's economic activity in the informal sector are scarce despite its importance both for the survival of women and their families and for the formal economy. Studies of the informal sector in Lima, Peru, for instance, show that it provides almost half the total employment for women and men and almost half of all working women are to be found in this sector (Scott, 1991; Bunster & Chaney, 1989). Indeed, women are overrepresented in the informal sector which, like the formal sector, is characterised by gender segregation of occupations (Humphrey, 1988; Stichter,

1990). Thus men monopolise the skilled and better remunerated activities in both sectors of the economy (Scott, 1991; Dennis, 1991; Feldman, 1991).

The under-representation of women in the formal sector and their confinement to the least skilled and lowest paid jobs has been taken as evidence of their 'marginalisation' from the process of industrialisation and modernisation (Boserup, 1989; Saffioti, 1978, 1986). However, this view has been criticised by those who argue that the informal sector itself is not marginal to capitalist industrialisation but provides the formal sector with essential goods and services; and, in addition, many informal sector activities are an integral part of the capitalist production process. Women's informal economic activity is therefore essential to the functioning of both the informal and formal sectors of the economy (Scott, 1986, 1990, 1991; Feldman, 1991).

The nature of women's work in the informal sector is illustrated by two studies of Andean women. One focuses on women in La Paz, Bolivia, who engage in petty commodity production (Buechler, 1986), the other looks at Andean market women in the city of Huaraz, the commercial and administrative centre of the Peruvian department of Ancash (Babb, 1986).

In Huaraz the main economic activity of women, given the domination of available wage work by men, is petty commerce. Babb notes that households often have members engaged in wage-labour, subsistence farming and petty production and commerce in order to survive. Women take to market articles that they can make in their homes, such as cooked food, drinks, knitted clothes, or that they can grow, such as fruit and vegetables. The time that is spent selling in the market is very flexible and children can be taken care of at the same time (Babb, 1986). Petty trading and commodity production are activities for which literacy is not a requirement. This is an important consideration given the literacy rates of men and women in some countries of Latin America. In La Paz, for instance, 4% of men aged between 10 and 70 were illiterate compared with 21% of the women. Another important consideration is that women who have children are able to engage in petty commodity production because much of the work takes place at home. Although the official economic activity rate for women in Bolivia is around 30% (this includes only women working for wages) Buechler found in her sample that only a very small percentage of wives 'did not work in non-domestic labour' and she argues that neither marriage nor motherhood prevents women from earning money (Buechler, 1986: 172). A similar finding was reported by Scott for Lima, Peru (Scott, 1990).

The conditions of the urban poor and their close connections with rural-dwelling kin are portrayed vividly in Oscar Lewis's *The Children of Sanchez* and related studies. The precariousness of existence and the incredible adaptability required to survive, as well as the flexibility of household composition noted by many others, come out clearly (Lewis, 1979, 1978, 1980).

It appears that women's informal economic activity takes place within existing gender divisions of labour and is shaped by the domestic division of labour as well as by gender divisions within the labour market (Scott, 1990). Thus, even in situations where women's economic activity is expected, as within the working class of Lima, Peru, an ideology of separate spheres and gender-appropriate activities ensures that men have privileged access to resources to further their economic activity and that women's economic activity is controlled by men and fits in with their domestic responsibilities (Scott, 1990). So although women may be economically active whatever their domestic responsibilities, the form that this economic activity takes is affected by the nature and extent of those responsibilities. As many feminists have pointed out, income generation that can be combined with child care and other domestic tasks is often the only option for women, and because of this much of women's economic activity takes place within the informal sector and is home-based (Feldman, 1991). It is therefore predicated upon existing gender divisions of labour rather than providing a challenge to them (Scott, 1991).

It is time now to explore the impact of female factory employment on gender divisions of labour, an issue which has received much attention in the literature and which has produced conflicting evidence (see, for example, Lim, 1990 for a summary of the debate). As we have already seen, the incorporation of Third World women into the industrial workforce has been facilitated by the adoption of export-led industrialisation strategies and the export of labour-intensive processes from the core to the periphery in which multinationals are now engaged. This, it is claimed, is resulting in the globalisation of production with different parts of a single production process being located in several geographical areas. Specifically, the labour-intensive parts of the production process have been relocated to low-wage areas of the Third World. Some Third World countries have enabled multinationals to set up these factories in Free Trade Zones where they are provided with very favourable operating conditions. Export-led industrialisation initially began in Puerto Rico (Ríos, 1990) and spread to the Caribbean, Mexico, Brazil and Colombia. It is also found in East and South-east Asia where the Newly Industrialised Countries (NICs) of Hong Kong, Singapore and Taiwan are located, and in North Africa and China. It has not developed in Sub-Saharan Africa (Stichter, 1990; Lim, 1990; Pearson, 1991, 1992).

The preferred workforce for these manufacturing processes is young, single, childless women, often migrants form rural areas and with no recognised skills (Stichter, 1990; Pearson, 1991; Wolf, 1991). However, although this is often the case when export processing factories are first set up, the longer established factories employ women who are older and who have children and other domestic responsibilities; this is particularly the case in Latin America and the Caribbean (Safa, 1986; Pearson, 1991). And there is evidence from Mexico that women may not reveal the extent of their domestic responsibilities because they know single, childless women are preferred (Pearson, 1991). In addition, women do not necessarily originate in rural areas (Bustamente, 1983; Fernandez-Kelly, 1983; Pearson, 1991) or may remain in rural areas while working in nearby factories (Wolf, 1990, 1991).

There is considerable disagreement as to whether female factory wage-labour provides an expansion of opportunities for women and the effect that it has on gender relations (Lim, 1990). This has produced a range of studies with contradictory findings.

Studies which focus on the employment of *young* women in world market factories suggest that it takes place within existing gender divisions and ideologies. For instance, a study of strawberry-export packing plants in Mexico found that most of the women employed were young (15 to 24 years of age) and were still living with their parents in rural areas (Arizpe & Aranda, 1981: 462). Their wages although low were seen as a contribution to a household in which they did not provide the sole income and in which their employment often met with opposition from their fathers. These young women still experienced 'subordination and restriction' within their parents' home. As Arizpe and Aranda comment, 'no modernisation of women's roles is evident in the region'; indeed, the fact that young women leave factory work on marriage can be seen as reinforcing the authority of husbands (Arizpe & Aranda, 1981: 472). Thus, employment in the capitalist sector, rather than challenging gender divisions which subordinate women, is predicated upon precisely this subordination which guarantees a supply of cheap, docile, flexible, female labour (Elson & Pearson, 1984; Safa, 1981; Heyzer, 1986; Ong, 1990; Mather, 1988).

Having said that, there is evidence that in some contexts female wage-labour tends to undermine women's subordination. Elson and Pearson distinguish three tendencies in the relation between this particular form of capitalist economic organisation, factory work, and the gender division of labour: 'a tendency to *intensify* the existing forms of gender subordination; a tendency to *decompose* existing forms of gender subordination; and a tendency to *recompose* new forms of gender subordination' (1984: 31). Indeed, although factory employment may replicate the patriarchal authority of the father within the factory (Heyzer, 1982, 1986; Stivens, 1984; Mather, 1988; Ong, 1990), it may also provide women with some room for manoeuvre as income earners and may even be seen as a means of 'partial liberation from the confines and dictates of traditional patriarchal social relations' (Lim, 1983: 83; 1990). Safa's study of Puerto Rican women factory workers found that, although for young women patriarchal authority remained unchallenged, for older women their paid employment had contributed to its erosion in the urban working-class context (Safa, 1986: 95; 1990).

Other studies that have been carried out in Indonesia and Taiwan also present conflicting evidence. One study compares women factory workers in Java, where women enjoy a good deal of autonomy and are expected to make an economic contribution throughout their lives, with those in Taiwan, where Confucian ideology enjoins young women to obey the authority of their parents and to repay them for having brought them up (Wolf, 1990, 1991). This comparison of young women working in export processing factories found that in the former case the opportunity to participate in wage-labour had given young women increased independence and control over their own wages and increased their status in the family. In the latter case young women worked at the behest of their parents, handing over all that they earned to them. This may have intensified gender divisions which disadvantage women because the money earned by young women was used to further the careers of their brothers (Wolf, 1990, 1991). Another study of young ethnic Chinese women in Singapore, Taiwan and Hong Kong found that young women benefited from earning wages in terms of their ability to buy consumer goods and participate in the consumer society generally, but that it did not enhance their status *vis-à-vis* their parents or brothers and their labour continued to be controlled by their parents (Salaff, 1990).

Evidence from a wider range of studies exploring changes in gender divisions within households consequent upon an increase in women's control over income suggests that the ability both to earn and control income enhances women's independence, self-reliance and self-respect and increases their say in household decision-making including fertility decisions (Safa, 1990; Blumberg, 1991: 114–15). It appears to be the amount of control exerted by women over their income rather than whether or not they earn an income in their own right that is significant. Thus, in the example above of Taiwan, most young women's wages are controlled by their parents not themselves, whereas in Java the young women controlled their own wages and this led to increased independence and status (Wolf, 1990).

Before leaving this topic it is useful to look at the experiences of the Newly Industrialised Countries (NICs) as they are held up as models of successful capitalist development and may offer more conclusive evidence of the effect of capitalist development on gender divisions. I shall focus on Hong Kong, Singapore and Taiwan which at first glance seem to confirm that women's status is radically altered by capitalist industrialisation. In all these societies fertility levels are low, age at marriage is high, women's participation in the workforce is high (just under half of all women work for wages full-time), education levels for women and men are relatively high and life expectancy is comparable to that in advanced capitalist countries. The state is involved in the provision of welfare in the form of health and housing in Singapore and Hong Kong (Salaff, 1990; Wong, 1981). In Singapore women are not only to be found in the labour-intensive and relatively low paid sectors of export-processing but also in more highly-skilled jobs in the more capital-intensive sectors (Phongpaichit, 1988). However, although figures indicate that over a third of married women are in the paid workforce it is likely that unless they are in relatively high paying jobs they will leave paid employment once they have children (Wong, 1981; Salaff, 1990). And in all three NICs it is young, unmarried women who dominate the workforce (Salaff, 1990; Heyzer, 1982, 1986; Wong, 1981). In Singapore, more than in Taiwan or Hong Kong, female employment is highly dependent on foreign capital and is thus very vulnerable to world economic recessions. Women can easily be laid off, particularly as large numbers of them are migrant workers with virtually no status in Singapore (Heyzer, 1982, 1986). Another important factor is that, apart from Taiwan, where land reform was carried out which prevented investment in land and freed the rural population to take part in the growing waged sector (Blumberg, 1981; Salaff, 1990), these societies are small and have no rural population to speak of. In this sense they are very different from most Third World societies where the majority of the population is rural. This has contributed to a 'tight' labour market and a need to recruit women as well as men into industry (Phongpaichit, 1988: 155). Women have benefited from this and in Singapore, for instance, women have equal pay with men and are afforded education and training opportunities. The incorporation of the population into wage-labour has also been facilitated by state measures which have reduced the possibility of alternative forms of income generation either in the informal economy or in the rural sector (Salaff, 1990). Thus the form taken by industrialisation in these societies has created a demand for labour and, in a situation of labour shortage, this has facilitated women's entry into the workforce. Because of industrialisation women's employment experience has changed and far more women are employed in the formal sector than previously, thus altering the form taken by gender divisions of paid employment. With the exception of Singapore, however, women are not found in the skilled and high paid sectors of the workforce and even though their economic activity rates are high they are concentrated in the low paid and least skilled jobs (Pearson, 1992). Within the domestic sphere it appears that the gender division of labour has not altered significantly although it may well do so in the future (Wong, 1981; Salaff, 1990).

From the evidence presented here it is not possible to argue that capitalist development in the Third World either undermines or reinforces women's subordination. Indeed it appears to do both, depending on the cultural and economic context. Thus, the employment of young women in low paid, labour-intensive assembly work does not appear to challenge patriarchal authority. Rather capitalism takes advantage of gender divisions which supply it with cheap, easily expendable labour and, in the process, reinforces women's subordination. On the other hand, where older, married women are employed and control their contribution to the household economy there is some evidence that male authority may be undermined (Safa, 1990; Blumberg, 1991). A third possibility also needs to be considered and that is that wage work increases women's workload and the expectation or necessity that they will participate in wage-labour is experienced as an added burden (Sharma, 1990). In rural areas capitalist development undermines patriarchal control by impoverishing the rural population and forcing large numbers of people to migrate in search of a living. This results in high numbers of female-headed households in which women may be only intermittently subject to male authority (Jacobs, 1991) or the absence of males altogether except for purposes of procreation (Bunster and Chaney, 1989). It also forces women as well as men into income generating activities and, where available, wage-labour (Deere & León de Leal, 1982). Industrialisation in most Third World societies is taking place in a situation of labour surplus. However, where labour markets are 'tight', as in some of the NICs, the demand for women's labour is high and this may lead to a lightening of their reproductive load within the domestic sphere, either through state intervention or a sharing of their domestic responsibilities with other members of their domestic unit, so that they are enabled to continue in paid employment (Phongpaichit, 1988; Salaff, 1990; Pearson, 1992).

SOCIALIST DEVELOPMENT

One of the issues which has been highlighted as having adverse effects both on women and on the development process is the assumption that production, particularly agricultural production, is household based and that family labour is under the control of the male head of household (Blumberg, 1991; Elson, 1991). This results in the neglect of women's productive activities and often in a deterioration of women's and children's nutritional status (Whitehead, 1991; Blumberg, 1991). Although attempts have been made to rectify this 'male bias' in development programmes it still prevails and is one of the ways in which women's independent access to productive resources is restricted. It might be thought that societies with an express commitment to socialism, such as Tanzania, Mozambique and Zimbabwe, would be following different policies which recognise and build on women's important and relatively independent productive activities and which do not reinforce or create women's dependence on men within domestic units. This assumption is justified by the commitment of such regimes to women's emancipation and their recognition that women's involvement in productive activity outside the domestic sphere is crucial to their liberation. However, a brief look at African socialism suggests that the processes occurring there share important features with those in other African societies.

All Third World societies which have been committed to socialism have implemented land reform, usually distributing land to the direct producers and taking over land which had previously been owned by the landowning classes (Deere, 1986). The result has been an agricultural sector with a mixture of state farms, cooperatively worked land and land worked by individual peasant households. As we saw in Chapter 4, in Cuba and Nicaragua women were entitled to land in their own right in the land reform. However, evidence from Zimbabwe, Mozambique, Ethiopia and Tanzania shows that land reform in those countries has distributed land to family units, specifically to adult men within those units who are designated head of household (Tadesse, 1982; Jacobs, 1984, 1990; Caplan, 1984; McCall, 1987). This is particularly significant in Africa where, prior to colonisation, women had extensive rights in land, and private property in land did not exist. In Tanzania, for instance, many societies were matrilineal and inheritance was either through the female line or cognatic, but colonial administrations imposed patterns of land ownership which were based on individual male ownership and male inheritance. A brief look at Tanzania and Mozambique and their rural development policies enables us to assess the ways in which socialist development differs from capitalist development in the Third World.

Tanzania began its socialist development programme in 1967,

aiming to introduce communal farming within ten years to the 94% of the population that lived in the countryside (Deere, 1986: 122). This process, known as villagisation, involved relocating the rural population in villages and allocating land to individual peasant households. This was done under compulsion (Deere, 1986: 122–4). In the villages each household had its own plot and was expected to provide labour for collective enterprises; these were either agricultural or to provide an infrastructure of services such as shops (Deere, 1986). Although plot allocation was supposed to be made to all members of a village, women and men alike, in practice plots were allocated to 'families'; that is, to 'male heads of households' (McCall, 1987: 205). This meant that women were dependent on men for access to land and it was only women who were themselves household heads who were allocated plots (McCall, 1987). Caplan's analysis of production and ownership on Mafia Island demonstrates how this policy reduces women's independent access to land, the main productive resource (Caplan, 1984). She shows that, prior to villagisation, women had access to land which was held by their descent group. Subsistence production was carried out on this land and shifting agriculture was practised. In addition, women were able to own coconut trees and under Islamic law they retained their property when they married. Couples often divided crops which had been jointly cultivated and stored their own halves separately. Men did not control their wives' labour (Caplan, 1984: 34). Women thus enjoyed a considerable degree of control and autonomy which would be undermined by the 'modernisation' policies adopted in the name of African socialism.

There are positive aspects to these policies such as improvements in access to health care and education (for girls as well as boys). But policies relating to land tenure, cash crops and villagisation disadvantage women. Cash cropping, which is being encouraged by the government, already benefits men more than women and its expansion is likely to exacerbate this. The government is changing patterns of land tenure and has declared all unoccupied land government land. This means that land may well be lost to the descent groups because their system of land use requires tracts of land to lie fallow for long periods and it is therefore officially defined as unoccupied. Because of this women will lose the rights to land use they held by virtue of their membership of a descent group independent of their husband. The assumptions underlying the policy of villagisation are that people live in households and consist of a man and his family (Caplan, 1984: 41). This is likely to have severe implications for societies in which households do not exist in that form and where co-residential groups are formed around women not men. As Caplan comments:

[I]n its construction of an entity which it terms 'the family', and in its assignation to such a unit of co-residential, productive, and reproductive functions, and above all, in its assignment of property-holding functions to this unit, the state seems likely to erode even further the autonomy which women previously enjoyed. (Caplan, 1984: 42)

It is ironic that in the name of socialism Tanzanian policy is to *establish* the family as an economic unit where it has not previously existed, when socialist theory clearly links the family to private property and the oppression of women and aims at its ultimate *abolition* as an economic unit. But Tanzania is not alone in this and similar processes are occurring in Mozambique.

Mozambique's liberation war against Portugal ended in 1975 and the Mozambique Liberation Front (FRELIMO) took power committed to socialism. A women's organisation, the Organisation of Mozambique (OMM), was founded in 1973 but is not independent of the party. Women have been granted legal equality with men and are encouraged to do 'men's' jobs. It appears that this encouragement is producing results in urban areas where the number of women working in the police force and in the skilled trades, for instance, is increasing (Hansen & Ashbaugh, 1991). However, most of Mozambique's population (90%), as is the case in Tanzania, is rural and it is FRELIMO's rural development policies which will affect the largest number of women.

In accordance with the socialist blueprint for women's emancipation FRELIMO has called upon women to participate in production. The problems of operationalising measures which were elaborated on the basis of an urban industrial society are particularly obvious in a situation where most rural women are already heavily involved in agricultural production. It underlines the need for a new analysis based on *existing* gender relations and relations of production rather than those which existed in capitalist industrial Britain in the nineteenth century. The call for women to participate in production is based on the assumption that such participation will empower women. However, rural development policies appear to be having the opposite effect and do not differ significantly from those pursued in other sub-Saharan African societies (Urdang, 1989).

Initially, policies aimed to establish communal villages, production co-operatives and state farms. The rural population was encouraged to relocate in villages where collective agricultural production would develop and services would be provided (Deere, 1986). However, most resources, which were very limited given the war of destabilisation being waged against FRELIMO by South Africa, went to the state farm sector which was the only employer of wage-labour in the rural areas and employed men (Urdang, 1989). The cooperative sector, on the other hand, was dominated by women. They formed 75% of cooperative members and they had equal access to economic resources; however, less than 2% of the economically active population was organised in this way (Arnfred, 1988; Deere, 1986).

This rural development policy together with natural disasters and the ending of migrant labour to South Africa, produced a crisis in agricultural production and, in 1984, the policy changed to one of encouraging family and private farming (Urdang, 1989; Deere, 1986). The emphasis was put on the development of cash cropping and surplus production rather than on ensuring the production of food necessary for daily survival. Urdang comments that this policy mirrors those adopted in other sub-Saharan African societies and is likely to marginalise women from agricultural production; they will continue in subsistence production while men are involved in cash crop production (Urdang, 1989: 26).

It also appears that FRELIMO and OMM are playing down the need to challenge the domestic division of labour, even calling for women not to rock the domestic boat (Urdang, 1989). The nuclear family and free-choice marriage are officially supported and encouraged in opposition to practices such as lobola (bride-price), polygyny and arranged marriages which are widespread in rural areas. This is problematic because there is significant support for these practices amongst both women and men, although it appears that younger women and men are more likely to be opposed to their continuance and that men are more likely than women to support polygyny (Urdang, 1989). Divorce, although legal, is officially frowned upon. It has been suggested that this reflects the predominance in FRELIMO and OMM of people from the south of the country who are patrilineal and where patrilocal marriage is practised. In the north, divorce has always been common amongst the matrilineal rural population (Urdang, 1989). Matriliny is attacked by FRELIMO while patriliny and the nuclear family are supported because they are 'functional to a modernising society' (Arnfred, 1988: 10). There is some evidence that women are organising independently into cooperatives and it has been suggested that they are combining 'the defence of women's traditional economic position with the struggle for a new identity' (Arnfred, 1988: 15). However, it is not clear how widespread this alternative strategy is nor how it will be able to counter the increasing capitalisation of agriculture which is occurring, particularly in the south, with the associated consequences for women (Roesch, 1988). Clearly the situation is complicated and Mozambique has extreme problems of civil war and famine to contend with. The adoption by FRELIMO of what amounts to a capitalist development policy for agriculture and their support for the nuclear family suggest that gender divisions are unlikely to be transformed in women's favour. On the contrary, women are likely to lose any independence they still enjoy as they are mobilised to work as family labour on their husbands' land.

In Zimbabwe, land reform policies have been based on the assumption of a male head of household and it is to households that unused and abandoned land has been allocated (Jacobs, 1984, 1991; Deere, 1986). Women are not entitled to land in their own right unless they are widows or divorced (Jacobs, 1991: 59). Thus for most women access to land is through a man. The farms of the white settler community were not expropriated after independence in 1980 and the state is attempting to create a sector of African farmers farming their own land; that is, a sector of small capitalist farmers (Deere, 1986; Jacobs, 1991). It has been argued that this process facilitates capitalist rather than socialist development in agriculture (Cliffe, 1988; Simon, 1985; Jacobs, 1991).

From this brief look at African socialism it is clear that it is not possible unambiguously to describe these rural development policies as socialist. For instance, both Zimbabwe and Mozambique are facilitating capitalist development in agriculture for reasons which relate to food shortages, the desperate need to integrate the rural population into the national economy and the need to implement the structural adjustment policies demanded by the IMF (Drakakis-Smith, 1987; Slater, 1987). This is particularly true in the case of Mozambique (Roesch, 1988). It is also the case that assumptions have been made about the nature of 'the family' and that these assumptions include a gender division of labour which, in the context of sub-Saharan Africa particularly, reduces women's economic independence considerably and underestimates their current contribution to production.

This evidence may support the view that socialist development in Third World societies has nothing to offer women and shares significant features with capitalist development. While this may be the case in some countries, it is important to remember the effect of socialist development policies in other Third World societies such as Cuba and Nicaragua where socialism has been a positive experience for many women (Molyneux, 1985, 1985a). Such a comparison suggests that the effect of socialist development policies on gender divisions depends partly on the nature of those societies prior to their revolutions. In pre-revolutionary Cuba and Nicaragua, women were subservient and subordinate to men in peasant households or were living in poverty in female-headed households with no access either to jobs or to a male wage. Socialist modernisation policies, as we have seen, involve the destruction of non-capitalist social forms. In the African context this may have negative consequences for women but in societies where feudal or semi-feudal forms of organisation predominate, as was the case in Cuba and Nicaragua and remains the case in much of Latin America and Asia, these policies may undermine author-itarian and patriarchal gender divisions. Such policies aim to eliminate the most oppressive aspects of gender divisions and by undermining the family as a productive unit, they challenge men's direct control of women's labour. That capitalist development does not necessarily do this is evidenced by Mies' data from India.

However, it may be that it is as members of the peasantry and working class that women benefit more from socialist development than from capitalist development (Urdang, 1989; Jacobs, 1991; Molyneux, 1985, 1985a). It should not be overlooked that the record of Third World socialist societies with regard to the provision of education, health care, housing, sanitation and so on is much better than that of most capitalist developing societies.

These measures, while not tackling gender divisions, improve the living conditions of women and men. The gender policies, although freeing women from patriarchal family control in societies which are characterised by family-based production, and thus changing gender divisions, do not result in their elimination. Indeed, the gender division of labour in socialist and capitalist Third World countries is remarkably similar, with women located in the labour-intensive sectors of agriculture and industry while men are in the more capital-intensive, technologically advanced sectors (Croll, 1981). Thus, socialist development may be better for women, not because it has managed to create gender equality, but because it improves material conditions for the majority of the population, while capitalist development improves them spectacularly for the élite few and considerably worsens them for the majority of the population.

In this and the preceding chapter the argument that the process of development worsens women's situation, intensifying their workload and leading to their impoverishment, has been subject to scrutiny. It has been shown that development, be it capitalist or socialist, transforms gender divisions of labour, but that the nature of this transformation is not unidirectional and depends on the nature of gender relations prior to colonisation and on the positions occupied by women in systems of stratification. Thus, in sub-Saharan Africa, colonialism, the subsequent development of capitalism and, in some societies, attempts to construct socialism, all seem to have undermined the material basis of women's autonomy which rested in pre-capitalist modes of production, although some women, precisely because of this autonomy and economic independence from men, have been able to take advantage of the opportunities provided by emergent capitalism. These women, however, are in a small minority. Generally, development has meant a transformation of gender divisions such that women are becoming dependent upon men, as well as upon their own income-generating activities, for access to cash which enables them to buy the means of subsistence that they are no longer able to produce for themselves.

In other regions of the Third World, particularly where pre-colonial societies were agrarian rather than horticultural or foraging, the development of capitalism and socialism have had contradictory effects on gender divisions, at one and the same time providing the possibility for women to achieve a measure of independence from patriarchal control through participation in wage-labour but also reinforcing and recreating gender divisions of labour which subordinate women.

It is, however, in those Third World societies which have successfully industrialised and modernised where the most significant transformation in gender divisions has occurred. This has gone along with a decline in fertility levels, increasing levels of education and workforce participation by women and the emergence of 'free-choice' marriage. However, gender divisions in such societies are still marked by women's subordination, it is the form taken by such subordination that has changed.

Clearly the process of development, whether capitalist or socialist, has contradictory effects on women and on gender divisions of labour. In some contexts it can undermine women's autonomy and independent access to resources, and in others it can undermine male control of female labour and patriarchal authority. It is therefore impossible to generalise about the effect of development on women as it depends on many variables besides that of gender. Indeed, feminist research in the past two decades has begun to demonstrate how important it is to look at changing gender divisions in the context of particular societies in particular historical periods in order to be able to understand the complexity of the relation between economic change and gender divisions of labour.

/ 8 /

WESTERN WOMEN'S LIBERATION MOVEMENTS AND GENDER DIVISIONS

The changing divisions of labour by gender that have been explored in the preceding chapters have been explained by changes in the mode of production and related processes of class formation, capitalist development and industrialisation. However, these changes also involve the active agency of women. Women are not passive in the face of social change but actively intervene, whether this be at the level of struggle for daily survival, organising to improve conditions for themselves and their communities, or participating in movements for more fundamental social, political and economic changes. Thus in Guayaquil, Ecuador, poor women have been instrumental in the formation of community organisations to press for improved housing and sanitation (Moser, 1987); in Honduras women are involved in land seizures by the peasantry and are in leadership positions (Benjamin, 1987); and in Bolivia tin miners' wives organised housewives' committees to press for improvements in the mines and in the treatment they receive from the company and the Bolivian government (Barrios de Chungara, 1978). In addition, the UN's decade for women has encouraged the setting up of women's organisations in many countries, and the heightened international awareness of women's social position has precipitated the emergence of women's liberation movements in countries such as Spain, Greece, Brazil and India (Threlfall, 1985; Sarti, 1989; Kabeer, 1988; Stamiris, 1986; Patel, 1985; Kumar, 1989; Gothaskar & Patel, 1982). However, although women are active in resisting exploitation and oppression and in organising to bring about change, this activity does not necessarily take the form of social

219

movements or have as its goal a transformation in the gender division of labour (Safa, 1990).

In Western Europe and North America during the 1970s, social movements emerged which had as their explicit goal a transformation in gender relations and an end to the subordination of women. Other social movements, such as socialist and nationalist movements, often incorporate into their programmes a commitment to women's emancipation and changes in the gender division of labour. Despite this express commitment on the part of such movements, they have been criticised by Western feminists for not being 'feminist' enough, for not prioritising gender struggles within the wider movement for social change, and for promoting a gender division of labour which continues to subordinate women (Molyneux, 1984a). Such criticisms often assume that the demands of Western women's liberation movements are essential for achieving women's liberation and are relevant to women everywhere, regardless of their social, economic and political circumstances. Such an assumption is problematic. For instance, demands for abortion to be freely available to women, which are put forward by women's liberation movements in Europe and North America, may be totally inappropriate in some countries of Latin America where forced sterilisation programmes are in operation and where the rights of the indigenous population to reproduce at all are being denied (Gilliam, 1991: 224). Similarly, an insistence on separatism and the necessity of struggle against men is regarded as inappropriate by women who are involved in struggles alongside men against imperialism or other forms of exploitation and oppression (Barrios de Chungara, 1978, 1983; Hendissi, 1986; Rowbotham & McCrindle, 1986; Stead, 1987). The priorities of women engaged in these sorts of struggle differ from the priorities of women involved in women's liberation movements in the West. Indeed, even within Western women's liberation movements priorities differ and there are profound disagreements over the way to achieve women's liberation and end sexism (Ramazanoglu, 1989). This suggests that the Western feminist agenda is not universally applicable and, further, that there is no essential feminism (Bacchi, 1990; Wilson, 1980: 165; 1986). Indeed, the assumption of a universally valid feminism rests on a notion of shared identity which, ultimately, given the extraordinary variety of social, economic and political circumstance in which women find themselves, can arise only from women's shared biology. And it ignores the very different circumstances in which women find themselves and which they are struggling to transform. It, therefore, seems a futile exercise to criticise social movements for not being feminist enough. What is important is to assess the nature of their impact on gender divisions. I have already discussed the impact of socialism on gender divisions and have briefly considered the relation between national liberation movements and women's emancipation. Here, I focus on Western women's liberation movements and their impact on gender divisions of labour.

THE EMERGENCE OF WOMEN'S LIBERATION MOVEMENTS

Women's liberation movements or second wave feminism began to emerge in Western Europe and North America at the end of the 1960s. These social movements were dubbed 'second wave' feminism because they were preceded by social movements demanding women's suffrage and legal rights at the end of the nineteenth and beginning of the twentieth centuries. And they were largely a phenomenon of advanced, capitalist societies (Chafetz & Dworkin, 1986). In the Eastern bloc, the USSR and Sweden (Kaplan, 1992: 71) and in most countries of the Third World there have not been comparable movements, although this is not to say that women are not involved in both practical and strategic gender struggles (Schirmer, 1989; Safa, 1990; Beall *et al.*, 1989; Kimble and Unterhalter, 1982; Kumar, 1989; Isis International, 1986).

The social circumstances which give rise to social movements are not fully understood, but it seems that different social movements emerge and decline together and it is certainly true that both first and second wave feminism arose along with other social movements (Brand, 1990). It is suggested that one of the factors giving rise to social movements is a feeling of relative deprivation amongst certain sections of the population. This explanation has been criticised because the so-called new social movements of the 1960s and 1970s were largely composed of middle-class radicals, the very people who benefit most from the current social and political arrangements of capitalist societies (Dalton *et al.*, 1990: 7; Brand, 1990: 25). This second point may not be so convincing, however, in the case of feminist social movements because it can be argued that women, even middle-class women, are excluded from many of the benefits and privileges enjoyed by middle-class men and that they may indeed feel relatively deprived (Freeman, 1975). There are various other explanations of the emergence of social movements but most of them remain at a high level of generality, and in order to understand the genesis of women's movements it is more useful to explore the context of the emergence of first and second wave feminist movements.

During the second part of the nineteenth century the ideology of female domesticity was at its height and middle-class women were confined to a domestic role, dependent upon their male relatives for support. At the time women outnumbered men in the population and many women could not expect to be supported by husbands. If their fathers were alive they looked to them for support but if not then they turned to their nearest male relative. This often put an intolerable strain on men who may have had a wife and children dependent upon them already. Thus there was pressure for single middle-class women to earn a living in order to support themselves. But the professions were barred to them and the only 'respectable' occupation was that of governess or, for some, writing (Lovell, 1987). It was out of this situation, in which single middle-class women had no respectable means of earning a living, that pressure grew to allow women to enter higher education and the professions and from which first wave feminism emerged. What is interesting about this is that no challenge to *married* women's domestic role was being made. It was accepted by middle-class feminists, and they were overwhelmingly from the middle classes, that motherhood was a full-time occupation and rightly so. What was being challenged was the exclusion of single women from the public world of the professions. And the campaign for women's suffrage was framed in terms that emphasised women's difference from men, their different values and greater capacity for nurturing, rather than their similarity. At the same time women's common humanity with men was stressed. It was argued that the injection of women's values into politics was necessary and would be of positive benefit to society. Thus, first wave feminism did not challenge the domestic division of labour and women's primary role as wives and mothers which contemporary feminism associates with women's subordination. And it was envisaged that only single women would want to take full advantage of women's increased educational and employment opportunities (Banks, 1986; Chafetz & Dworkin, 1986; Bacchi, 1990).

Second wave feminism arose first in the USA then in Britain at the end of the 1960s. Women's liberation movements of varying strengths emerged in most other European countries during the 1970s; Sweden provides a notable exception which will be looked at more closely below (Chafetz & Dworkin, 1986; Randall, 1987; Lovenduski, 1986; Gelb, 1990; Kaplan, 1992). Their emergence was associated with that of other social movements, most notably the civil rights movement in the USA, the student movements, the peace movement and the ecology movement, some of which pre-date and some of which post-date the women's liberation movement. It has been argued that Western women's liberation movements emerged as a response to the post-war increase in the numbers of women entering further and higher education and the gulf that existed between their aspirations and the life of domesticity that awaited them after graduation; this is the relative deprivation thesis mentioned earlier (Freeman, 1975; Banks, 1986). This relative deprivation was termed 'the problem that has no name' by Betty Friedan in *The Feminine Mystique*, the publication of which marked the beginning of the women's liberation movement in the USA (Friedan, 1965). Also important was the continuing decline in fertility levels, which meant that women were spending far fewer years than previously in child care, and the steady increase in the numbers of *married* women entering the workforce (Chafetz & Dworkin, 1986). Working-class women solved the problem of combining paid employment with child care by working part time. But this option was neither available to nor seen as desirable by middle-class women wanting to pursue careers. The tension experienced by middle-class women between their domestic roles and their opportunities in paid employment seems to have been the spark that ignited a movement for women's liberation.

Another factor in the emergence of women's liberation movements may be the extent of labour movement involvement in government and the resulting importance attached to policies which benefit the working class (Ruggie, 1987). It is argued that where workers' interests are prioritised by a state committed to socialism, and where this takes the institutional form of working-class representation at governmental level, policies result which are beneficial to women as workers. For instance, policies which are developed to improve the position of low-paid workers, as in Sweden, are likely to benefit women simply because women are disproportionately represented among low-paid workers. Additionally, parties with a commitment to socialism usually have a commitment to improving women's status, a commitment which often requires pressure from women party members before it is implemented but which, nevertheless, differentiates them from parties with other political orientations. Thus in Sweden, and formerly in Eastern Europe and the USSR, women workers' interests are represented and catered for in measures such as equal pay, raising the wages of low-paid workers relative to other workers, the provision of child-care facilities, paid parental or maternity leave and so on (Bassnett, 1986; Ruggie, 1987; see also Chapter 4 above). Such measures remove the obvious causes of much of the discontent voiced in the early stages of the women's liberation movements and, by having already catered for many of the needs of women workers, restrict the possibility of channelling women's remaining grievances into a social movement (Lovenduski, 1986). This is particularly likely to be the case where it is perceived that political parties are responsive to women's needs and introduce appropriate measures. The impetus for political change, given these circumstances, is more likely to be channelled through the existing political parties than to take the form of a social movement which often, at least in its early stages, perceives the political parties as part of the opposition and not to be trusted to take women's issues seriously (Costain & Costain, 1987). Social movements are, after all, aimed at political change and if the current political arrangements are able to incorporate, in this case, women's interests there is no basis for the formation of a social movement.

In the absence of a strong labour movement with a real and continuing influence on government policies, measures which benefit women as workers are less likely to be in evidence. In a situation where increasing numbers of women with children are entering or wish to enter paid employment, this lack gives rise to tensions and contradictions which may result in the emergence of women's liberation movements. As will be seen below, once these contradictions begin to be solved, by political parties' incorporating women's demands and legislating (partially) to meet them, the impetus for the social movement disappears and the movement eventually fragments.

To understand the nature of social movements it is also important to look at the social characteristics of the participants. The women who became involved in the women's liberation movement in both the USA and Britain were, in the main, young and highly educated (Freeman, 1975; Banks, 1986; Rowbotham, 1989; Wilson, 1986; Coote & Campbell, 1982). This meant that they were likely to be white and middle class. For many of them, joining the local women's liberation group was a response to the extreme sexism that they had encountered in the civil rights, student or anti-Vietnam war movements or in the New Left. As with first wave feminism, women were taking the arguments of other liberatory social movements and demanding that those principles be applied to women.

Because of their genesis in the sexually permissive 1960s and the radical movements of the time, Western women's liberation movements are marked by libertarian ideologies. This anti-authoritarian, anti-hierarchical heritage found expression in the organisational forms adopted by the movement. It eschewed formal organisation and, instead, women came together in small groups which became known as consciousness-raising groups. The basic form of organisation of the movement remained small groups, although whether they were solely consciousness-raising groups or were involved in campaigns locally and nationally varied. Many groups combined all these activities in the early years (Freeman, 1975; Wilson, 1986; Banks, 1986; Rowbotham, 1989). Formal structures within the groups were avoided in the interests of democracy and maximum participation and, very early on, it was decided that groups would be women only. The decision to exclude men was based on an assumption that if men were present they would dominate the proceedings and define the agenda. Research has shown that men do indeed tend to dominate conversations in mixed groups and that this may reflect the power differential between women and men (Spender, 1985). The creation of women-only groups thus served to build up the confidence of women as well as enabling them to explore the political and social causes of their seemingly unique personal problems (Freeman, 1975; Banks, 1986). The small group, women-only structure also resulted in generating considerable solidarity among group members which participants found enormously supportive (Rowbotham, 1989; Segal, 1987; Freeman, 1975).

It has been noted that women's groups were generally an urban phenomenon (Hellman, 1987a; Lovenduski, 1986; Dahlerup, 1986) and proliferated during the early years of the movement, new groups forming and old groups disappearing very rapidly (Rowbotham, 1989). Many groups disappeared because of internal conflicts and, in the face of structurelessness, individual women with strong personalities were easily able to dominate (Freeman, 1975; Rowbotham, 1989). It has also been suggested that these small, consciousness-raising groups were well suited to raising women's political awareness and providing a support network, but once the need for political intervention became apparent, their capacity to mobilise in support of demands was less than adequate (Freeman, 1975). This problem was circumvented in different ways in different societies. In some, such as Italy, the left-wing political parties took up and organised on issues which had been raised by the women's movement, often through their women's organisations. In others, organisations were set up which were not aligned to any political party and were a constituent part of the movement (Hellman, 1987, 1987a; Freeman, 1975; Banks, 1986).

In the USA, for instance, the women's liberation movement had no natural constituency in the political parties and in 1966 a national organisation was set up; it was called NOW, the National Organisation for Women (Freeman, 1975). NOW initially campaigned on equal rights issues, particularly the equal rights amendment to the American constitution, but later, under pressure from the small groups of the movement, or the younger branch as Jo Freeman calls them, it took up issues relating to fertility control, sexuality and male violence against women (Freeman, 1975; Banks, 1986). Interestingly, trade union women who initially supported NOW left the organisation over the issue of the equal rights amendment (Freeman, 1975; Banks, 1986). This was because its ratification would automatically nullify all the measures for which the trade union movement had fought to protect working-class women from the harsher aspects of capitalist exploitation, such as night work and compulsory overtime. In the

USA the argument has been put and accepted by feminists that such protective measures are actually restrictive and prevent women from deciding for themselves such things as what hours they will work and what weights they are prepared to lift. However, the benefits of such legislation have been sacrificed on the altar of equality rather than retained and extended to men (Bacchi, 1990: 136–7). American feminists accept the argument that equality necessarily rules out special treatment for women, and that women must expect to be treated exactly as men are if they want equality. Thus, in the interests of equality, no concessions can be made to the fact that women become pregnant and carry the burden of child care. The admission of difference or special needs is guarded against as it is seen as opening the door to discrimination and unequal treatment. Childbearing and rearing are thus defined as private issues to be solved by individuals outside the workplace and pregnancy is defined as a disability in terms of employment law. The logic behind this is that disabilities can affect either sex, so if pregnancy is treated as a disability rather than something that affects only women, it reduces the likelihood of discrimination against women employees. However, defining pregnancy in this way means that women have to return to work after the birth of a child as soon as they are physically able and no maternity leave is available (Bacchi, 1990: 114). Not all feminists in the USA adopt this position, but the view that any admission of women's special needs would be a fatal weakness in the case for equality is dominant and has been most influential in terms of policy.

THE BRITISH EXPERIENCE

In order to explore these issues in more detail I want to look at the women's liberation movement as it emerged in Britain. Here, unlike in the USA, there is a relatively strong labour movement and there was a strong commitment on the part of large sections of the women's movement, particularly in the early years, to creating links with working-class women and raising 'women's' issues in the trade union movement (Rowbotham, 1989; Segal, 1987). This orientation was apparent in the genesis of the women's liberation movement. As Banks reminds us, 1968 was the fiftieth anniversary of women's suffrage and it was the year of the Ford women machinists' strike (Banks, 1986). What was significant about this strike is that it was for equal pay and there was a woman Secretary of State for Employment at the time who took the women's case seriously and used it to press the Labour government to implement their manifesto pledge. At the same time women trade unionists, disappointed at the failure of the government to implement equal pay, set up a National Joint Action Committee for Women's Equal Rights (NJACWER). It adopted a five-point charter and in May 1969 held a rally in London (Coote & Campbell, 1982). The starting point of the autonomous women's movement is, however, marked by the holding of the first national women's liberation conference at Ruskin College, Oxford, organised by a group of women who had attended the Ruskin history workshops. It had been anticipated that three hundred women would attend but twice that number turned up, including women from newly formed local women's liberation groups, women from the NJACWER, from left-wing political groups and from equal rights organisations which dated from the suffrage era. As in the USA the women's movement in Britain linked local autonomous groups to a national structure. A National Women's Coordinating Committee was set up at the first conference and the structure was to be 'small autonomous groups based on localities or special interests, each with equal status, loosely coordinated through national meetings, to which each group could send two delegates' (Coote & Campbell, 1982: 23). There were three levels of organisation: local groups, national conferences and nationally coordinated campaigns. The local groups were small and concentrated on consciousness-raising and/or organising political activity at local level. They were linked through a national network and held national conferences which were relatively unstructured and, at least formally, non-hierarchical. There were also national campaigns such as the National Abortion Campaign which organised to prevent attempts to undermine the 1967 Abortion Act; the refuge movement which set up refuges for women escaping domestic violence, and campaigns to preserve family allowances. Such campaigns were nationally organised and co-ordinated to a greater or lesser extent, and local groups considered themselves part of them by organising around the issues and, if appropriate, affiliating.

This first national conference took place in 1970. It was followed by the disruption of the Miss World competition later that year and in 1971 by the formulation of four demands which were carried on banners on the International Women's Day demonstration in March. The demands were for equal pay now; equal education and job opportunities; free contraception and abortion on demand; and free, 24-hour nurseries. In 1975 two further demands were added to the original four. They were for financial and legal independence, and an end to all discrimination against lesbians and a woman's right to define her own sexuality. In 1978 the seventh demand was adopted: freedom from intimidation by threat or use of violence or sexual coercion, regardless of marital status and an end to all laws, assumptions and institutions which perpetuate male dominance and men's aggression towards women (Coote & Campbell, 1982). Thus, issues of the social organisation of child care, women's ability to control their fertility, and sexuality and male violence were identified as crucial for women's liberation.

The women's liberation movement was united around the notion that the 'personal is political' which had implications for the politics of the movement. Firstly, it was taken as axiomatic that all women were sisters, united by their shared experience of oppression. Secondly, the organisational form that arose from the stress on the 'personal is political' was that of consciousness-raising groups where the emphasis was on the shared nature of women's personal experiences and their social and political causes. The fact that personal problems were socially located meant that women could organise collectively and politically to overcome them. And, thirdly, women tried to live their politics in their personal lives. So, for instance, if they were living with men they battled with them to try to get them to share child care and housework; and in left-wing organisations they refused any longer to make the tea, take minutes and type correspondence.

The analysis of the personal as political is associated with libertarian and anarchist traditions and the women's movement applied it to the social position of women. They linked the state to the organisation of gender divisions within the household, arguing that domestic tasks are constructed as women's work through social and economic policies and that it is not simply a matter of personal choice that women give up their jobs to look after children; and neither is such a division of labour natural. In this sense the personal is political because the state intervenes in the so-called private sphere of personal relations, at that time still sanctioning men's unlimited sexual access to the women they marry (McIntosh, 1978). Feminism thus questions the notion of a private sphere altogether and questions the way woman's place has been constructed by the state as the private sphere of the home and family and man's as the public sphere of employment and politics (Evans *et al.*, 1986).

The seven demands reflect the mixture of political influences on the women's liberation movement at that time. An analysis which located women's subordination in the domestic division of labour and women's responsibility for child care, as well as in discriminatory practices on the part of employers and in education, was apparent, as was recognition of the importance of women's being able to control their fertility. Such an analysis, and the demands which arise from it, have more in common with the analysis of women's oppression and the measures seen as necessary to end it adopted by the socialist women's movements of the early twentieth century than they do with liberal demands for equal rights. The influence of the socialist tradition and marxism is clearly in evidence, although so also is the liberal feminist or equal rights tradition. Demands for equal pay and opportunities can be regarded as liberal demands since they are about treating women the same as men and eliminating discrimination. Demands for child care, however, recognise that women have special needs which have to be met before equal rights can be meaningful and they locate women's subordination within the social arrangements for bearing and rearing children. The sixth demand is also aimed at eliminating women's dependence on men which is an integral part of the domestic division of labour. These demands, therefore, represent the influence of socialism on the women's liberation movement. Control of fertility – the demand for contraception and abortion – is an issue which is important to all second wave feminists and is not associated with a particular ideological or political standpoint.

The last two demands raise issues of sexuality and male violence towards women and, although sexuality had been an issue in first wave feminism and in socialist movements (Banks, 1986), it had not been raised in quite this way before. These demands addressed directly issues of male domination and control of women's sexuality; issues of power and domination on an inter-personal as well as societal level. They were to become associated with radical feminism which, eventually, dominated the women's movement in Britain. In its early years, though, the movement concerned itself with public policy as well as emphasising the politics of the personal. The demands focused on the state, attacking its control of women's fertility, its construction of women as dependants of men and its control of female sexuality and implicit support for male violence against women.

The activities of the women's movement, irrespective of the analysis underpinning them, took the form of campaigns and of setting up alternative services run by women for women. Thus, women's groups set up refuges for women escaping domestic violence and pressurised local authorities to provide suitable premises, which many eventually did. Women's centres which provided advice of all kinds to women were set up in many towns and cities. Some groups set up and ran pregnancy testing services; this underlined the failure of the National Health Service to meet women's needs. The provision of such services on a self-help basis also challenged the monopoly of knowledge and skills by professionals. For instance, pregnancy testing is a simple procedure which can be carried out by anyone with a certain amount of care; a nursing or medical qualification is not required. In Italy and the USA the challenge to the medical profession was more threatening in that women's groups set up and ran abortion services, often illegally, challenging both the law and the monopoly of skills enjoyed by the medical profession. One of the aims of the women's movement and an important part of its philosophy was to demystify these skills and to demonstrate that ordinary women were quite capable of doing the most extraordinary things.

Most of the new women's movements were composed of a similar political mixture as the British women's liberation movement although the relative strengths of the contending political traditions varied. Thus, in the USA liberal feminism dominated; in Italy, the women's movement remained closely tied to socialist feminism due to close links with left-wing parties and the trade union movement; and in Germany the movement was dominated from fairly early on by radical feminists (Haug, 1986; Hellman, 1987a; Freeman, 1975).

In the British movement the socialist-feminist influence was strong, although there is disagreement as to whether it was dominant in the early 1970s or whether the movement was liberal feminist in character (Bassnett, 1986; Barrett, 1980). What is interesting about the British movement in comparison with that in the USA is that women's special needs were recognised and not seen as detracting from the anti-discrimination lobby. Thus, child-care facilities were demanded from the inception of the movement, and the abolition of protective legislation in the interests of equality was not supported. On the contrary, the movement argued for the retention of protective legislation and its extension to men. As the 1970s wore on the socialist-feminist influence declined and radical feminist influence became dominant, resulting in the 1978 national conference which split the movement (Barrett, 1980; Segal, 1987). The issues which led to this split are important as they indicate that the assumption of sisterhood concealed many differences between women that could lead to division rather than solidarity.

Between 1970 and 1978 there were annual national women's liberation conferences and between 1973 and 1975 the socialist-feminist current held five national conferences followed by a further two in 1978 and 1979 (Segal, 1987: 44). In the mid 1970s socialist-feminists were active in various campaigns including the National Abortion Campaign to defend the 1967 Abortion Act; the Working Women's Charter Campaign which was aimed at persuading trade unions to take up many of the demands of the women's movement; and campaigns for child-care provision. Socialist-feminists were active theoretically as well as politically. They regarded it as crucial to develop an analysis of the causes of women's subordination and its links with capitalism and, as we have already seen, this analysis underpinned many of their campaigns. Some local groups managed to combine activities on all these fronts throughout the 1970s but others split into specialist groups concerned with single issues. As the decade wore on the latter pattern prevailed.

By the time of the last socialist-feminist conference socialist-feminism was coming under increasing attack, both for giving too much attention to developing complicated theoretical analyses of women's subordination, and for taking up racist and reformist positions; the latter because it was making demands on the state. In the wider movement it was also being attacked for minimising the significance of sexuality and male violence to women's subordination and it was this issue which proved so divisive at the last national conference in 1978. In Segal's words, 'Opposing attitudes to heterosexuality and to the significance of male violence blew apart the women's movement of the seventies' (Segal, 1987: 65).

The tension which had been apparent over issues of sexuality within the women's liberation movement came to a head in 1978. The issue which proved so divisive at the conference was the relation of sexuality and male violence to women's oppression. Radical feminists saw this as the most important issue facing the women's movement whereas liberal and socialist-feminists did not. The debate arose from differing analyses of women's oppression but came to be seen (and experienced) as a conflict between heterosexual women and lesbians. The former were condemned politically by the latter on the basis of their sexual orientation and sexuality became the central issue of the women's movement. A motion was passed which made ' "the right to define our sexuality" the over-riding demand of the women's movement, preceding all other demands' (Segal, 1987: 96). Ironically, many heterosexual women felt that their right to define their own sexuality was being questioned as heterosexuality was being defined as 'consorting with the enemy' and a strategy of 'political lesbianism' was being argued for. Thus, the conference identified men's sexual domination of women and the resulting inability of women to define their own sexuality as the pivot of women's oppression. Women's oppression was located in the institution of heterosexuality. This weighting of heterosexuality as the main cause of women's oppression split the movement and that conference was the last national conference.

As Coote and Campbell point out, the split was based on different analyses of women's oppression and although sexuality was the major issue the split was not simply between lesbian and heterosexual women (Coote & Campbell, 1982: 31). The differences stemmed from the differing socialist and radical feminist analyses of women's oppression. Socialist-feminist analysis of sexuality argues that women's sexuality arises from social and economic arrangements which divide production from reproduction and assign to women responsibility for reproduction within the domestic sphere. Radical feminists argue that male control over female sexuality is located in differences in physiology between women and men and underlies all other forms of oppression and exploitation. In the early years of the women's movement there was no prioritising of a single issue. After the last conference the analysis became much more simple; the enemy was men.

The growing influence of radical feminism within the movement has to be set in the context of the changing political environment. In the early 1970s the working class and the labour movement were still on the offensive. But by the end of the decade public expenditure cuts, rising unemployment and the recession made demands involving greater state expenditure on social provision seem impossibly utopian; the battle was now on to defend the gains represented by the Welfare State and this was increasingly where socialist-feminists directed their energies. It is in the context of defensive struggles on the part of socialist-feminism and the working class that radical feminism, seeming to involve a total onslaught on the system, came into its own (Bouchier, 1983; Segal, 1987).

FRAGMENTATION

Ironically, the election of the first woman Prime Minister in 1979 coincided with the fragmentation and demise of the women's movement. Hailed by some feminists as a victory for feminism, the dominant view within the movement was that Margaret Thatcher was a representative of the capitalist class and that her election would do nothing to further the cause of women's liberation. In fact, her election is a clear example of the limitations of liberal feminism and its compatibility with bourgeois democracy and capitalism. Margaret Thatcher is a highly educated, wealthy woman, who managed to combine motherhood with a demanding political career by paying other women to look after her children and take over her domestic responsibilities. For middle-class women with the money to enable them to find an individual solution to the problems of child care and domestic labour there are no barriers, except those of discrimination, to equality in education and employment. For women who do not have these resources, working-class and many ethnic minority women, individual solutions are not available. Equal rights in education and employment cannot be taken advantage of if the range of potential jobs available is already severely limited by the requirement that hours of work fit in with children's school hours and school holidays. Most of the jobs involving such hours are low paid, offering no security and minimal benefits.

There is disagreement as to whether the fragmentation of women's liberation movements in Western Europe and North America marked the demise of women's liberation as a social movement. The continued existence of groups with feminist interests is often taken to be an indication that women's movements are still alive and kicking. It is important, however, to distinguish between groups which may be working around one or another issue which is feminist, and a movement which has as its aim a profound social transformation and takes organisational form, not only in a variety of women's interest groups, but also has an autonomous existence at both local and national level. This was the case during the 1970s in Britain but not subsequently.

The situation which exists now is similar to that which existed between the first and second waves of feminism. During that period women who were feminists could be found in many different organisations pressing for improvements in women's social position (Pugh, 1992). Thus women were active in the trade union movement, the Labour Party, the peace movement and women's organisations, such as the National Council of Women and The Six Point Group. During this period that strand of feminism which stressed women's special virtues and the importance of motherhood, sometimes referred to as welfare feminism (Banks, 1986), was in evidence. Vera Brittain hailed the Welfare State as recognising women's 'unique value', for instance, though today this recognition, enshrined in the Beveridge report and subsequent Social Security legislation, is attacked as a means of confining women to domesticity, financial dependence and subordination (Wilson, 1977, 1980: 164). Women's special values were similarly invoked to explain their greater commitment to peace and many feminists were centrally involved in the Campaign for Nuclear Disarmament (CND) when it emerged in the 1950s (Wilson, 1980: 178–9). There is therefore something almost *déjà vu* about developments within feminism since the fragmentation of the women's movement at the end of the 1970s.

An appeal for the merger of the women's liberation movement and the labour movement or, rather, for the creation of a new socialist movement, was published at this time (Rowbotham *et al.*, 1980). The women's liberation movement did not merge, but many individual women activists did; moving to work within the labour movement, either in their trade unions or the Labour Party (Segal, 1987: 56; Perrigo, 1986; Elliott, 1984; Labour Party Feminists, 1984). The impact of feminism on local Labour Party politics in some areas became apparent with the election of left-wing Labour councils such as the Greater London Council (GLC) in the early 1980s. These councils were committed to the provision of child-care facilities and the implementation of equal opportunities policies, both for their own employees and within the voluntary organisations that they funded (Mackintosh & Wainwright, 1987).

Radical feminism continued to dominate what remained of the women's liberation movement and, indeed, has become the dominant form of popular feminism, along with equal rights feminism, to survive into the 1990s. Feminists are active in groups which provide services to women, such as refuges for women escaping domestic violence, rape crisis lines, incest survivors' support groups and so on; and, at the end of the 1970s and beginning of the 1980s, there continued to be anti-pornography actions and 'reclaim the night' marches, both of which challenged men's sexual violence towards women.

The 'feminist' issue of the 1980s, however, was peace, with the women's camp at Greenham Common and 30,000 women ringing the American nuclear base in the winter of 1982 (Neustatter, 1990: 51). The arguments put forward by feminists defining peace as a feminist issue bear a striking similarity to those advanced by women active in the peace movement in the 1950s. Peace is seen as a feminist issue because of women's special values of caring and non-aggression. And women are more committed than are men to peace because they are the ones who create life. Ecology is likewise defined as a feminist issue because of women's closer relationship to nature and commitment to preserving the planet, hence 'ecofeminism' (Ferree, 1987; Collins, 1991). Similarly, courses on women's studies, feminist publishing houses and so on have been established with the aim of rediscovering and revalidating women's culture.

The problem with notions of women's essential difference from men, which underlie these arguments, is that they are locked within the dichotomies which are part and parcel of Western liberalism. Far from challenging ideologies of masculinity and femininity, which are themselves linked to notions of the public and the private, men's rationality and women's emotionality, men's rights and women's virtue, this celebration of women's difference accepts the dichotomies of Western liberal thought which the women's movement was seeking to transcend (Kennedy & Mendus, 1987; Ramazanoglu, 1989: 61, 89; Collins, 1991). This is not to detract from the achievements of the women's peace movement and the courage and vision of the women permanently camped at Greenham, but simply to point out the distance that has been travelled from the transformative vision of the women's liberation movement and its goals of ending women's oppression. As Lynne Segal warns, 'The real problem with the "new feminism" which sees women as essentially virtuous and men as essentially vicious is that it serves the forces of reaction as surely as it serves the forces of progress' (Segal, 1987: 246) and it remains imprisoned within the 'ideas of sexual polarity which feminism originally aimed to challenge' (Segal, 1987: xii). And on this basis such unholy alliances can be built as that between feminist anti-pornography campaigners and Mary Whitehouse. Demands for greater state control of pornography easily lend themselves to legitimating greater state control of sexuality, thus limiting freedoms which the women's liberation movement has supported in the past and reducing women's ability to define their own sexuality (Segal, 1990).

Significantly, liberal feminist conceptions of equality have also retained currency and are particularly evident in the field of employment and education under the aegis of the Equal Opportunities Commission. This ideology argues that women and men should be treated equally because they are the same and it has accepted arguments that gender equality is impossible as long as special treatment for women continues. Thus, protective legislation has been repealed and, as in the USA, the door is now open for women to work underground in Britain for the first time since

1842. It is a moot point whether it is a victory for women that they, as well as men, may now work underground or fight in wars as American women did in the Gulf in 1991. But this is the logic of liberal feminism, a feminism which has found support in right-wing political parties in both Britain and the USA (Freeman, 1987).

The result of the fragmentation of the women's liberation movement in Britain and elsewhere has been the co-option and absorption of the struggle for women's liberation. The transformative goals of the movement have disappeared and in their place is a multiplicity of organisations and individuals working around various separate aspects of women's liberation (Haug, 1986, 1989; Hellman, 1987a; Segal, 1987). Thus, feminists are active in trade unions and political parties, some of which have taken on board demands which will help women to compete equally with men in the world of work, and others are providing much needed services for women. However, the exploitative and competitive structures of the world of work, which the women's movement challenged, remain intact rather than being transformed. And piecemeal change and support for individual women – the value of which is not to be underestimated – have taken the place of a revolutionary transformation of society.

This is not to say, however, that the women's movements of Europe and North America have not had an impact on the societies in which they emerged. Before looking at this, though, I wish to explore the issue of difference and the effect it has had on the women's movement.

DIFFERENCE

The fragmentation of the women's liberation movement coincided with the emergence of differences among women and the recognition that differences lead to different women prioritising different issues (Ramazanoglu, 1989). This realisation grew out of a trenchant critique of the racism and élitism of Western women's movements. Initially the movement had assumed an unproblematic sisterhood which linked all women in their common oppression. Despite the fact that many women's movements tried to include working-class women such attempts were rarely successful and black women's participation was significant by its absence. Older women, too, felt excluded from the predominantly youthful, white, middle-class women's movement. In the early years of the movement it was easy to ignore differences between women as most of the women who were 'different' were not participating anyway.

There is another dimension to the issue of difference and that is that strategies adopted by the women's movement seek to stress either women's similarity to or difference from men (Bacchi, 1990). For instance, the demands of the British women' movement are underpinned by assumptions about sameness and difference. The demands for equal rights assume two similarities: first, that women are the same as men and should therefore enjoy the same rights and responsibilities; differences between them are irrelevant. Second, that all women are the same and will be able to take advantage of equal rights in the same way. Clearly, in capitalist societies women do not all share the same social status; they are divided by class, 'race' and age. Defining feminist aims in terms of equality with men is therefore limited; it masks the social inequalities that exist between women and it excludes women who are not white and middle class. It may have the effect of improving the status of white, middle-class women, but is likely to have only marginal impact on other women and, in fact, may be detrimental to them. Demands for equality do not have the same meaning if all that equality will provide is the chance to be as exploited as are men. As Bell Hooks puts it:

The working class or poor woman ... knows that being discriminated against or exploited because one is female may be painful and dehumanising, but it may not necessarily be as painful, dehumanising, or threatening as being without food or shelter, as starvation, as being deathly ill but unable to obtain medical care. Had poor women set the agenda for feminist movement, they might have decided that class struggle would be a central feminist issue; that poor and privileged women would work to understand class structure and the way it pits women against one another. (Hooks, 1986: 136)

Stressing issues of equality, therefore, obscures both differences between women and interests that women may share with men, and is most appropriate for white, middle-class women for whom gender inequality is the only inequality they experience (Ramaza-noglu, 1989: 125; Chafetz, 1990: 197).

The racism of Western women's movements emerged around the issues of reproduction, sexuality and male violence against women. Black feminists have pointed out that campaigns against male sexual violence can have racist overtones. In the words of Angela Davis: 'When white women raised the strategic demand for more police, longer prison sentences, the Black community would bear the brunt of this' (Davis, 1989: 72). And in the context of an Asian woman's facing deportation from Britain because she has left her husband due to domestic violence, priorities for black women may differ from those of white women. In a particular instance the priority for black women was to campaign against the immigration rules and to ensure that the woman was granted leave to stay in Britain. However, some white women 'tried to centre the campaign around male violence, rape, and general violence against women' and in the process obscured the main issues (Trivedi 1984: 46). This is not to say that domestic violence is an issue of no concern to Asian women; it clearly is and refuges for Asian women have been set up; but in the context of a fight for leave to stay in Britain male violence is not a priority issue.

The National Abortion Campaign in Britain was similarly attacked for its racist assumptions and, in 1983, the Campaign for Reproductive Rights was set up. It focused on a wider range of issues including strategies for population control and the profligate use of dangerous contraceptives such as Depo Provera which are more likely to be used on poor, black women (Segal, 1987: 64). Similarly, analyses which located women's oppression in the family and argued that the state supports a woman's dependence within the family were accused of ignoring the positive solidarity against racist oppression that can be provided by black families (Bhavnani & Coulson, 1986: 89).

The racism and racist assumptions of the women's movement, both on an individual and on an organisational level, alienated many black women from it. The priority of the movement was to combat sexism, whereas for black women, racism and imperialism as well as sexism were identified as targets (Davis, 1989: 69). Thus, for black and working-class women oppression was not identified simply as sexist oppression but was compounded by living in a racist and class-divided society. The women's liberation movement did not encompass these differences and they, rather than the assumed identity of interests among women, became dominant towards the end of the 1970s, contributing to its fragmentation.

Another contributory factor was the lifestyle and identity politics of the women's liberation movement and its concentration on personal liberation (Davis, 1989; Harriss, 1989; Parmar, 1989). While at the beginning of the 1970s the focus on personal experience was in the context of raising awareness of the social, economic and political structures which shape and constrain personal lives, latterly politics has come to be interpreted in purely personal terms. Political consciousness is assumed to be given directly by experience, and the more oppressions a woman suffers from the more valid is her experience. It is forgotten that know-ledge does not arise spontaneously from experience but requires the intervention of theory and analysis (Barrett, 1987: 36; Ramazanoglu, 1989: 53). Many feminists now choose to ignore this, reducing politics to personal experience and defining political problems in subjective terms. Men – individual men – are identified as the oppressors of women, and women as individuals have become identified as the oppressors of other women. Heterosexual women are accused of ignoring the interests of lesbian women, white women have ignored black women's interests, young women have ignored older women's interests – the list is endless. Thus, instead of challenging the structure of oppression and domination in society the challenge is reduced to an individual level. It has been suggested that this fragmentation of women's interests and the proliferation of competing interest groups *obscures* the structure of exploitation in a racist, capitalist society and creates the possibility of co-option and absorption into 'the pluralism of capitalist democracy' (Harriss, 1989).

POLICY OUTCOMES OF THE WOMEN'S LIBERATION MOVEMENT

If social movements are difficult to define so too is their impact at the level of policy. It is sometimes implied that the coincidence of policies which address issues raised by women's movements with the movements themselves is evidence of a direct relationship between the two (Gelb, 1990). However, it is not necessarily as straightforward as this (Lovenduski, 1986; Randall, 1987; Beck-with 1987; Hellman, 1987; Banks, 1986; Gelb & Palley, 1987).

Women's liberation movements and legislation which addresses 'women's' issues may both be the result of other social processes. What can be said with more certainty is that second wave feminism emerged at a time when the contradictions between women's increasing participation in the workforce and their continuing responsibility for child rearing and home making had become acute. Both the women's liberation movement and policy changes were a response to this situation and have resulted in women's participation in the workforce becoming ideologically and politically more acceptable. In some countries the role of the women's movement in precipitating policy changes seems to have been significant. In others, although similar policy changes have occurred, it seems not to have been a direct result of the women's liberation movement. Indeed, on issues such as equal pay, there seems to have been far more effective and long-term pressure for the implementation of legislation from the labour movement and social democratic parties. This is truer for Europe than for the USA (Bouchier, 1983: 39).

An example of this is provided by Britain. After the Second World War pressure built up, particularly in the white collar unions such as the civil service and teaching unions which had a high female membership, for equal pay to be awarded to women (Wilson, 1980; Banks, 1986; Pugh, 1992). A demonstration for equal pay was organised in 1951 by a Conservative Party feminist with support of women MPs from both parties (Wilson, 1980: 172). At Labour Party conferences in 1947, 1952, 1963 and 1968 resolutions were passed committing the party to implementing equal pay (Craig, 1982). But it was the Conservatives who legislated for equal pay in the Civil Service and teaching in 1954. It was to be introduced in stages up to 1961 (Wilson, 1980: 173; Pugh, 1992). Other unions subsequently committed themselves to equal pay, and there was increasing pressure on governments to implement equal pay because Britain was applying to join the European Common Market which required member states to legislate for equal pay for women. The Labour Party won the election in 1964 committed to implementing equal pay but, as we have already seen, made good its promise only under pressure from women trade unionists. The Equal Pay Act was passed in 1970 but equal pay was not fully implemented until 1975. This enabled many employers to reorganise their workforces in such a way as to ensure that gender segregation minimised the overlap between men's and women's jobs and, consequently, the ability of women to claim equal pay (Snell, 1986). Similarly, pressure for anti-discrimination legislation did not emanate from the women's liberation movement but was in evidence prior to its emergence. Women within the Labour Party in the 1960s were pressing for such legislation, which eventually reached the statute books in 1975. As Olive Banks comments:

The British equal rights legislation of the early 1970s, therefore . . . does not owe its origin to the new feminism, even if a new feminist awareness helped create the mood in which such legislation could be better achieved. (Banks, 1986: 219–20)

This point is important. Many authors have pointed to one of the lasting effects of the women's movements of the 1970s as being a change in consciousness which is still apparent in the 1990s (Segal, 1987; Lovenduski, 1986: Neustatter, 1990; Gelb, 1990; Flammang, 1987; Mueller, 1987; Freeman, 1987). And it is through this change in consciousness that some of the policy changes have been effected. There is thus a complex relationship between the emergence of women's movements, the influence of feminist ideas on women (and men) who are active politically but may not be directly involved in the women's movement, and the implementation of policies which are related to the demands of the movement. The intermediate stage may also consist of women who are active in the movement involving or re-involving themselves in trade unions and political parties and pushing for them to adopt feminist policies (Freeman, 1987; Mueller, 1987; Perrigo, 1986).

Although this process may result in the adoption and implementation of policies that are feminist inspired, it usually involves a change in emphasis such that the original demands are only partially met (Beckwith, 1987; Petchesky, 1986). And this implementation of watered-down feminist demands is part of the process of co-option noted by several authors (Hellman, 1987a: 48–9; Lovenduski, 1986; Haug, 1989). This process removes the dynamism from the women's movement and absorbs the energies of many of its activists, resulting in accommodation to the existing political system rather than its transformation (Offe, 1990).

Let us look a little more closely at the sorts of policy developments that accompanied women's liberation movements in

Europe and North America. As we have already seen, the demands raised by women's movements covered issues of equal rights; women's control of sexuality and reproduction; child-care arrangements and violence towards women. It appears that in the USA and Britain equal rights were granted later than in Western Europe; consequently pressure for their implementation was greater. In Western Europe the central issues were contraception and abortion and, in the Catholic countries, divorce reform. In many countries legislation liberalising abortion was passed as a direct result of pressure from women's movements (Lovenduski, 1986; Threlfall, 1985; Beckwith, 1987). In Italy, for instance, the demand of the women's movement for a woman's right to choose resulted in all the left political parties presenting their own version of abortion legislation. This has resulted in one of the most liberal abortion laws in Western Europe although, because of the lack of adequate provision, it still does not fulfil the movement's demand that a woman has the right to choose (Beckwith, 1987; Hellman, 1987, 1987a; Morgan & Lee, 1991: 34–5). In West Germany, on the other hand, women's access to abortion is hedged around with limitations although abortion is now legal. In Britain, legislation legalising abortion was put on the statute books in 1967, before the emergence of the women's movement but in a climate of sexual liberalisation, and coincided with legislation that legalised homosexual acts between consenting adults. It also coincided with legislation which enabled local authorities to provide advice on contraception (the Family Planning Act) and was preceded by the thalidomide scare in 1962 (Bouchier, 1983: 27, 39). The women's movement in Britain was, throughout the 1970s and into the 1980s, involved in campaigns to prevent the passage through parliament of a series of Private Members' Bills designed to restrict women's access to abortion. The most recent legislation has, in effect, lowered the upper time limit for termination to 24 weeks but liberalised it in certain circumstances (Morgan & Lee, 1991). Every time there is a threat to the abortion legislation support for the 1967 act is mobilised through the Abortion Law Reform Association, an organisation which long pre-dates the women's liberation movement, and the National Abortion Campaign (NAC). The success of the NAC was manifest in the TUC demonstration in 1979 in defence of the 1967 Abortion Act against John Corrie's attempt to restrict it. In 1978 the TUC had made a commitment to organise such a demonstration should the need arise, and the result was the biggest-ever demonstration in defence of a woman's right to choose with 100,000 participants (Lovenduski, 1986: 81; Coote & Campbell, 1982: 147–8). The support of the TUC had been won by women trade unionists working within their unions to organise support for the 1967 Act. The NAC was an example of a women's movement organisation building links with the labour movement, it set up the Labour Abortion Rights Campaign within the Labour Party and gained the support of the trade unions and Labour Party. It also established itself as a centrally co-ordinated national organisation with a presence at national level which was recognised by government (Lovenduski, 1986: 80).

Women's liberation movements also mobilised around the issue of male violence, particularly domestic violence and rape (Lovenduski, 1986; Randall, 1987). In Britain the first refuge for women escaping domestic violence was set up in 1972 in Chiswick, and since that time many local refuge groups have opened refuges for women run on a self-help basis with minimal state funding. They are affiliated to Women's Aid Federations in England, Scotland and Wales. During the early 1970s the Department of Health and Social Security sponsored research into domestic violence and the government set up a Select Committee on violence within marriage which made recommendations as to minimum levels of provision (Select Committee, 1975). At the same time two pieces of legislation were passed which recognised domestic violence as a serious problem. The Domestic Violence Act of 1976 gave women limited legal protection from domestic violence for the first time, and the Housing (Homeless Persons) Act 1977 recognised domestic violence or threat of domestic violence as a legitimate cause of homelessness. The actions of the women's movement and the setting up of refuges with attendant publicity quite clearly contributed to raising the awareness of domestic violence as a problem. Much of the work of Women's Aid is educational and is aimed at those professionals, such as the police, who may come into contact with women who are being abused. Similarly, rape crisis lines have been set up by the women's movement and the groups that run them also perform an educational function. There are perceptible changes in this area also. In 1976 the Sexual Offences (Amendment) Act preserved the anonymity of women during rape trials and, in 1991, rape within marriage was criminalised. Previously, rape within marriage had been deemed not to exist in law in England and Wales (*Guardian*, 15 February 1991; Lovenduski, 1986: 78–9).

Equal rights campaigns were a more important part of the women's movement in the USA than in Britain and Europe, although equal rights legislation was passed by many European governments during the 1970s. For instance, equal rights for women were enshrined in the Italian constitution in 1946 but, in the 1970s, legislation on equal pay and sex discrimination was introduced to bring Italian law in line with the Treaty of Rome (Lovenduski, 1986: 265). Thus, in the USA much of the activity of the women's movement has centred on the Equal Rights Amendment, equal pay having become law in 1963 (Banks, 1986: 210). However, in the USA as in Britain, pressure for equal rights had been present and had affected policies long before the emergence of the women's movement and dating from first wave feminism (Gelb & Palley, 1987). It may be that labour shortages, combined with economic growth after the Second World War in both countries, were important factors in generating pressure and a sympathetic climate for introducing more gender equality into employment practice, particularly in the context of the need to attract women into the workforce.

In the USA sex discrimination was outlawed, along with discrimination on grounds of 'race', in 1964 with the passing of the Civil Rights Act (Banks, 1986: 212). The National Organisation of Women was set up in order to ensure the implementation of anti-discrimination measures of the Civil Rights Act as they affected women. This was because the Equal Employment Opportunities Commission had refused to enforce the gender aspects of the act (Banks, 1986: 212). In some respects, in the USA and Britain, the women's movement was acting not to get policies onto the statute books but to make sure that a paper commitment was turned into something more tangible.

In Europe it is from the EEC that much of the impetus for implementing and enforcing equal rights has come, particularly in the area of employment. Thus, joining the EEC has increased pressure for change in this area and it periodically issues equality directives with which member nations are required to comply. In the 1970s it issued directives covering equal pay, equal treatment in employment and training and equal treatment in Social Security (Lovenduski, 1986: 283). It is no coincidence that Britain's equal pay legislation came into effect in 1975, the year the equal pay directive was issued. More recently, women have been able to take cases of discrimination in social security matters to the European Court and have effected changes to some of the more discriminatory aspects of the British social security legislation. It is significant that the 1975 Sex Discrimination Act covered employment and education but did not cover social security. Therefore, redress is not available in British law for discrimination within the social security system which is grounded in assumptions of women's financial dependence on men within the family (Wilson, 1977). This legislation has so far survived although the British taxation laws were reformed in 1990 in the direction of greater gender equality.

Although reform has occurred in most of Western Europe and North America such that women have equal rights in terms of employment and education and have access to the means of fertility control, success in increasing the provision of child care has not been marked. This is despite the importance attached to it by women's movements and the campaigns around its provision which took place in the 1970s (Charles, 1979). In fact, child-care provision in Britain is amongst the worst in Europe. It is only now, with the projected downturn in the supply of young people coming onto the labour market and employers' need to look toward married women to supply their demand for skilled labour, that child-care provision is beginning to receive any government attention. The Labour Party is committed to some form of state provision of child care if it is returned to office, but the Conservative government has made it clear that it is up to employers and women themselves to find a solution to their mutual problem (Moss, 1991). The high cost of child-care provision is likely to mean that employers who need to retain professional and skilled women workers will invest in such provision, whereas, for most women, employers will not be prepared to make the necessary investment, and the solution to combining employment with child-care responsibilities will remain part-time, flexible and low paid hours of work for women.

The adoption of equal opportunities policies by many employers during the 1980s, in response to the anti-discrimination legislation and under pressure from trade unions, has also raised the issue of child care and it now has a higher public profile. During the early 1980s, as we have already seen, the GLC and other metropolitan authorities introduced comprehensive equal opportunities policies for their employees and priority was attached to the provision of child-care facilities. Many also set up women's committees to advise on the effects of policies on women and to involve ordinary women in the policy-making process (Wainwright, 1987; Goss, 1984). These developments were partly a result of the influx of women's movement activists into local Labour Party branches after 1979, but women within the Labour Party who had not necessarily been active in the women's liberation movement were also instrumental in getting such policies adopted (Wainwright, 1987).

Before leaving this discussion of the policy impact of women's movements it is important to note that similar policies have also been adopted in societies where no women's movement has been in existence. Thus, Sweden was in advance of Europe and North America in legislating for women's rights, as were the countries of the Eastern bloc and the USSR. There are two factors which are important here and which these countries share. The first is a labour shortage and a resulting need to encourage women to enter the workforce; and the second is a strong collectivist or socialist orientation (Lovenduski, 1986: 100). Thus, it seems possible to argue that policies which give women equal rights in employment and education, which outlaw discrimination on grounds of sex and which allow women to limit the number of children they have, are necessary if women are to be able and willing to participate in the workforce. And increased participation of women, particularly married women, in the workforces of Western Europe and North America has certainly occurred throughout the twentieth century and particularly since the end of the Second World War.

Most of the legislation and policy changes we have looked at relate to women's employment and facilitate their entry into the workforce. It is even possible to regard legislation on rape and domestic violence as part of this process. Male violence towards women has been identified by feminists as a means of controlling women's access to public space (Hanmer & Maynard, 1987; Brownmiller, 1986; Hanmer & Saunders, 1984; Pahl, 1985). If women are required in the workforce then any restriction on their movements is potentially problematic. For instance, if women are working a late shift as telephonists or nurses they risk attack in leaving their work place late at night. This is a serious concern for employers as well as for women themselves.

What I am suggesting is that both the women's liberation movements and changes in public policy and legislation which affect gender divisions can be seen as responses to changes in the pattern of women's employment. Changes in the economy, which have increased the demand for female labour, have been occurring since the beginning of the twentieth century and in societies where there has been a strong and consistent working-class influence on the state, legislation has kept pace with these changes and facilitated women's entry into the workforce. In other countries this has not happened and it is there that women's movements have emerged. Their emergence seems to have had the effect of accelerating changes that would probably sooner or later have occurred anyway. Thus, it could be argued that the women's movements have played a part in changing legal and social policies such that they are more in line with economic developments. Supporting this analysis is the continuing influence of the EEC on member countries to introduce measures which will enable women to participate on an equal basis with men of their own social class in employment. This development cannot be seen in any direct way as a result of second wave feminism (Lovenduski, 1986: 284).

It is also argued that women's movements have been important in changing consciousness (Gelb, 1990). Indeed, the continued existence of women's groups and the public visibility of feminist ideology stems from the women's movements of the 1970s. An example of this is provided by such things as the BBC's commitment to using gender-free language, an outcome of consistent campaigns waged by women within the media unions. The feminist ideologies which retain currency, however, are: an individualistic equal rights feminism which, in Britain at least, has been strengthened by Margaret Thatcher's long period as Prime Minister and which fits very comfortably with an increasingly competitive society where individual initiative and assertiveness are highly valued; and a feminism which emphasises women's unique qualities which makes them different from and better than men. This feminism, stressing women's connectedness with one another and with humanity as a whole, is to be found in movements such as the peace movement and ecofeminism. Socialist-feminism is not part of popular feminism. The feminist ideologies which retain currency are compatible with the values of capitalist societies, stressing either competition and individualism or connectedness and difference. Within liberal thought, the former is defined as part of the public realm and the latter as part of the private. The two feminisms thus retain this duality and do not challenge the underlying categories. What has happened, though, is that women's participation in the public realm has become more accepted, while their special responsibility and aptitude for caring and nurturing remains intact. This is despite the challenge to the domestic division of labour which was central to the women's movement. As Gelb and Palley put it, role equity issues have found support amongst policy makers while role change issues, which involve redistributing power and resources, have not (Gelb & Palley, 1987: 210).

The goal of the women's liberation movement was a transformation of society such that gender divisions which subordinated women no longer existed. In order for this to come about, a restructuring of both the public and the private spheres was essential. This has not yet happened. The reforms that have taken place have facilitated women's involvement in public life without significantly altering the domestic division of labour. And feminists identified this division of labour as being central to women's subordination. Women's dependence on men within the family still underpins much social policy and legislation and their responsibility for the home and children has hardly been touched. This is reflected in the lack of commitment to social provision of child care in most capitalist countries, with the notable exception of Sweden, although this may change with the increased need to attract women to the workforce and to retain them. This lack is more marked in the USA and Britain than in other Western European countries (Melhuish & Moss, 1991).

The women's movement has not, therefore, achieved its aims. But this does not mean that it has had no impact on gender divisions. During the 1970s, when the women's movements were at their height, there was a spate of legislation throughout Western Europe and North America which improved women's position as workers and made discrimination on grounds of gender or pregnancy unlawful. This does not, of course, mean that such discrimination no longer exists, especially as much of the legislation excluded many categories of women workers. The move towards greater gender equality in employment is continuing but is contradictory. On the one hand, efforts are being made to retain skilled women workers by providing career breaks, crèche facilities and allowing women to work from home; on the other, employers are providing flexible, part-time hours for women employees, but this goes hand in hand with low pay, lack of entitlement to maternity leave and much of the legislation protecting workers from arbitrary dismissal, and total lack of job security. There is now an expectation that women will work in paid employment for most of their lives, taking a relatively short time out when their children are of pre-school age. However, it is still women who will take time out to look after young children rather than men, and men's pay is still higher than women's, the gap having hardly changed since pre-women's movement days (Gelb & Palley, 1987: 210).

It is possible to argue that the women's movements and women's increasing participation in the workforce and accompanying legislation are part of a process of social transition (Harris, 1987). Juliet Mitchell suggests that the women's movement may have contributed to a process of deskilling and casualisation of the workforce, a substitution of part-time insecure employment for full-time secure employment, which characterised Western capitalist economies throughout the 1980s (Mitchell, 1986). She suggests that women's demands for equal employment opportunities and an end to discrimination have to be set in the context of rising male unemployment and rising female employment. This has led to women's being in the vanguard of an economic transition that involves: the substitution of part-time workers for full-time workers, under the guise of providing employment which is suitable for women; the deskilling and cheapening of labour through employing women on 'new' jobs using new technology which then renders the old, skilled jobs redundant; and a third stage which has not yet been reached, of reasserting women's domestic role and withdrawing or excluding married women from the workforce. This third stage may not happen, but Mitchell's assessment of the long-term effects of the women's liberation movement provides a counter-balance to analysts who argue that it is all progress and, importantly, situates those effects in the context of capitalist economic development and class struggle, a context which is ignored by liberal and radical feminism and their popular variants. She also suggests that feminism, by emphasising the common experience of women and counterposing this to men, has contributed to the creation of the myth of the classless society; a necessary ideological prelude to the redrawing of the class map and the redefining of class boundaries. The fate of women's liberation movements and their impact on gender divisions of labour seem to depend to a considerable extent on the vagaries of capitalist economies and their changing labour requirements, and they need to be assessed within this context (Chafetz & Dworkin, 1986).

From this discussion it seems evident that the women's movements of Western Europe and North America have had an impact on the societies in which they emerged. But the impact is not unidirectional nor has it resulted in the transformation of society that was envisaged by women activists in the early days of the movements. The women's liberation movements of the 1970s may be understood as a means of bringing gender ideologies into line with economic developments and facilitating a restructuring of the gender division of labour. This restructuring has changed the distribution of women and men within the workforce and has made it more acceptable for men to be seen pushing prams and hanging out the washing; but it has not resulted in the elimination of women's subordination and may have contributed to the fragmentation of the working class and the undermining of its resistance to capitalist exploitation.

CONCLUSIONS

In these final pages I propose to draw together the theoretical arguments that have been presented in the book rather than to recapitulate the main points of each chapter. It will be remembered that three issues of theoretical importance were discussed in the introduction and have formed a leitmotif throughout the chapters which followed. These are the control of women's labour by men; the seemingly universal involvement of women in reproductive activities; and the relationship between gender divisions of labour and modes of production.

It appears, from the evidence presented here, that there is a strong argument to be made that different gender divisions of labour are associated with different modes of production. Thus, egalitarian gender divisions of labour characterise hunter-gatherer or foraging societies while extremely inegalitarian and hierarchical gender divisions characterise agrarian societies. Inequalities between women and men do not exist in isolation from other inequalities, and the link between the emergence of gender inequality and exploitative relations of production identified by Engels seems to be supported by contemporary ethnographic evidence. The emergence of inegalitarian gender divisions is located in the sphere of production rather than reproduction and it is argued that it is the ability of men to control the labour of women that led to the emergence of male domination. Labour is, of course, a productive resource, or part of the means of production, and the ability to control female labour emerged alongside unequal access to other productive resources. This control may have developed from the distinction between owner-producers (men and women) and producers (women) that emerged in patrilineal, patrilocal societies. Control over female labour eventually led to control over female sexuality and reproduction. This argument prioritises production over reproduction in explaining changes in gender divisions of labour and the emergence of male dominance.

Biological reproduction does, however, have a part to play in this type of explanation because it is recognised that fertility levels may affect the nature of women's participation in production. However, changes in levels of fertility are themselves linked to changes in the mode of production which lead to improvements in diet, for instance, or changes from nomadic to sedentary modes of existence or changes in the demand for labour. Thus, in hunter-gatherer societies, where women's participation in production is high and gender divisions of labour are egalitarian, women space births so that their role in productive activities is not curtailed. And in industrial societies means of fertility control are sanctioned to enable women to control their fertility and participate in the labour force. It seems then that changes in the mode of production may affect levels of fertility as well as gender divisions of labour.

Male control over female labour is important to the subsequent development of male control of female sexuality and male domination. As we have seen, male control over female labour could have emerged from changes in the labour process associated with the emergence of stratification. It has also been argued that increased control over female labour is one of the results of colonialist expansion and disruption of pre-colonial economies. Capitalist development, however, has contradictory effects on women. In some contexts it may increase their autonomy and reduce male control and in others it may reduce their autonomy and increase the potential for male control. However, nowhere has capitalist development led to egalitarian gender divisions of labour and, in most circumstances where it has reduced male control over women, it has done this through disrupting systems of production which are household based and impoverishing the mass of the population. Male control of female labour appears to be most marked in agrarian societies which are characterised also by high levels of fertility and repressive gender ideologies. An important exception to this is provided by the wet-rice growing regions of the world where women enjoy relatively high degrees of autonomy and where, importantly, their contribution to production is not only essential but visible. This evidence suggests that women's status is related to the amount of control that they themselves exercise over their own labour, an important aspect of the means of production.

Industrialisation, particularly in its labour-intensive early stages, has the potential to undermine male control of female labour by enabling women's participation in wage-labour. This may be because, historically, the process of industrialisation has undermined labour processes which are household based and which are predicated upon specific gender divisions of labour. For example, within peasant households women's labour is controlled by the head of household who also exercises control over their sexuality and reproductive capacities. With the move to factory-based production these two types of control are separated. And although men occupy positions of authority and control within the capitalist labour process, the personal and intimate tyranny of the male head of household is separated from control of the workforce and women's labour within the workforce. This argument is supported by historical evidence which shows that, during the period of capitalist industrialisation in Europe, struggles were waged in order to reconstitute within the work-place the male–female authority relations which were being undermined by the development of industrialisation and the destruction of the household as a productive unit. These struggles have resulted in the reconstitution of male–female authority relations within the labour process. Similar processes can be observed in developing societies. The development of wage-labour and women's participation in it, although it may disconnect control of women's labour from control of their sexuality, does not mean that women exercise control over their own labour. The extent to which this occurs partly depends on gender ideologies and practices within family households and kinship systems. Where practices which reinforce women's subordination are eliminated and patriarchal authority undermined by state measures, or when pre-existing gender ideologies allow a degree of female autonomy, women are more likely to control the product of their labour (in this case the wage) than in circumstances where repressive gender ideologies and family structures are not challenged. Similarly, with capitalist development both women and men become free to sell their labour power and, in this sense, exercise control over it, but control within the labour process is exercised by the capitalist class and, within enterprises, usually by men. Women, therefore, may escape the control of their male head of household only to find it replaced by male authority within the work-place. Thus, although industrialisation and modernisation disrupt and transform existing gender divisions, the potential challenge that this poses to women's subordination may simply result in its reconstitution in different forms.

This process of disruption and reconstitution has also occurred in societies attempting to construct socialism. Socialism, while promising an end to women's subordination, has given rise to a gender division of labour which is similar to the gender divisions characterising capitalist society. This outcome, that women are responsible for domestic labour and child care within the family household and are therefore disadvantaged in the world of paid work and politics, is not, however, inevitable. Struggles were waged in the early years in the USSR, for instance, between those who wanted to transform this domestic division of labour and those who wanted to preserve 'the family'. Those wanting to preserve it won and the first and subsequent socialist regimes have supported the family as the basic unit of society. It is argued that retaining women's responsibility for domestic labour within the family is the cheapest way of ensuring the reproduction of the working class. This is crucial in societies which are characterised by class exploitation and where capital accumulation is the driving force. The constant pressure to maximise accumulation leads to a constant struggle between the working class and the capitalist class over the distribution of the cost of reproducing the workforce. Hence the struggle in capitalist societies over welfare provision, important to the reproduction of the working class, and the provision of social facilities, wages and so on. A gender division of labour within the household that assigns to women responsibility for child care and domestic labour is cheaper for capital than providing social facilites such as nurseries and dining-rooms. It is therefore in the interests of capital accumulation that such a gender division of labour exists within the working class. However, the extent to which this occurs varies between societies and at different historical periods within societies. This variation appears to be the outcome of class and gender struggles.

Despite the evidence that socialist modernisation has much in common with capitalist modernisation and that the effects of both on gender divisions are similar, there are important differences. In particular, socialist regimes are likely to introduce measures which raise the standard of living of the poorest sectors of society. Such measures are of benefit to women as workers, as peasants and as members of the poorest strata of society among which women are likely to be overrepresented. This is an important point and illustrates that class struggle is not irrelevant to women. As we have seen, socialist societies and societies such as Sweden, where there is a strong working-class influence on the state, are more likely to pursue policies which benefit the working class. Such policies often include the provision of social facilties, such as nurseries, and a commitment to equal pay for women and men. They benefit the working class because they raise the standard of living of the class and reduce their personal expenditure on social reproduction. But they also benefit women. The collective organisation of the working class therefore affects women as workers and peasants by improving their living and working conditions. However, what is clear from the material presented is that, although the influence of the working class on state policies may benefit women, nowhere has it succeeded in eliminating women's subordination.

The persistence of gender divisions which disadvantage women and their existence in many different societies have led marxist-feminists to conclude that it is women's responsibility for reproductive activities which explains their subordination. This analysis has been developed in order to explain gender divisions of labour in both the developed and developing worlds and in socialist and capitalist societies. According to this analysis, women's secondary status in the world of paid employment can be explained by their responsibility for reproduction. This is not simply, or even mainly, biological reproduction, but those activities that ensure the daily and generational survival of themselves and other members of their households. Such activities produce use-values rather than exchange values and have, hitherto, not been regarded as productive. They have not been regarded as productive because they do not attract a wage but, nevertheless, they are of crucial importance to the economy because they contribute to the reproduction of the workforce. The recognition of the importance of women's unpaid labour is an important outcome of feminist research and analysis. Thus, in advanced capitalist societies women engage in domestic labour within the home in order to feed and clothe themselves and their families. Similarly, women in Third World societies engage in subsistence agriculture and activities such as food processing and preparation; these activities are conceptualised as reproductive activities. In both types of society women may also participate in wage-labour. The significance of these activities for the formal economy is substantial although immeasurable as they take place outside the capital-wage labour relation. The responsibility of women for reproduction is also a feature of socialist societies and, it is argued, limits the ability of women to participate in the labour force. However, although such an explanation is appealing it seems to be a tautology. It is surely women's responsibility for reproductive activities and the associated undervaluing of their work which is in need of explanation, and it cannot be explained simply by observing that it is a common feature of developing and developed societies and must therefore be the cause of women's subordination. To assert that women's responsibility for such tasks explains their secondary status within the workforce is to explain one aspect of the gender division of labour by recourse to another, a position with was examined in Chapter 2 and found wanting, and which has as its basis a reproductive or biological model, the ultimate explanation for women's responsibility for reproductive activities being their role in biological reproduction. A second problem is that the categories mobilised are the same categories as are mobilised by classical sociological theory and which led feminists to berate it for its inability to conceptualise gender divisions of labour. Women's timeless responsibility for reproduction rendered them uninteresting to the project of sociology. Instead production, which changed over time and varied from society to society, was chosen as the object of study. Thirdly, and most importantly, there is considerable confusion about the way in which reproduction is conceptualised. Is it to refer to those tasks that are carried out by women within the domestic sphere? Is it all those activities which produce use-values rather than exchange values? Or does it refer to the process of social reproduction whereby a society reproduces the conditions which are necessary to its continued existence? Within much of the feminist literature, reproduction seems to have become synonymous with child care and other domestic activities, those activities which ensure that individuals survive from day to day. Undoubtedly such survival is an important part of social reproduction, but it is not all that is involved, even in the reproduction of labour power.

A more fruitful way of approaching the problem is to define clearly what is meant by social reproduction and then to assess whether it can explain women's subordination. Social reproduction is taken to refer to the processes by which a society reproduces itself through time. Part of this process is the reproduction of the workforce or labour power which necessarily involves the biological reproduction of human beings but cannot be reduced to it. Thus, in advanced industrial societies the reproduction of the workforce involves women in bearing and rearing children but it also involves education and training and a certain level of health care, all provided outside the family household. Clearly this involves far more than unpaid domestic labour and men as well as women participate in social reproduction. However, it is true that all over the world women retain the responsibility for non-waged aspects of social reproduction. This needs explaining because this is the form taken by women's subordination.

It has already been said that within societies characterised by class exploitation and the drive for capital accumulation there is a constant struggle over the distribution of the costs of social reproduction. And one of the ways of keeping down the costs to capital is to support a gender division of labour which makes women responsible for child care and other domestic tasks within the family household. Although the burden of unpaid reproductive tasks on women may be less in societies where the working class is able to shift responsibility for the costs of social reproduction more in its favour, it is still women who carry that burden. In order to explain this, concepts such as patriarchy and gender ideology have been mobilised, as have variations in levels of fertility (Chapter 3). It seems possible to argue that struggles are waged over the distribution of the costs of social reproduction, both between classes and between genders, and that these struggles are associated with levels of fertility and gender ideologies, both of which bear a relation to the mode of production. However, the nature of the relationship between modes of production, gender divisions, fertility levels and gender ideologies requires further analysis. What is clear is that the concept of social reproduction on its own is not sufficient to explain gender divisions of labour which subordinate women, and that underlying its use lurks a reproductive model.

Feminists have also argued that gender ideologies are important in maintaining and reproducing gender divisions. The evidence presented here suggests that certain types of gender ideology are associated with certain types of society and may be an important means of legitimating gender divisions of labour. Thus, gender ideologies which stress male authority over women are associated with agrarian societies where male control over female labour is an important aspect of production. In industrial societies naturalistic gender ideologies predominate which legitimate existing gender inequalities in the name of natural, biological differences between women and men. This is linked to the association of capitalism and industrialisation with secularisation and the emergence of science. Science thus replaces religion as the legitimating ideology.

It has also been suggested that ideologies are important in the constitution or reconstitution of gender divisions of labour. Thus, during the industrial revolution in Britain, struggles were waged in order to reconstitute male authority within the factory when its basis in household-based production was being undermined. Similarly, after the revolution in the USSR and with the support of the peasantry, a new form of the family was established as the basic unit of society in the face of attempts to abolish it altogether. Gender ideologies are therefore important both in preserving and legitimating existing gender divisions of labour and in mobilising social groups to challenge or defend existing gender divisions of labour. An example of the former is provided by the women's liberation movement which fought for gender equality and for the recognition of women's difference from men. Conflicting gender ideologies are apparent here, both of which have a place in capitalist, industrial society.

Finally, I have tried to demonstrate that gender divisions cannot be understood in isolation from the rest of society. They are part of the social and economic structure of societies and different types of society are characterised by different forms of gender division and different gender ideologies. Similarly, social movements which challenge gender divisions and gender ideologies are part of wider processes of social and economic change. Indeed, gender divisions and gender ideologies are often challenged precisely to facilitate processes such as modernisation and economic development. Perhaps unsurprisingly, when this is so, social movements and the regimes resulting from them have not eliminated women's subordination. But neither have social movements which have women's liberation as their sole aim. Such movements have emerged with capitalist society and are both a product of and contributor to the social and economic changes associated with capitalism. However, despite the express commitment of these movements to women's liberation and the changes in gender divisions that are associated with them, women's subordination persists. It is hoped that the analysis presented in the preceding pages may contribute to an understanding of why this is so.

BIBLIOGRAPHY

Acosta-Belén, Edna and Bose, Christine E.: 'From structural subordination to empowerment: women and development in Third World contexts', *Gender and Society*, vol. 4 no. 3, 1990, pp. 299–320.

ACTT (Association of Cinematograph, Television and Allied Technicians): *Patterns of Discrimination against Women in the Film and Television Industries*, ACTT: London, 1975.

Afonja, Simi: 'Changing modes of production and the sexual division of labour among the Yoruba', *Signs*, 7 (2), 1981, pp. 299–313.

Afonja, Simi: 'Women, power and authority in traditional Yoruba society', in Dube, L., Leacock, E. and Ardener, S. (eds): *Visibility and Power: Essays on women in society and development*, Oxford University Press: Oxford, 1986, pp. 136–57.

Afonja, Simi: 'Land control: a critical factor in Yoruba gender stratification', in Robertson, C. and Berger, I. (eds): *Women and Class in Africa*, Africana Publishing Company: New York, 1986a, pp. 78–91.

Afonja, Simi: 'Changing patterns of gender stratification in West Africa' in Tinker, I. (ed.): *Persistent Inequalities: Women and world development*, Oxford University Press: Oxford, 1990, pp. 198–209.

Afshar, Haleh: 'The position of women in an Iranian Village', in Afshar, H. (ed.): *Women, Work and Ideology in the Third World*, Tavistock: London, 1985, pp. 66–82.

Afshar, Haleh: 'Women and reproduction in Iran', in Yuval-Davis, N. and Anthias, F. (eds): *Woman–Nation–State*, Macmillan: Basingstoke, 1989, pp. 110–25.

Agarwal, Bina: 'Women and technological change in agriculture: the Asian and African experience', in Ahmed, I. (ed.): *Technology and Rural Women: Conceptual and empirical issues*, Allen and Unwin: London, 1985, pp. 67–114.

Ahmed, Leila: 'Women and the advent of Islam', *Signs*, 11 (4), 1986, pp. 665–91.

Akeroyd, Anne V.: 'Gender, food production and property rights: constraints on women farmers in southern Africa', in Afshar, A. (ed.): *Women, Survival and Development in the Third World*, Longman: Harlow, 1991, pp. 139–71.

Alavi, Hamza: 'The structure of peripheral capitalism', in Alavi, H. and Shanin, T. (eds): *Introduction to the Sociology of 'Developing' Societies*, Macmillan: London, 1982, pp. 172–92.

Albers, Patricia C.: 'From illusion to illumination: anthropological studies of American Indian women', in Morgen, S. (ed.): *Gender and Anthropology: Critical reviews for research and teaching*, American Anthropological Association: Washington DC, 1989, pp. 132–70.

Alexander, Sally: 'Women's work in nineteenth century London: a study of the years 1820–50', in Mitchell, J. and Oakley, A. (eds): *The Rights and Wrongs of Women*, Penguin: Harmondsworth, 1979, pp. 59–111.

Althusser, Louis: *Lenin and Philosophy*, New Left Books: London, 1971.

Anderson, Karen: 'Commodity exchange and subordination: Montagnais-Naskapi and Huron women, 1600–1650', *Signs*, 11 (1), 1985, pp. 48–62 .

Ardener, Edwin: 'Belief and the problem of women', in Ardener, S. (ed.), *Perceiving Women*, Dent: London, 1975, pp. 1–18.

Ardener, Edwin: 'The "Problem" revisited', in Ardener, S. (ed.): *Perceiving Women*, Dent: London, 1975a, pp. 19–28.

Aries, Philippe: *Centuries of Childhood*, Random House: New York, 1962.

Arizpe, Lourdes: 'Women in the informal labour sector: the case of Mexico City', *Signs*, 3 (1), 1977, pp. 25–37.

Arizpe, Lourdes and Aranda, Josefina: 'The "Comparative Advantages" of women's disadvantages: women workers in the strawberry export agribusiness in Mexico', *Signs*, 7 (2), 1981, pp. 453–73.

Arnfred, Signe: 'Women in Mozambique: gender struggle and politics', *Review of African Political Economy*, 41, 1988, pp. 5–16.

Awe, Bolanle and Ezumah, Nkoli N.: 'Women in West Africa: a Nigerian case study', in Gallin, R.S. and Ferguson, A. (eds): *The Women and International Development Annual*, vol. 2, Westview: Boulder, CO, 1991, pp. 177–204.

Babb, Florence E: 'Producers and reproducers: Andean market women in the economy', in Nash, J., Safa, H. and contributors: *Women and Change in Latin America*, Bergin and Garvey: South Hadley, MA, 1986, pp. 53–64.

Bacchi, Carol Lee: *Same Difference: Feminism and sexual difference*, Allen and Unwin: London, 1990.

Bakker, Isabella: 'Women's employment in comparative perspective',

Feminisation of the Labour Force: Paradoxes and promises, Jenson, J., Hagen, E. and Reddy, G. (eds), Polity: Oxford, 1988, pp. 17–44.

Banks, Olive: *Faces of Feminism*, Blackwell: Oxford, 1986.

Barash, David P.: *Sociobiology and Behaviour*, Heinemann: London, 1978.

Barrett, Michele: *Women's Oppression Today*, Verso: London, 1980.

Barrett, Michele: 'Rethinking women's oppression: a reply to Brenner and Ramas', *New Left Review*, 146, 1984, pp. 123–8.

Barrett, Michele and Hamilton, Roberta (eds): *The Politics of Diversity*, Verso: London, 1986.

Barrett, Michele: 'The concept of difference', *Feminist Review*, no. 26, 1987, pp. 29–41.

Barrett, Michele and McIntosh, Mary: 'The "Family wage": some problems for socialists and feminists', *Capital and Class*, 11, 1980.

Barrios de Chungara, Domitila: *Let me speak*, Monthly Review Press: New York, 1978.

Barrios de Chungara, Domitila: 'Women and Organisation', in Davies, M. (ed.): *Third World, Second Sex: Women's struggles and national liberation*, Zed: London, 1983, pp. 39–59.

Bassnett, Susan: *Feminist Experiences: The women's movement in four cultures*, Allen and Unwin: London, 1986.

Beall, Jo, Hassim, Shireen and Todes, Alison: ' "A bit on the side"?: gender politics in the politics of transformation in South Africa', *Feminist Review*, 33, 1989, pp. 30–56.

Bebel, August: *Woman under Socialism*, Schocken: New York, 1975.

Beckwith, Karen: 'Response to feminism in the Italian Parliament: divorce, abortion, and sexual violence legislation', in Katzenstein, M., Mueller, C. (eds): *The Women's Movements of the United States and Western Europe*, Temple University Press: Philadelphia, 1987, pp. 153–71.

Beechey, Veronica: 'On Patriarchy', *Feminist Review*, 3, 1979, pp. 66–82.

Beechey, Veronica: 'What's so special about women's employment?: a review of some recent studies of women's paid work', *Feminist Review*, 15, 1983, pp. 23–46.

Beechey, Veronica: *Unequal Work*, Verso: London, 1987.

Beechey, Veronica and Perkins, Tessa: *A Matter of Hours*, Polity: Oxford, 1987.

Beechey, Veronica and Whitelegg, Ann (eds): *Women in Britain Today*, Open University: Milton Keynes, 1986.

Behrend, Hanna: 'Women catapulted into a different social order: women in East Germany', *Women's History Review*, vol. 1, no. 1, 1992, pp. 141–53.

Bell, Diane: *Daughters of the Dreaming*, McPhee Gribble/Allen and Unwin: Melbourne, 1983.

Benería, Lourdes: 'Accounting for women's work', in Benería, L. (ed.): *Women and Development: The sexual division of labour in rural societies*, Praeger: New York, 1982, pp. 119–48.

Benería, Lourdes and Sen, Gita: 'Accumulation, reproduction, and women's role in economic development: Boserup revisited', *Signs*, 7 (2), 1981, pp. 279–98.

Benjamin, Medea (trans. and ed.): *Don't be afraid, Gringo: A Honduran woman speaks from the heart. The story of Elvia Alvarado*, Food First: San Francisco, CA, 1987.

Bennholdt-Thomsen, Veronika: 'Subsistence production and extended reproduction', in Young, K., Wolkowitz, C. and McCullagh, R. (eds): *Of Marriage and the Market*, Routledge and Kegan Paul: London, 1984, pp. 41–54.

Berger, Brigitte and Berger, Peter L.: *The War over the Family*, Penguin: Harmondsworth, 1984.

Bettelheim, Charles: 'Economic reform in China', *The Journal of Development Studies*, 24 (4), 1988, pp. 15–49.

Bhavnani, Kum-kum and Coulson, Margaret: 'Transforming socialist-feminism: the challenge of racism' *Feminist Review*, 23, 1986: pp. 81–92.

Bleier, Ruth: *Science and Gender*, Pergamon: Oxford, 1984.

Bloch, Maurice and Bloch, Jean H.: 'Women and the dialectics of nature in eighteenth-century French thought', in MacCormack, C.P. and Strathern, M. (eds): *Nature, Culture and Gender*, Cambridge University Press: Cambridge, 1980, pp. 25–41.

Blumberg, Rae Lesser: 'Females, farming and food: rural development and women's participation in agricultural production systems', in Lewis, B.C. (ed.): *Invisible Farmers*, Agency for International Development: Washington, DC, 1981.

Blumberg, Rae Lesser: 'Toward a feminist theory of development', in Wallace, R. (ed.): *Feminism and sociological theory*, Sage: London, 1989, pp. 161–99.

Blumberg, Rae Lesser: 'Income under female versus male control: hypotheses from the theory of gender stratification and data from the Third World', in Blumberg, R.L. (ed.): *Gender, Family and Economy: The triple overlap*, Sage: London, 1991, pp. 97–127.

Bolles, A. Lynn: 'Economic crisis and female-headed households in urban Jamaica', in Nash, J., Safa, H. and contributors: *Women and Change in Latin America*, Bergin and Garvey: South Hadley, MA, 1986, pp. 65–83.

Boserup, Ester: *Woman's Role in Economic Development*, Earthscan: London, 1989 (1st edn 1970).

Boserup, Ester: 'Economic change and the roles of women', in Tinker, I. (ed.): *Persistent Inequalities: Women and world development*, Oxford University Press: Oxford, 1990, pp. 14–24.

Boston, Sarah: *Women Workers and the Trade Unions*, Lawrence and Wishart: London, 1987.

Bouchier, David: *The Feminist Challenge: The movement for women's liberation in Britain and the USA*, Schocken: New York, 1983.

Bradley, Harriet: *Men's Work, Women's Work: A sociological history of the sexual division of labour in employment*, Polity: Oxford, 1989.

Branca, Patricia: 'Image and reality: the myth of the ideal Victorian woman', in Hartman, M.S. and Banner, L. (eds): *Clio's Consciousness Raised*, Octagon: New York, 1976, pp. 179–91.

Brand, Karl-Werner: 'Cyclical aspects of new social movements: waves of cultural criticism and mobilisation cycles of new middle-class radicalism', in Dalton, R.J. and Kuechler, M. (eds): *Challenging the Political Order: New social and political movements in Western democracies*, Polity: Oxford, 1990, pp. 23–42.

Brannen, Julia and Wilson, Gail (eds): *Give and Take in Families*, Allen and Unwin: London, 1987.

Braverman, Harry: *Labour and Monopoly Capital*, Monthly Review Press: New York, 1974.

Brenner, Johanna and Ramas, Maria: 'Rethinking women's oppression', *New Left Review*, 144, 1984, pp. 33–71.

Breugel, Irene: 'Women's employment, legislation and the labour market', in Lewis, J. (ed.): *Women's Welfare Women's Rights*, Croom Helm: London, 1983, pp. 130–69.

Bridger, Sue: 'Women and agricultural reform' in Buckley, M. (ed.): *Perestroika and Soviet Women*, Cambridge University Press: Cambridge, 1992, pp. 39–53.

Britten, Nicky and Heath, Anthony: 'Women, men and social class', in Gamarnikow, E. *et al.* (eds): *Gender, Class and Work*, Heinemann: London, 1983, pp. 46–60.

Brown, George W. and Harris, Tirril: *Social Origins of Depression*, Tavistock: London, 1978.

Brown, Judith K.: 'Iroquois women: an ethnohistoric note', in Reiter, R.R. (ed.): *Toward an Anthropology of Women*, Monthly Review Press: New York, 1975, pp. 235–51.

Browning, Genia K: *Women and politics in the USSR*, Harvester Wheatsheaf: Hemel Hempstead, 1987.

Brownmiller, Susan: *Against Our Will: Men, women and rape*, Penguin: Harmondsworth, 1986.

Broyelle, Claudie: *Women's Liberation in China*, Harvester Wheatsheaf: Hemel Hempstead, 1977.

Brydon, Lynne and Chant, Sylvia: *Women in the Third World: Gender issues in rural and urban areas*, Edward Elgar: Cheltenham, 1989.

Buckley, Mary: 'Women in the Soviet Union', *Feminist Review*, 8, 1981, pp. 79–106.

Buckley, Mary: 'Soviet interpretation of the woman question', in Holland, B. (ed.): *Soviet Sisterhood*, Fourth Estate: London, 1985, pp. 24–53.

Buckley, Mary: *Women and Ideology in the Soviet Union*, Harvester Wheatsheaf: Hemel Hempstead, 1989.

Buckley, Mary: 'The "Woman Question" in the contemporary Soviet Union', in Kruks, S., Rapp, R. and Young, M.B. (eds): *Promissory Notes: Women in the transition to socialism*, Monthly Review Press: New York, 1989a, pp. 251–81.

Buckley, Mary: 'Perestroika and the woman question', in Deacon, B. and Szalai, J. (eds): *Social Policy in the New Eastern Europe*, Avebury: Aldershot, 1990, pp. 212–25.

Buckley, Mary: 'Political reform', in Buckley, M. (ed.): *Perestroika and Soviet Women*, Cambridge University Press: Cambridge, 1992, pp. 54–71.

Buechler, Judith-Maria: 'Women in petty commodity production in La Paz, Bolivia', in Nash, J., Safa, H. and contributors: *Women and Change in Latin America*, Bergin and Garvey: South Hadley, MA, 1986, pp. 165–188.

Buenaventura-Posso, Elisa and Brown, Susan E.: 'Forced transition from egalitarianism to male dominance: the Bari of Colombia', in Etienne, M. and Leacock, E. (eds): *Women and Colonisation: Anthropological perspectives*, Praeger: New York, 1980, pp. 109–33.

Bujra, Janet: ' Introductory: female solidarity and the sexual division of labour' in Caplan, P. and Bujra, J.M. (eds): *Women United, Women Divided*, Tavistock: London, 1978.

Bujra, Janet: ' "Urging women to redouble their efforts . . .": class, gender and capitalist transformation in Africa', in Robertson, C. and Berger, I. (eds): *Women and Class in Africa*, Africana Publishing Company: New York, 1986, pp. 117–40.

Bunster, Ximena and Chaney, Elsa M.: *Sellers and Servants: Working women in Lima, Peru*, Bergin and Garvey: South Hadley, MA, 1989.

Burton, Clare: *Subordination*, Allen and Unwin: London, 1985.

Bustamante, Jorge A.: '*Maquiladoras*: a new face of international capitalism on Mexico's northern frontier' in Nash, J. and Fernandez-Kelly, M.P. (eds): *Women, Men, and the International Division of Labour*, State University of New York Press: Albany, 1983, pp. 224–56.

Bystydzienski, Jill M.: 'Women and socialism: a comparative study of women in Poland and the USSR', *Signs*, 14 (3), 1989, pp. 669–84.

Caplan, Patricia: 'Cognatic descent, Islamic law and women's property on the East African coast', in Hirschon, R. (ed.) *Women and Property, Women as Property*, Croom Helm: London, 1984, pp. 23–43.

Cardoso, Fernando Henrique: 'Dependency and development in Latin America', in Alavi, H. and Shanin, T. (eds): *Introduction to the Sociology of 'Developing' Societies*, Macmillan: Basingstoke, 1982, pp. 112–27.

Cavendish, Ruth: *On the Line*, Routledge and Kegan Paul: London, 1982.

Chafetz, Janet S.: *Gender Equity: An integrated theory of stability and change*, Sage: London, 1990.

Chafetz, Janet S. and Dworkin, Anthony G.: *Female Revolt: Women's movements in world and historical perspective*, Rowman and Allanheld: Totowa, NJ, 1986.

Chaney, Elsa M.: 'Women's components in integrated rural development projects', in Deere, C.D. and León, M. (eds): *Rural Women and State Policy*, Westview: Boulder, CO, 1987, pp. 191–211.

Charles, Lindsey and Duffin, Lorna (eds): *Women and Work in Pre-industrial England*, Croom Helm: London, 1985.

Charles, Nicola: *An Analysis of the Ideology of Woman's Domestic Role and its Social Effects in Britain*, unpublished PhD thesis, University of Keele, 1979.

Charles, Nicola: 'Women and trade unions in the workplace', *Feminist Review* (ed.): *Waged Work: A reader*, Virago: London, 1986, pp. 160–85.

Charles, Nicola: 'Women and class: a problematic relationship?', *Sociological Review*, 38 (1), 1990, pp. 43–89.

Charles, Nickie and Brown, David: 'Women, shiftwork and the sexual division of labour, *Sociological Review*, 29 (4), 1981, pp. 685–704.

Charles, Nickie and Kerr, Marion: *Women, Food and Families*, Manchester University Press: Manchester, 1988.

Charlton, Sue Ellen M.: *Women in Third World Development*, Westview: Boulder, CO, 1984.

Chen, Pi-chao: 'Birth control methods and organisation in China' in Croll, E., Davin, D. and Kane, P. (eds): *China's One-child Family Policy*, Macmillan: Basingstoke, 1985, pp. 135–48.

Chinchilla, Norma S.: 'Industrialisation, monopoly capitalism and women's work in Guatemala', *Signs*, 3 (1), 1977, pp. 38–56.

Chinchilla, Norma S.: 'Revolutionary popular feminism in Nicaragua: articulating class, gender and national sovereignty', *Gender and Society*, vol. 4, no. 3, 1990, pp. 370–97.

Chinery-Hesse, Mary *et al.*: *Engendering Adjustment for the 1990s:*

Report of a Commonwealth expert group on women and structural adjustment, Commonwealth Secretariat: London, 1989.

Chodorow, Nancy: *The Reproduction of Mothering*, University of California Press: Berkeley, 1978.

Cliffe, Lionel: 'Zimbabwe's agricultural success and food security', *Review of African Political Economy*, 43, 1988, pp. 4–25.

Cockburn, Cynthia: *Machinery of Dominance*, Pluto: London, 1985.

Collier, Jane F. and Rosaldo, Michelle Z.: 'Politics and gender in simple societies', in Ortner, S.B. and Whitehead, H. (eds): *Sexual Meanings*, Cambridge University Press: Cambridge, 1981, pp. 275–329.

Collins, Jane L.: 'Women and the environment: social reproduction and sustainable development', in Gallin, R.S. and Ferguson, A. (eds): *The Women and International Development Annual*, vol. 2, Westview: Boulder, CO, 1991, pp. 33–58.

Collinson, Helen (ed.): *Women and Revolution in Nicaragua*, Zed: London, 1990.

Coontz, Stephanie and Henderson, Peta: 'Property forms, political power and female labour in the origins of class and state societies', in Coontz, S. and Henderson, P. (eds): *Women's Work, Men's Property: The origins of gender and class*, Verso: London, 1986, pp. 108–55.

Coontz, Stephanie and Henderson, Peta: 'Introduction', in Coontz, S. and Henderson, P. (eds): *Women's Work, Men's Property: The origins of gender and class*, Verso: London, 1986a, pp. 1–42.

Coote, Anna and Campbell, Beatrix: *Sweet Freedom: The struggle for women's liberation*, Picador: London, 1982.

Corrin, Chris: 'The situation of women in Hungarian society', in Deacon, B. and Szalai, J. (eds): *Social Policy in the New Eastern Europe*, Avebury: Aldershot, 1990, pp. 179–91.

Costain, Anne N. and Costain, W. Douglas: 'Strategy and tactics of the women's movement in the US: the role of political parties', in Katzenstein, M. and Mueller, C. (eds): *The Women's Movements of the United States and Western Europe*, Temple University Press: Philadelphia, PA, 1987, pp. 196–214.

Craig, F.W.S.: *Conservative and Labour Party Conference Decisions 1945–81*, Parliamentary Research Services, Gower: Chichester, 1982.

Crehan, Kate: 'Women and development in North Western Zambia: from producer to housewife', *Review of African Political Economy*, 27/28, 1984, pp. 51–66.

Croll, Elisabeth J.: *Feminism and Socialism in China*, Routledge and Kegan Paul: London, 1980.

Croll, Elisabeth J.: 'Women in rural production and reproduction in the Soviet Union, China, Cuba and Tanzania: socialist development experiences', *Signs*, 7 (2), 1981, pp. 361–74.

Croll, Elisabeth J.: 'Women in rural production and reproduction in the Soviet Union, China, Cuba and Tanzania: case studies', *Signs*, 7 (2), 1981a, pp. 375–99.

Croll, Elisabeth J.: *Chinese Women since Mao*, Zed: London, 1983.

Croll, Elisabeth J.: 'Introduction: fertility norms and family size in China', in Croll, E., Davin, D. and Kane, P. (eds): *China's One-child Family Policy*, Macmillan: Basingstoke, 1985, pp. 1–36.

Croll, Elisabeth J.: 'The household, family and reform', in Benewick, R. and Wingrove, P. (eds): *Reforming the Revolution: China in transition*, Macmillan: Basingstoke, 1989, pp. 161–78.

Crompton, Rosemary: 'Women and the "service class" ', in Crompton, R. and Mann, M. (eds): *Gender and Stratification*, Polity: Oxford, 1986, pp. 119–36.

Dahlerup, Drude (ed.): *The New Women's Movement: Feminism and political power in Europe and the USA*, Sage: London, 1986.

Dale, Jennifer and Foster, Peggy: *Feminists and State Welfare*, Routledge and Kegan Paul: London, 1986.

Dalla Costa, Mariarosa: *The Power of Women and the Subversion of the Community*, Falling Wall: Bristol, 1973.

Dalton, Russell J., Kuechler, Manfred and Burklin, Wilhelm: 'The challenge of the new movements', in Dalton, R.J. and Kuechler, M. (eds): *Challenging the Political Order: New social and political movements in Western democracies*, Polity: Oxford, 1990, pp. 3–20.

Davin, Anna: 'Imperialism and motherhood', *History Workshop Journal*, 5, 1978, pp. 9–65.

Davin, Delia: 'Engels and the making of Chinese family policy', in Sayers, J., Evans, M. and Redclift, N. (eds): *Engels Revisited*, Tavistock: London, 1987, pp. 145–63.

Davin, Delia: 'Gender and population in the People's Republic of China', in Afshar, H. (ed.): *Women, State and Ideology*, Macmillan: Basingstoke, 1987a, pp. 111–29.

Davin, Delia: 'Of dogma, dicta and washing machines: women in the People's Republic of China' in Kruks, S., Rapp, R. and Young, M. (eds): *Promissory Notes: Women in the transition to socialism*, Monthly Review Press: New York, 1989, pp. 354–8.

Davin, Delia: 'Women, work and property in the Chinese peasant household of the 1980s', in Elson, R. (ed.): *Male Bias in the Development Process*, Manchester University Press: Manchester, 1991a, pp. 29–50.

Davin, Delia: 'Chinese models of development and their implications for women' in Afshar, H. (ed.): *Women, Development and Survival in the Third World*, Longman: Harlow, 1991b, pp. 30–52.

Davis, Angela Y.: 'Complexity, activism, optimism: an interview with Angela Y. Davis', *Feminist Review*, 31, 1989, pp. 66–81.

Dawkins, R.: *The Selfish Gene*, Oxford University Press: New York, 1976.

de Beauvoir, Simone: *The Second Sex*, Penguin: Harmondsworth, 1972.

Deere, Carmen Diana: 'Agrarian reform, peasant participation, and the organisation of production in the transition to socialism', in Fagen, R.R., Deere, C.D. and Coraggio, J.L. (eds): *Transition and Development: Problems of Third World socialism*, Monthly Review Press: New York, 1986, pp. 97–142.

Deere, Carmen Diana: 'Rural women and agrarian reform in Peru, Chile, and Cuba', in Nash, J., Safa, H. and contributors: *Women and Change in Latin America*, Bergin and Garvey: South Hadley, MA, 1986a, pp. 189–207.

Deere, Carmen Diana: 'The division of labour by sex in agriculture: a Peruvian case study', in Archetti, E.P., Cammack, P. and Roberts, B. (eds): *Sociology of 'Developing' Societies: Latin America*, Macmillan: Basingstoke, 1987, pp. 196–212.

Deere, Carmen Diana: 'The Latin American agrarian reform experience', in Deere, C.D. and León, M. (eds): *Rural Women and State Policy*, Westview: Boulder, CO, 1987a, pp. 165–90.

Deere, Carmen Diana and León de Leal, Magdalana: 'Peasant production, proletarianisation, and the sexual division of labour in the Andes', in Benería, L. (ed.): *Women and Development: The sexual division of labour in rural societies*, Praeger: New York, 1982, pp. 65–94.

Deere, Carmen Diana and León, Magdalena: 'Introduction', in Deere, C.D. and León, M. (eds): *Rural Women and State Policy: Feminist perspectives on Latin American agricultural development*, Westview: Boulder, CO, 1987, pp. 1–17.

Deighton, Jane, Horsley, Rossana, Stewart, Sarah and Cain, Cathy: *Sweet Ramparts: Women in revolutionary Nicaragua*, War on Want Nicaragua Solidarity Campaign: London, 1983.

de Lattes, Zulma Recchini and Wainerman, Catalina H.: 'Unreliable account of women's work: evidence from Latin American census statistics', *Signs*, 11 (4), 1986, pp. 740–50.

de los Angeles Crummett, Maria: 'Rural women and migration in Latin America', in Deere, C.D. and León, M. (eds): *Rural Women and State Policy*, Westview: Boulder, CO, 1987, pp. 239–60.

Delphy, Christine: 'Women in stratification studies', in Roberts, H. (ed.): *Doing Feminist Research*, Routledge and Kegan Paul: London, 1981, pp. 114–28.

Delphy, Christine: *Close to Home*, Hutchinson: London, 1984.

Delphy, Christine and Leonard, Diana: 'Class analysis, gender analysis and the family', in Crompton, R. and Mann, M. (eds): *Gender and Stratification*, Polity: Oxford, 1986, pp. 57–73.

Dennis, Carolyne: 'Capitalist development and women's work: a Nigerian case study', *Review of African Political Economy*, 27/28, 1984, pp. 109–19.

Dennis, Carolyne: 'The limits to women's independent careers: gender in the formal and informal sectors in Nigeria', in Elson, D. (ed.): *Male Bias in the Development Process*, Manchester University Press: Manchester, 1991, pp. 83–104.

Dennis, Carolyne: 'Constructing a "career" under conditions of economic crisis and structural adjustment: the survival strategies of Nigerian women', in Afshar, H. (ed.): *Women, Survival and Development in the Third World*, Longman: Harlow, 1991a, pp. 88–106.

Dennis, Norman, Henriques, Fernando and Slaughter, Clifford: *Coal is Our Life*, Tavistock: London, 1969 (1st edn 1956).

Department of Employment: *Women and Work: A statistical survey*, Manpower Paper 9, HMSO: London, 1974.

Dex, Shirley: *The Sexual Division of Work: Conceptual revolutions in the social sciences*, Harvester Wheatsheaf: Hemel Hempstead, 1985.

Dodge, Norton T.: 'Women in the professions', in Atkinson, D., Dallin, A., Lapidus, G. (eds): *Women in Russia*, Harvester Wheatsheaf: Hemel Hempstead, 1978, pp. 205–24.

Dolling, Irene: 'Between hope and helplessness: women in the GDR after the "Turning Point" ', *Feminist Review*, 39, 1991, pp. 3–15.

Donzelot, Jacques: *The Policing of Families*, Hutchinson: London, 1979.

Doyal, Lesley: *The Political Economy of Health*, Pluto: London, 1981.

Drakakis-Smith, David: 'Urban and regional development in Zimbabwe', in Forbes, D. and Thrift, N. (eds): *The Socialist Third World: Urban development and territorial planning*, Blackwell: Oxford, 1987, pp. 194–213.

Draper, Patricia: '!Kung women: contrasts in sexual egalitarianism in foraging and sedentary contexts', in Reiter, R.R. (ed.): *Toward an Anthropology of Women*, Monthly Review Press: New York, 1975, pp. 77–109.

Dwyer, Daisy and Bruce, Judith (eds): *Women and Income in the Third World*, Stanford University Press: Stanford, California, 1988.

Economic Survey 1947, HMSO: London, Cmd 7046.

Edholm, Felicity, Harris, Olivia and Young, Kate: 'Conceptualising women', *Critique of Anthropology*, 3 (9 & 10), 1977, pp. 101–30.

Einhorn, Barbara: 'Socialist emancipation: the women's movement in the German Democratic Republic', in Kruks, S., Rapp, R. and Young, M. (eds): *Promissory Notes: Women in the transition to socialism*, Monthly Review Press: New York, 1989, pp. 282–305.

Einhorn, Barbara: 'Where have all the women gone?: women and the women's movement in East Central Europe', *Feminist Review*, 39, 1991, pp. 16–36.

Eisenstein, Hester: *Contemporary Feminist Thought*, Unwin: London, 1984.

Elliott, Ruth: 'How far have we come?: women's organisation in the unions in the United Kingdom', in Cockburn, C. (ed.): 'Trade unions and the radicalising of socialist feminism', *Feminist Review*, 16, 1984, pp. 64–73.

el Sadaawi, Nawal: *The Hidden Face of Eve: Women in the Arab world*, Zed: London, 1980.

Elson, Diane: 'Male bias in the development process: an overview', in Elson, D. (ed.) *Male Bias in the Development Process*, Manchester University Press: Manchester, 1991, pp. 1–28.

Elson, Diane and Pearson, Ruth: ' "Nimble fingers make cheap workers": an analysis of women's employment in Third World export manufacturing', *Feminist Review*, 7, 1981, pp. 87–107.

Elson, Diane and Pearson, Ruth: 'The subordination of women and the internationalisation of factory production', in Young, K., Wolkowitz, C. and McCullagh, R. (eds): *Of Marriage and the Market*, Routledge and Kegan Paul: London, 1984, pp. 18–40.

Elson, Diane and Pearson, Ruth: 'Third World Manufacturing', in *Feminist Review* (ed.) *Waged Work: A reader*, Virago: London, 1986.

El-Wathig, Kamier, El-Bakri, Zeinab, Salim, Idris, El-Ngar, Samiya: 'The state of women's studies in the Sudan', *Review of African Political Economy*, 27/28, 1984, pp. 130–7.

Ember, Carol R.: 'The relative decline in women's contribution to agriculture with intensification', *American Anthropologist*, 85, 1983, pp. 285–304.

Employment Gazette, August 1986.

Engel, Barbara Alpern: 'Women in Russia and the Soviet Union', *Signs*, 12 (4), 1987, pp. 761–80.

Engels, Frederick: *The Condition of the Working Class in England*, Panther: London, 1969.

Engels, Frederick: *The Origin of the Family, Private Property and the State*, Lawrence and Wishart: London, 1972.

Engels, Frederick: 'Principles of Communism', in Marx, K. and Engels, F.: *Selected Works*, vol. 1, Progress Publishers: Moscow, 1973.

Equal Opportunities Commission: *Women and Men in Britain 1991*, HMSO: London, 1991.

Errington, Frederick and Gewertz, Deborah: 'The remarriage of Yebiwali: a study of dominance and false consciousness in a non-Western society', in Strathern, M. (ed.): *Dealing with Inequality*, Cambridge University Press: Cambridge, 1987, pp. 63–88.

Errington, Shelly: 'Recasting sex, gender and power: a theoretical and regional overview', in Atkinson, J.M. and Errington, S. (eds): *Power and Difference: Gender in island Southeast Asia*, Stanford University Press: Stanford, CA, 1990, pp. 1–58.

Etienne, Mona: 'Women and men, cloth and colonisation: the transformation of production-distribution relations among the Baule (Ivory Coast)', in Etienne, M. and Leacock, E. (eds): *Women and Colonisation: Anthropological perspectives*, Praeger: New York, 1980, pp. 214–38.

Etienne, Mona and Leacock, Eleanor: 'Introduction. Women and anthropology: conceptual problems', in Etienne, M. and Leacock, E. (eds): *Women and Colonisation*, Praeger: New York, 1980, pp. 1–24.

Evans, Judith *et al.*: *Feminism and Political Theory*, Sage: London, 1986.

Evans Clements, Barbara: 'Working-class and peasant women in the Russian revolution, 1917–1923', *Signs*, 8 (2), 1982, pp. 215–35.

Fagen, Richard R., Deere, Carmen D. and Coraggio, Jose Luis: 'Introduction', in Fagen, R. Deere, D. and Coraggio, J.L. (eds): *Transition and Development: Problems of Third World socialism*, Monthly Review Press: New York, 1986, pp. 9–27.

Fapohunda, Eleanor R.: 'The nonpooling household: a challenge to theory', in Dwyer, D. and Bruce, J. (eds): *A Home Divided: Women and income in the Third World*, Stanford University Press: Stanford, CA, 1988, pp. 143–54.

Farnsworth, Beatrice Brodsky: 'Bolshevik alternatives and the Soviet family: The 1926 marriage law debate', in Atkinson, D., Dallin, A. and Lapidus, G.W. (eds): *Women in Russia*, Harvester Wheatsheaf: Hemel Hempstead, 1978, pp. 139–65.

Farnsworth, Beatrice Brodsky: *Aleksandra Kollontai; Socialism, feminism and the Bolshevik revolution*, Stanford University Press: Stanford, CA, 1980.

Feldman, Rayah: 'Women's groups and women's subordination: an analysis of policies towards rural women in Kenya', *Review of African Political Economy*, 27/28, 1984, pp. 67–85.

Feldman, Shelley: 'Still invisible: Women in the informal sector' in Gallin, R.S. and Ferguson, A. (eds): *The Women and International Development Annual*, vol. 2, Westview: Boulder, CO, 1991, pp. 59–86.

Feminist Review (ed.): *Waged Work: A reader*, Virago: London, 1986.

Fernandez-Kelly, Maria Patricia: 'Mexican border industrialisation, female labour force participation and migration', in Nash, J. and Fernandez-Kelly, M.P. (eds): *Women, Men and the International*

Division of Labour, State University of New York Press: Albany, 1983, pp. 205–23.

Ferree, Myra Marx: 'Equality and autonomy: feminist politics in the US and West Germany', in Katzenstein, M. and Mueller, C. (eds): *The Women's Movements of the United States and Western Europe*, Temple University Press: Philadelphia, 1987, pp. 172–95.

Finch, Janet and Groves, Dulcie (eds): *A Labour of Love*, Routledge and Kegan Paul: London, 1983.

Finch, Janet and Groves, Dulcie: 'Community care and the family: a case for equal opportunities?', in Ungerson, C. (ed.): *Women and Social Policy*, Macmillan: Basingstoke, 1985, pp. 218–42.

Fineman, Stephen: *Unemployment: Personal and social consequences*, Tavistock: London, 1987.

Firestone, Shulamith: *The Dialectic of Sex*, Paladin: London, 1971.

Flammang, Janet A: 'Women made a difference: comparable worth in San Jose', in Katzenstein, M.F. and Mueller, C.M. (eds): *The Women's Movements of the United States and Western Europe*, Temple University Press: Philadelphia, 1987, pp. 290–309.

Folbre, Nancy: 'The black four of hearts: towards a new paradigm of household economics', in Dwyer, D. and Bruce, J. (eds): *A Home Divided: Women and income in the Third World*, Stanford University Press: Stanford, CA, 1988, pp. 248–64.

Folbre, Nancy: 'Women on their own: global patterns of female headship', in Gallin, R.S. and Ferguson, A. (eds): *The Women and International Development Annual*, vol. 2, Westview: Boulder, CO, 1991, pp. 89–126.

Foster-Carter, Aidan: 'Sociology of development' in Haralambos, M. (ed.): *Sociology: New directions*, Causeway: Ormskirk, Lancs, 1985, pp. 91–213.

Freeman, Jo: *The Politics of Women's Liberation*, David McKay: New York, 1975.

Freeman, Jo: 'Whom you know versus whom you represent: feminist influences in the Democratic and Republican Parties', in Katzenstein, M.F. and Mueller, C.M. (eds): *The Women's Movements of the United States and Western Europe*, Temple University Press: Philadelphia, 1987, pp. 215–44.

Friedan, Betty: *The Feminine Mystique*, Penguin: Harmondsworth, 1965.

Friedl, Ernestine: *Women and Men: An anthropologist's view*, Holt Reinhart and Winston: New York, 1975.

Friszara, Malgorzata: 'Will the abortion issue give birth to feminism in Poland?', in Maclean, M. and Groves, D. (eds): *Women's Issues in Social Policy*, Routledge: London, 1991, pp. 205–28.

Fu, Gangzhan, Hussain, Athar, Pudney, Stephen and Wang, Limin:

Unemployment in Urban China: An analysis of survey data from Shanghai, CP no. 21, SICERD, 1992.

Gaitzkell, Deborah, Kimble, Judy, Maconachie, Moira and Unterhalter, Elaine: 'Class race and gender: domestic workers in South Africa', *Review of African Political Economy*, 27/28, 1984, pp. 86–108.

Gardiner, Jean: 'Political economy of domestic labour in capitalist society', in Barker, D.L. and Allen, S. (eds): *Dependence and Exploitation in Work and Marriage*, Longman: London, 1976, pp. 109–20.

Gelb, Joyce: 'Feminism and political action', in Dalton, R.J. and Kuechler, M. (eds): *Challenging the Political Order*, Polity: Oxford, 1990, pp. 137–55.

Gelb, Joyce and Palley, Marian Lief: *Women and Public Policies* (2nd edn), Princeton University Press: Princeton, New Jersey, 1987.

Ghoussoub, Mai: 'Feminism – or the eternal masculine – in the Arab world', *New Left Review*, 161, 1987, pp. 3–18.

Gilliam, Angela: 'Women's equality and national liberation', in Mohanty, C.T., Russo, A. and Torres, L. (eds): *Third World Women and the Politics of Feminism*, Indiana University Press: Bloomington, IN, 1991, pp. 215–36.

Ginsberg, Norman: *Class, Capital and Social Policy*, Macmillan: Basingstoke, 1979.

Gittins, Diana: *The Family in Question*, Macmillan: Basingstoke, 1985.

Glendinning, Caroline and Millar, Jane (eds): *Women and Poverty in Britain*, Harvester Wheatsheaf: Hemel Hempstead, 1987.

Glucksmann, Miriam: 'In a class of their own?: Women workers in the new industries in inter-war Britain', *Feminist Review*, 24, 1986, pp. 7–39.

Goldberg, Steven: *Male Dominance: The inevitability of patriarchy*, Abacus Sphere Books: London, 1979.

Goldman, Wendy Seva: 'Women, the family and the new revolutionary order in the Soviet Union', in Kruks, S., Rapp, R. and Young, M. (eds): *Promissory notes: Women in the transition to socialism*, Monthly Review Press: New York, 1989, pp. 59–81.

Goldthorpe, John H.: 'Women and class analysis: in defence of the conventional view', *Sociology*, 17 (4), 1983, pp. 465–88.

Goldthorpe, John H.: 'Women and class analysis: a reply to the replies', *Sociology*, 18 (4), 1984, pp. 491–9.

Goldthorpe, John H., Lockwood, David, Bechhofer, Frank and Platt, Jennifer: *The Affluent Worker*, Cambridge University Press: Cambridge, 1970.

Gough, Ian: *The Political Economy of the Welfare State*, Macmillan: Basingstoke, 1983.

Goss, Sue: 'Women's initiatives in local government', in Boddy, M. and Fudge, C. (eds): *Local Socialism?: Labour Councils and New Left Alternatives*, Macmillan: Basingstoke, 1984.

Gothaskar, Sujata and Patel, Vithubai: 'Documents from the Indian women's movement', Introduction by Carol Wolkowitz, *Feminist Review*, 12, 1982, pp. 92–103.

Graham, Hilary: 'Do her answers fit his questions?: Women and the survey method', in Gamarnikow, E., Morgan, D., Purvis, J. and Taylorson, D. (eds): *The Public and the Private*, Gower: London, 1986, pp. 132–46.

Griffin, Christine: *Typical Girls?: Young women from school to the job market*, Routledge and Kegan Paul: London, 1985.

Guardian, East is Best for Women, Letters, 2 August 1990, 15 February 1991.

Guyer, Jane: 'Household and community in African studies', *African Studies Review*, vol. 24, nos. 2/3, 1981, pp. 87–137.

Guyer, Jane: 'Intra-household processes and farming systems research: perspectives from anthropology', in Moock, J.L. (ed.): *Understanding Africa's Rural Households and Farming Systems*, Westview: Boulder, CO, 1986, pp. 92–104.

Guyer, Jane: 'Dynamic approaches to domestic budgeting: a challenge to theory', in Dwyer, D. and Bruce, J. (eds): *A Home Divided: Women and income in the Third World*, Stanford University Press: Stanford, CA, 1988, pp. 155–72.

Guyer, Jane and Peters, Pauline: 'Introduction', *Development and Change*, vol. 18, no. 2, 1987, pp. 197–214.

Hakim, Catherine: *Occupational Segregation*, Research paper no. 9, Department of Employment: London, 1979.

Hall, Catherine: 'The early formation of Victorian domestic ideology', in Burman, S. (ed.): *Fit Work for Women*, Croom Helm: London, 1979, pp. 15–32.

Hall, Catherine: 'The home turned upside down?: The working-class family in cotton textiles 1780–1850', in Whitelegg, E. *et al.* (ed.): *The Changing Experience of Women*, Basil Blackwell: Oxford, 1982, pp. 17–29.

Hanmer, Jalna and Maynard, Mary (eds): *Women, Violence and Social Control*, Macmillan: Basingstoke, 1987.

Hanmer, Jalna and Saunders, Sheila: *Well-founded Fear: A community study of violence to women*, Hutchinson: London, 1984.

Hansen, Karen Tranberg and Ashbaugh, Leslie: 'Women on the front line: development issues in Southern Africa', in Gallin, R.S. and Ferguson, A. (eds): *The Women and International Development Annual*, vol. 2, Westview: Boulder, CO, 1991, pp. 177–204.

Harris, C.C.: *The Family and Industrial Society*, Allen and Unwin: London, 1983.

Harris, C.C.: *Redundancy and Recession*, Basil Blackwell: Oxford, 1987.

Harris, Olivia: 'Households as natural units', in Young, K., Wolkowitz, C. and McCullagh, R. (eds): *Of Marriage and the Market*, Routledge and Kegan Paul: London, 1984, pp. 136–56.

Harris, Olivia and Young, Kate: 'Engendered structures: some problems in the analysis of reproduction', in Kahn, J.S. and Llobera, J.R. (eds): *The Anthropology of Pre-capitalist Societies*, Macmillan: London, 1981, pp. 109–47.

Harriss, Kathryn: 'New alliances: socialist-feminism in the eighties', *Feminist Review*, 31, 1989, pp. 34–54.

Hartmann, Heidi: 'The unhappy marriage of marxism and feminism: towards a more progressive union', in Sargent, L. (ed.): *The Unhappy Marriage of Marxism and Feminism*, Pluto: London, 1986, pp. 1–41.

Haug, Frigga: 'The women's movement in West Germany', *New Left Review*, 155, 1986, pp. 50–74.

Haug, Frigga: 'Lessons from the women's movement in Europe', *Feminist Review*, 31, 1989, pp. 107–16.

Haug, Frigga: 'The end of socialism in Europe: a new challenge for socialist feminism?', *Feminist Review*, 39, 1991, pp. 37–48.

Heath, Anthony and Britten, Nicky: 'Women's jobs do make a difference', *Sociology*, 18 (4), 1984, pp. 475–90.

Heitlinger, Alena: *Women and State Socialism*, Macmillan: Basingstoke, 1979.

Heinen, Jacqueline: 'The impact of social policy on the behaviour of women workers in Poland and East Germany', *Critical Social Policy*, 29, 1990, pp. 79–91 .

Hellman, Judith Adler: 'Women's struggle in a workers' city: feminist movements in Turin', in Katzenstein, M. and Mueller, C. (eds): *The Women's Movements of the United States and Western Europe*, Temple University Press: Philadelphia, 1987, pp. 111–31.

Hellman, Judith Adler: *Journeys among Women: Feminism in five Italian cities*, Oxford University Press: Oxford, 1987a.

Hendissi, Mandana: 'Fourteen thousand women meet: report from Nairobi', *Feminist Review*, 23, 1986, pp. 147–56.

Henn, Jeanne Koopman: 'The material basis of sexism: a mode of production analysis', in Stichter, S.B. and Parpart, J.L. (eds): *Patriarchy and Class: African women in the home and workforce*, Westview: Boulder, CO, 1988, pp. 27–60.

Henwood, Melanie, Rimmer, Lesley and Wicks, Malcolm: *Inside the Family: Changing roles of men and women*, Family Policy Studies Centre: London, Occasional Paper 6, 1987.

Hettne, Bjorn: *Development Theory and the Three Worlds*, Longman Scientific and Technical: Harlow, 1990.

Heyzer, Noeleen: 'From rural subsistence to an industrial peripheral workforce: an examination of female Malaysian migrants and capital accumulation in Singapore', in Benería, L. (ed.): *Women and Development: The sexual division of labour in rural societies*, Praeger: New York, 1982, pp. 179–202.

Heyzer, Noeleen: *Working Women in South-East Asia: Development, subordination and emancipation*, Open University: Milton Keynes, 1986.

Hillier, Sheila: 'Women and population control in China: issues of sexuality, power and control', *Feminist Review*, 29, 1988, pp. 101–13.

Holcombe, Lee: *Victorian Ladies at Work*, Archon Books: Hamden, Conn., 1973.

Hong, Lawrence K.: 'Potential effects of the one-child policy on gender equality in the People's Republic of China', *Gender and Society*, 1 (3), 1987, pp. 317–26.

Hooks, Bell: 'Sisterhood: political solidarity between women', *Feminist Review*, 23, 1986, pp. 125–38.

Hooks, Bell: 'Feminism: a movement to end sexist oppression' in Phillips, A. (ed.): *Feminism and Equality*, Blackwell: Oxford, 1987, pp. 62–76.

Hubbard, Ruth: 'Social effects of some contemporary myths about women', in Lowe, M. and Hubbard, R. (eds): *Woman's Nature*, Pergamon: Oxford, 1983, pp. 2–8.

Huber, Joan: 'A theory of family, economy, and gender' in Blumber, R.L. (ed.): *Gender, Family and Economy: The triple overlap*, Sage: London, 1991, pp. 35–51.

Humphrey, John: *Gender and Work in the Third World*, Macmillan: Basingstoke, 1988.

Humphries, Jane: 'The working class family, women's liberation and class struggle: the case of nineteenth-century British history', *The Review of Radical Political Economics*, 9 (3), 1977a.

Humphries, Jane: 'Class struggle and the persistence of the working-class family', *Cambridge Journal of Economics*, 1, 1977b, pp. 241–58.

Humphries, Jane: 'Protective legislation, the capitalist state, and working-class men: the case of the 1842 Mines Regulation Act', *Feminist Review*, 7, 1981, pp. 1–34.

Humphries, Jane: 'The origin of the family: born out of scarcity not wealth', in Sayers, J., Evans, M. and Redclift, N. (eds): *Engels Revisited*, Tavistock: London, 1987, pp. 11–36.

Hunt, Audrey: *A Survey of Women's Employment*, Government Social Survey, HMSO: London, 1968.

Hunt, Felicity: 'Opportunities lost and gained: mechanisation and women's work in the London bookbinding and printing trades', in John, A.V. (ed.): *Unequal Opportunities: Women's employment in England 1800–1918*, Blackwell: Oxford, 1986, pp. 71–93.

Hunt, Pauline: *Gender and Class Consciousness*, Macmillan: Basingstoke, 1980.

Hussain, Athar, Lanjouw, Peter and Stern, Nicholas: *Income Inequalities in China: Evidence from household survey data*, CP no. 18, SICERD, 1991.

Huxley, Aldous: *Brave New World*, Penguin: Harmondsworth, 1955.

International Labour Organisation: *Yearbook of Labour Statistics*, International Labour Organisation: Geneva, 1991.

ISIS International: *The Latin American Women's Movement: Reflections and actions*, *Women's Journal*, no. 5, ISIS International: Rome, Santiago, 1986.

Jabbra, Nancy: 'Women and development: the Middle East and North Africa', in Parpart, J. (ed.): *Women and development in Africa: Comparative perspectives*, Dalhousie African Studies Series 7, University Press of America: Lanham, MD, 1989, pp. 115–38.

Jacobs, Susie: 'Women and land resettlement in Zimbabwe', *Review of African Political Economy*, 27/28, 1984, pp. 33–50.

Jacobs, Susie: 'Changing gender relations in Zimbabwe: the case of individual family resettlement areas', in Elson, D. (ed.): *Male Bias in the Development Process*, Manchester University Press: Manchester, 1991, pp. 51–82.

Jancar, Barbara Wolfe: *Women under Communism*, Johns Hopkins University Press: Baltimore, 1978.

Jayawardena, Kumari: *Feminism and Nationalism in the Third World*, Zed: London, 1986.

Jelin, Elizabeth: 'Migration and labour force participation of Latin American women: the domestic servants in the cities', *Signs*, 3 (1), 1977, pp. 129–41.

Jenkins, Stephen P: 'Poverty measurement and the within-household distribution: agenda for action', *Journal of Social Policy*, 20(4) pp. 457–83, 1991.

Jenson, Jane: 'Changing discourse, changing agendas: political rights and reproductive policies in France', in Katzenstein, K.F. and Mueller, C.K. (eds): *The Women's Movements of the United States and Western Europe*, Temple University Press: Philadelphia, 1987, pp. 64–88.

Jenson, Jane, Hagen, Elizabeth, Reddy, Ceallaigh (eds): *Feminisation of the Labour Force: Paradoxes and promises*, Polity: Oxford, 1988.

Jephcott, Pearl, Seear, Nancy, Smith, John H.: *Married Women Working*, Allen and Unwin, 1962.

John, Angela V.: *By the Sweat of their Brow: Women workers at Victorian coal mines*, Croom Helm: London, 1980.

John, Angela V. (ed.): *Unequal Opportunities: Women's employment in England 1800–1918*, Blackwell: Oxford, 1986.

Johnson, Cheryl: 'Class and gender: a consideration of Yoruba women during the colonial period', in Robertson, C. and Berger, I. (eds): *Women and Class in Africa*, Africana Publishing Company: New York, 1986, pp. 237–54.

Jowell, Roger and Witherspoon, Sharon (eds): *British Social Attitudes*, Gower: London, 1985.

Judd, Ellen: 'Alternative development strategies for women in rural China', *Development and Change*, vol. 21 (1), 1990, pp. 21–42.

Kabeer, Naila: 'Subordination and struggle: women in Bangladesh', *New Left Review*, 168, 1988, pp. 95–121.

Kandal, Terry K.: *The Woman Question in Classical Sociological Theory*, Florida International University Press: Miami, 1988.

Kandiyoti, Deniz: 'Sex roles and social change: a comparative appraisal of Turkey's women', *Signs*, 3 (1), 1977, pp. 57–73.

Kandiyoti, Deniz: 'Women and the Turkish state: political actors or symbolic pawns?', in Yuval-Davis, N. and Anthias, F. (eds): *Woman–Nation–State*, Macmillan: Basingstoke, 1989, pp. 126–49.

Kandiyoti, Deniz: 'Women and rural development policies: the changing agenda', *Development and Change* vol. 21, no. 1, 1990, pp. 5–22.

Kaplan, Gisela: *Contemporary Western European Feminism*, UCL Press, Allen & Unwin: London, 1992.

Keesing, Roger M: 'Ta'a geni: women's perspectives in Kwaio society', in Strathern, M. (ed.): *Dealing with Inequality*, Cambridge University Press: Cambridge, 1987, pp. 33–62.

Kelkar, Govind: '. . . Two steps back?: New agricultural policies in China and the woman question', in Agarwal, B. (ed.): *Structures of Patriarchy: The state, the community and the household*, Zed: London, 1988, pp. 121–50.

Kennedy, Ellen and Mendus, Susan: *Women in Western Political Philosophy*, Harvester Wheatsheaf: Hemel Hempstead, 1987.

Kerr, Marion and Charles, Nicola: 'Servers and providers: the distribution of food within the family', *Sociological Review*, 34 (1), 1986, pp. 115–57.

Kimble, Judy and Unterhalter, Elaine: ' "We opened the road for you, you must go forward": ANC women's struggles, 1912–1982', *Feminist Review*, 12, 1982, pp. 11–36.

Kiss, Yudit: 'The second "No": women in Hungary', *Feminist Review*, 39, 1991, pp. 49–57.

Kruks, Sonia, Rapp, Rayna and Young, Marilyn B. (eds): *Promissory Notes: Women in the transition to socialism*, Monthly Review Press: New York, 1989.

Kumar, Radha: 'Contemporary Indian feminism', *Feminist Review*, 33, 1989, pp. 20–9.

Labour Party Feminists: 'The women's movement and the Labour Party: an interview with Labour Party feminists', *Feminist Review*, 16, 1984, pp. 75–87.

Lampland, Martha: 'Biographies of liberation: testimonials to labour in socialist Hungary', in Kruks, S. Rapp, R. and Young, M. (eds): *Promissory Notes: Women in the transition to socialism*, Monthly Review Press: New York, 1989, pp. 306–22.

Land, Hilary: 'Women: supporters or supported?', in Barker, K.L. and Allen, S. (eds): *Sexual Divisions and Society: Process and change*, Tavistock: London, 1976, pp. 108–32.

Lane, Christel: 'Women in socialist society with special reference to the German Democratic Republic', *Sociology*, 171 (4), 1983, pp. 489–505.

Lapidus, Gail: *Women in Soviet Society: Equality, development and social change*, University of California Press: Berkeley, 1978.

Lapidus, Gail: 'Sexual equality in Soviet policy: a developmental perspective', in Atkinson, D., Dallin, A. and Lapidus, G. (eds): *Women in Russia*, Harvester Wheatsheaf: Hemel Hempstead, 1978a, 115–38.

Leacock, Eleanor: 'Introduction', in Engels F.: *The Origin of the Family, Private Property and the State*, Lawrence and Wishart: London, 1972, pp. 7–68.

Leacock, Eleanor: 'Women's status in egalitarian society: implications for social evolution', *Current Anthropology*, 19 (2), 1978, pp. 247–75.

Leacock, Eleanor: 'History, development, and the division of labour by sex: implications for organisation', *Signs*, 7 (2), 1981, pp. 474–91.

Leacock, Eleanor: *Myths of Male Dominance*, Monthly Review Press: New York, 1981a.

Leacock, Eleanor: 'Women, power and authority', in Dube, L., Leacock, E. and Ardener, S. (eds): *Visibility and Power: Essays on women in society and development*, Oxford University Press: Bombay, 1986, pp. 107–35.

Leacock, Eleanor and Lee, Richard: 'Introduction', in Leacock, E. and Lee, R. (eds): *Politics and History in Band Societies*, Cambridge University Press: Cambridge, 1982, pp. 1–20.

Leahy, Margaret E.: *Development Strategies and the Status of Women : A comparative study of United States, Mexico, Soviet Union, Cuba*, Lynne Rienner: Boulder, CO, 1986.

Lee, Richard: 'Politics, sexual and non-sexual, in an egalitarian society', in Leacock, E. and Lee, R. (eds): *Politics and History in Band Societies*, Cambridge University Press: Cambridge, 1982, pp. 37–60.

Leeson, Joyce and Gray, Judith: *Women and Medicine*, Tavistock: London, 1978.

Lenin, V.I.: *The Development of Capitalism in Russia*, Collected Works, vol. 3, Lawrence and Wishart: London, 1964.

Lenin, V.I.: *A Great Beginning*, Collected Works, vol. 29, Lawrence and Wishart: London, 1965.

León de Leal, Magdalena and Deere, Carmen Diana: 'Rural women and the development of capitalism in Colombian agriculture', *Signs*, 5 (1), 1979, pp. 60–77.

Lévi-Strauss, Claude: *The Elementary Structures of Kinship*, Eyre and Spottiswoode: London, 1969.

Lewenhak, Sheila: *Women and Trade Unions*, Ernest Benn: London, 1977.

Lewis, Barbara C. (ed.): *Invisible Farmers: Women and the crisis in agriculture*, Agency for International Development: Washington DC, 1981.

Lewis, Jane: *Women in England 1870–1950*, Harvester Wheatsheaf: Hemel Hempstead, 1984.

Lewis, Jane: 'The debate on sex and class', *New Left Review*, 149, 1985, pp. 108–20.

Lewis, Oscar: *A Death in the Sanchez family*, Penguin: Harmondsworth, 1978.

Lewis, Oscar: *The Children of Sanchez*, Penguin: Harmondsworth, 1979.

Lewis, Oscar: *Pedro Martinez*, Penguin: Harmondsworth, 1980.

Liebowitz, Lila: 'Perspectives on the evolution of sex differences', in Reiter, R.R. (ed.): *Toward an Anthropology of Women*, Monthly Review Press: New York, 1975, pp. 36–50.

Liebowitz, Lila: 'Origins of the sexual division of labour', in Lowe, M. and Hubbard, R. (eds): *Woman's Nature*, Pergamon: Oxford, 1983, pp. 123–47.

Liebowitz, Lila: 'In the beginning . . .: The origins of the sexual division of labour and the development of the first human societies', in Coontz, S. and Henderson, P. (eds): *Women's Work, Men's Property*, Verso: London, 1986, pp. 43–75.

Lim, Linda Y.C.: 'Capitalism, imperialism, and patriarchy: the dilemma of Third World women workers in multinational factories', in Nash, J. and Fernandez-Kelly, M.P. (eds): *Women, Men and the Inter-*

national Division of Labour, State University of New York Press: Albany, 1983, pp. 70–91.

Lim, Linda Y.C.: 'Women's work in export factories: the politics of a cause', in Tinker, I. (ed.): *Persistent Inequalities: Women and world development*, Oxford University Press: Oxford, 1990, pp. 101–19.

Longhurst, Richard: 'Resource allocation and the sexual division of labour: a case study of a Moslem Hausa village in northern Nigeria', in Benería, L. (ed.): *Women and Development: The sexual division of labour in rural societies*, Praeger: New York, 1982, pp. 95–118.

Lovell, Terry: *Consuming Fiction*, Verso: London, 1987.

Lovenduski, Joni: *Women and European Politics: Contemporary feminism and public policy*, Harvester Wheatsheaf: Hemel Hempstead, 1986.

Lovibond, Sabina: 'Feminism and postmodernism', *New Left Review*, 178, 1989, pp. 5–28.

Lowe, Graham S.: *Women in the Administrative Revolution*, Polity: Oxford, 1987.

Lowe, Marian and Hubbard, Ruth (eds): *Woman's Nature: Rationalisation of inequality*, Pergamon: Oxford, 1983.

Lown, Judy: 'Not so much a factory, more a form of patriarchy: gender and class during industrialisation', in Gamarnikow, E. *et al.* (eds): *Gender, Class and Work*, Heinemann: London, 1983, pp. 28–45.

Luz Padilla, Martha, Murguialday, Clara and Criquillon, Ana: 'Impact of the Sandinista agrarian reform on rural women's subordination', in Deere, C.D., León, M. (eds): *Rural Women and State Policy*, Westview: Boulder and London, 1987, pp. 124–41.

MacCormack, Carol P. and Strathern, Marilyn (eds): *Nature, Culture and Gender*, Cambridge University Press: Cambridge, 1980.

Mack, Joanna and Lansley, Stewart: *Poor Britain*, Allen and Unwin: London, 1985.

Mackintosh, Maureen: 'Gender and economics: the sexual division of labour and the subordination of women', in Young, K., Wolkowitz, C. and McCullagh, R. (eds): *Of Marriage and the Market*, Routledge: London, 1984, pp. 3–17.

Mackintosh, Maureen and Wainwright, Hilary: *A Taste of Power: The politics of local economics*, Verso: London, 1987.

McAuley, Alastair: *Women's Work and Wages in the Soviet Union*, Allen and Unwin: London, 1981.

McCall, Michael: 'Carrying heavier burdens but carrying less weight: some implications of villagization for women in Tanzania', in Momsen, J.H. and Townsend, J.G. (eds): *Geography of Gender in the Third World*, State University of New York Press/Hutchinson: London, 1987, pp. 192–214.

McIntosh, Mary: 'The state and the oppression of women', in Kuhn, A. and Wolpe, A. (eds): *Materialism and Feminism*, Routledge and Kegan Paul: London, 1978, pp. 254–89.

McRae, Susan: *Cross-class families*, Clarendon Press: Oxford, 1986.

McRobbie, Angela and Garber, Jenny: 'Girls and subcultures: an exploration', in Hall, S. and Jefferson, T. (eds): *Resistance through Rituals*, Hutchinson: London, 1976, pp. 209–22.

Maher, Vanessa: 'Work, consumption and authority within the household: a Moroccan case', in Young, K., Wolkowitz, C. and McCullagh, R. (eds): *Of Marriage and the Market*, Routledge and Kegan Paul: London, 1984, pp. 117–35.

Mandle, Joan D.: 'Comment on Hong', *Gender and Society*, 1 (3), 1987, pp. 327–31.

Marnini, Margaret: *The Position of Women in the Labour Market: Trends and developments in the 12 member states of the European Community, 1983–1990*, Women of Europe Supplements, no. 36, Commission of the European Communities, March 1992.

Marshall, Gordon, Newby, Howard, Rose, David and Vogler, Carolyn: *Social Class in Modern Britain*, Hutchinson Educational: London, 1988.

Martin, Jean and Roberts, Ceridwen: *Women and Employment: A lifetime perspective*, Department of Employment/OPCS, 1984.

Marx, Karl: *Capital*, vol. 1, Lawrence and Wishart: London, 1974.

Marx, Karl and Engels, Frederick: 'Manifesto of the Communist Party', in Marx, K. and Engels, F.: *Selected Works*, vol. 1, Progress Publishers: Moscow, 1973.

Mather, Celia: 'Subordination of women and lack of industrial strife in West Java', in Taylor, J.G. and Turton, A. (eds): *Sociology of 'Developing' Societies: South East Asia*, Macmillan: Basingstoke, 1988, pp. 147–57.

Mead, Margaret: *Sex and Temperament in Three Primitive Societies*, William Morrow: New York, 1935.

Mead, Margaret: *Male and Female: A study of the sexes in a changing world*, Penguin: Harmondsworth, 1970 (1st edn 1950).

Meillassoux, Claude: 'From reproduction to production: a marxist approach to economic anthropology', *Economy and Society*, 1 (1), 1972, pp. 91–105.

Meillassoux, Claude: *Maidens, Meal and Money*, Cambridge University Press: Cambridge, 1981.

Melhuish, Edward C. and Moss, Peter (eds): *Day Care for Young Children: International perspectives*, Routledge: London, 1991.

Mernissi, Fatima: *Beyond the Veil: Male–female dynamics in a modern Muslim society*, John Wiley: Chichester, 1975.

Messick, Brinckley: 'Subordinate discourse: women, weaving, and gender relations in North Africa', *American Ethnologist*, 14 (2), 1987, pp. 210–25.

Meyer, Alfred G.: 'Marxism and the women's movement' in Atkinson, D., Dallin, A. and Lapidus, G.W. (eds): *Women in Russia*, Harvester Wheatsheaf: Hemel Hempstead, 1978, pp. 85–112.

Middleton, Chris: 'Women's labour and the transition to pre-industrial capitalism', in Charles, L. and Duffin, L. (eds): *Women and Work in Pre-industrial England*, Croom Helm: London, 1985, pp. 181–206.

Mies, Maria: 'The dynamics of the sexual division of labour and integration of rural women into the world market', in Benería, L. (ed.): *Women and Development: The sexual division of labour in rural societies*, Praeger: New York, 1982, pp. 1–28.

Mies Maria: *Patriarchy and Accumulation on a World Scale*, Zed: London, 1986.

Mies, Maria, Bennholdt-Thomsen, Veronika and von Werlhof, Claudia: *Women: The last colony*, Zed: London, 1988.

Mill, John Stewart: 'The subjection of women', *On Liberty, Representative Government, the Subjection of Women*, Oxford University Press: London, 1971, pp. 427–548.

Mills, C. Wright: *The Sociological Imagination*, Penguin: Harmondsworth, 1970.

Millett, Kate: *Sexual Politics*, Sphere: London, 1971.

Mitchell, Juliet: 'Reflections on twenty years of feminism', in Mitchell, J. and Oakley, A. (eds): *What is Feminism?*, Blackwell: Oxford, 1986, pp. 34–48.

Moir, Anne and Jessel, David: *BrainSex.: The real difference between men and women*, Michael Joseph: London, 1989.

Molyneux, Maxine: 'Beyond the domestic labour debate', *New Left Review*, 116, 1979, pp. 3–27.

Molyneux, Maxine: 'Socialist societies old and new: progress towards women's emancipation', *Feminist Review*, 8, 1981, pp. 1–34.

Molyneux, Maxine: 'Women in socialist societies: problems of theory and practice', in Young, K., Wolkowitz, C. and McCullagh, R. (eds): *Of Marriage and the Market*, Routledge and Kegan Paul: London, 1984, pp. 55–90.

Molyneux, Maxine: 'Mobilisation without emancipation?: women's interests, state and revolution in Nicaragua', *Critical Social Policy*, Issue 10, 4 (1), 1984a, pp. 59–75.

Molyneux, Maxine: 'Family reform in socialist states: the hidden agenda', *Feminist Review*, 21, 1985, pp. 47–64.

Molyneux, Maxine: 'Women', in Walker, T.W. (ed.): *Nicaragua: The first five years*, Praeger: New York, 1985a.

Molyneux, Maxine: 'The politics of abortion in Nicaragua: revolutionary pragmatism – or feminism in the realm of necessity', *Feminist Review*, 29, 1988, pp. 114–32.

Momsen, Janet Henshall: *Women and Development in the Third World*, Routledge: London, 1991.

Moore, Barrington: *Social Origins of Dictatorship and Democracy*, Allen Lane, Penguin Press: Harmondsworth, 1967.

Moore, Henrietta L.: *Feminism and Anthropology*, Polity: Oxford, 1988.

Morgan, Derek and Lee, Robert G.: *Blackstone's Guide to the Human Fertilisation and Embryology Act 1990*, Blackstone: London, 1991.

Morsy, Soheir A: 'Women and contemporary social transformation in North Africa' in Gallin, R.D. and Ferguson, A. (eds): *The Women and International Development Annual*, vol. 2, Westview: Boulder, CO, 1991, pp. 129–76.

Morris, Lydia: *The Workings of the Household*, Polity: Oxford, 1990.

Morris, Lydia: 'The household and the labour market', in Harris, C.C. (ed.): *Family, Economy and Community*, University of Wales Press: Cardiff, 1990a, pp. 79–98.

Moser, Caroline: 'The experience of poor women in Guayaquil', in Archetti, E.P., Cammack, P., Roberts, B. (eds): *Sociology of 'Developing' Societies: Latin America*, Macmillan: Basingstoke, 1987, pp. 305–20.

Moss, Peter: 'Day care for young children in the United Kingdom', in Melhuish, E.C. and Moss, P. (eds): *Day Care for Young Children*, Routledge: London, 1991, pp. 121–41.

Mueller, Carol McLurg: 'Collective consciousness, identity transformations and the rise of women in public offices in the US', in Katzenstein, M. and Mueller, C. (eds): *The Women's Movements of the United States and Western Europe*, Temple University Press: Philadelphia, 1987, pp. 89–108.

Mukhopadhayay, Carol C. and Higgins, Patricia J.: 'Anthropological studies of women's status revisited: 1977–1987', *Annual Review of Anthropology*, vol. 17, 1988, pp. 461–95.

Murray, Nicola: 'Socialism and feminism: women and the Cuban revolution', *Feminist Review*, 2 and 3, 1979, pp. 57–73 (no. 2), 99–108 (no. 3).

Myrdal, Alva and Klein, Viola: *Women's Two Roles: Home and work*, Routledge: London, 1968.

NALGO (National Association of Local Government Officers): *Equal Rights Working Party Report*, NALGO, 1975.

NBPI (National Board for Prices and Incomes): *Hours of Work, Overtime and Shiftworking*, Cmnd 4554, HMSO: London, 1970.

Nash, June: 'Aztec women: the transition from status to class in Empire and Colony', in Etienne, M. and Leacock, E. (eds): *Women and Colonisation: Anthropological perspectives*, Praeger: New York, 1980, pp. 134–48.

Nash, June: 'The impact of the changing international division of labour on different sectors of the labour force', in Nash, J. and Fernandez-Kelly, M.P. (eds): *Women, Men and the International Division of Labour*, State University of New York Press: Albany, 1983, pp. 3–38.

Nash, June: 'A decade of research on Latin America', in Nash, J., Safa, H. *et al.*: *Women and Change in Latin America*, Bergin and Garvey: South Hadley, MA, 1986, pp. 3–21.

Nash, June: 'Gender studies in Latin America', in Morgen, S. (ed.): *Gender and Anthropology: Critical reviews for research and teaching*, American Anthropological Association: Washington, DC, 1989, pp. 228–45.

Nash, June and Fernandez-Kelly, Maria Patricia: *Women, Men, and the International Division of Labouor*, State University of New York Press: Albany, 1983.

Navarro, Marysa: 'Research on Latin American women', *Signs*, 5 (1), 1979, pp. 111–20.

Nazzari, Muriel: 'The "woman question" in Cuba: an analysis of material constraints on its solution', *Signs*, 9 (2), 1983, pp. 246–63.

Nazzari, Muriel: 'The "woman question" in Cuba: an analysis of material constraints on its resolution', in Kruk, S. Rapp, R. and Young, M. (eds): *Promissory Notes: Women in the transition to socialism*, Monthly Review Press: New York, 1989, pp. 109–26.

Neustatter, Angela: *Hyenas in Petticoats*, Penguin: Harmondsworth, 1990.

Nicaragua Solidarity Campaign: *Current Situation Briefing*, 27 August 1992.

Nye, Andrea: *Feminist Theory and the Philosophies of Man*, Croom Helm: London, 1988.

Oakley, Ann: *Sex, Gender and Society*, Temple Smith: London, 1972.

Oakley, Ann: *The Sociology of Housework*, Martin Robertson: London, 1974.

Oakley, Ann: 'Wisewoman and medicine man: changes in the management of childbirth', in Mitchell, J. and Oakley, A. (eds): *The Rights and Wrongs of Women*, Penguin: Harmondsworth, 1979, pp. 17–58.

Oakley, Ann: 'Interviewing women: a contradiction in terms', in Roberts, H. (ed.): *Doing Feminist Research*, Routledge and Kegan Paul: London, 1981, pp. 30–61.

Oakley, Ann: 'Women and health policy', in Lewis, J. (ed.): *Women's Welfare Women's Rights*, Croom Helm: London, 1983, 103–30.

Oakley, Ann: *Housewife*, Penguin: Harmondsworth, 1985.

Oakley, Ann: 'Women's studies in sociology: to end at our beginning?', *British Journal of Sociology*, 40 (3), 1989, pp. 442–70.

Offe, Claus: 'Reflections on the institutional self-transformation of movement politics: a tentative stage model', in Dalton, R.J. and Kuechler, M. (eds): *Challenging the Political Order: New social and political movements in Western democracies*, Polity: Oxford, 1990, 232–50.

Okeyo, Achola Pala: 'Daughters of the lakes and rivers: colonisation and the land rights of Luo women', in Etienne, M. and Leacock, E. (eds): *Women and Colonisation: Anthropological perspectives*, Praeger: New York, 1980, pp. 186–213.

Ong, Aihwa: 'Centre, periphery and hierarchy: gender in South East Asia', in Morgen, S. (ed.): *Gender and Anthropology: Critical reviews for research and teaching*, American Anthropological Association: Washington, DC, 1989, pp. 294–312.

Ong, Aihwa: 'Japanese factories, Malay workers: class and sexual metaphors in West Malaysia', in Atkinson, J.M. and Errington, S. (eds): *Power and Difference: Gender in island South East Asia*, Stanford University Press: Stanford, CA, 1990, pp. 385–422.

Oren, L: 'The welfare of women in laboring families: England, 1860–1950', in Hartman, M.S. and Banner, L. (eds): *Clio's Consciousness Raised*, Octagon: New York, 1976, pp. 226–44.

Ortner, Sherry B.: 'Is female to male as nature is to culture?', in Rosaldo, M.Z. and Lamphere, L. (eds): *Woman, Culture and Society*, Stanford University Press: Stanford, CA, 1974, pp. 67–88.

Ortner, Sherry B. and Whitehead, Harriet: 'Introduction', in Ortner, S.B. and Whitehead, H. (eds): *Sexual Meanings*, Cambridge University Press: Cambridge, 1981, pp. 1–28.

Osterud, Nancy Grey: 'Gender divisions and the organisation of work in the Leicester hosiery industry', in John, A.V. (ed.): *Unequal Opportunities: Women's employment in England 1800–1910*, Blackwell: Oxford, 1986, pp. 45–70.

Pahl, Jan: 'Patterns of money management within marriage', *Journal of Social Policy*, 9 (3), 1983, pp. 313–35.

Pahl, Jan: *Private Violence and Public Policy: The needs of battered women and the response of the public services*, Routledge and Kegan Paul: London, 1985.

Pahl, Jan: *Money and Marriage*, Macmillan: Basingstoke, 1989.

Papanek, Hanna and Schwede, Laurel: 'Women are good with money: earning and managing in an Indonesian city', in Dwyer, D. and Bruce, J. (eds): *A Home Divided: Women and income in the Third World*, Stanford University Press: Stanford, CA, 1988, pp. 71–98.

Parmar, Pratibha: 'Other kinds of dreams', *Feminist Review*, no. 31, 1989, pp. 55–65.

Parsons, Talcott: 'The social structure of the family', in Anshen, R.N. (ed.): *The Family: Its function and destiny*, Harper and Row: New York, 1949.

Parsons, Talcott: *Essays in Sociological Theory*, Free Press: New York, Collier Macmillan: London, 1954.

Pascall, Gillian: *Social Policy: A feminist analysis*, Tavistock: London, 1986.

Patel, Pragna: 'Women living under Muslim laws dossiers 1–6 : review essay', *Feminist Review*, 37, 1991, pp. 95–102.

Patel, Vibhuti: 'Women's liberation in India', *New Left Review*, 153, 1985, pp. 75–86.

Pavlychko, Solomea: 'Between feminism and nationalism: new women's groups in the Ukraine', in Buckley, M. (ed.): *Perestroika and Soviet women*, Cambridge University Press: Cambridge, 1992, pp. 82–96.

Pearson, Ruth: 'Male bias and women's work in Mexico's border industries', in Elson, D. (ed.): *Male Bias in the Development Process*, Manchester University Press: Manchester, 1991, pp. 133–63.

Pearson, Ruth: 'Questioning perestroika: a socialist-feminist interrogation', *Feminist Review*, 39, 1991a, pp. 91–6.

Pearson, Ruth: 'Gender issues in industrialisation', in Hewitt, T. Johnson, H. and Wield, D. (eds): *Industrialisation and Development*, Oxford University Press: Oxford, 1992, pp. 222–47.

Pember Reeves, Maud: *Round about a Pound a Week*, Virago: London, 1979.

Perrigo, Sarah: 'Socialist-feminism and the Labour Party: some experiences from Leeds', *Feminist Review*, 23, 1986, pp. 101–8.

Petchesky, Rosalind Pollack: *Abortion and Woman's Choice*, Verso: London, 1986.

Phillips, Anne and Taylor, Barbara: 'Sex and skill: notes towards a feminist economics', *Feminist Review*, 6, 1980, pp. 79–88.

Phizachlea, Annie: *Unpacking the Fashion Industry: Gender, racism and class in production*, Routledge: London, 1990.

Phongpaichit, Pasuk: 'Two roads to the factory: industrialisation strategies and women's employment in South East Asia', in Agarwal, B. (ed.): *Structures of Patriarchy: The state, the community and the household*, Zed: London, 1988, pp. 151–63.

Piachaud, David: *Round about 50 hours a Week*, Child Poverty Action Group: London, 1984.

Pinchbeck, Ivy: *Women Workers and the Industrial Revolution 1750–1850*, Virago: London, 1981.

Pine, Frances: 'Family structure and the division of labour: female roles in urban Ghana', in Alavi, H. and Shanin, T. (eds): *Introduction to the Sociology of 'Developing' Societies*, Macmillan: Basingstoke, 1982, pp. 387–405.

Pollert, Anna: *Girls, Wives, Factory Lives*, Macmillan: Basingstoke, 1981.

Porter, Marilyn: 'Standing on the edge: working class housewives and the world of work', in West, J. (ed.): *Work, Women and the Labour Market*, Routledge and Kegan Paul: London, 1982, pp. 117–34.

Pringle, Rosemary: *Secretaries Talk*, Verso: London, 1988.

Pugh Martin: *Women and the Women's Movement in Britain 1914–1959*, Macmillan: Basingstoke, 1992.

Ramazanoglu, Caroline: *Feminism and the Contradictions of Oppression*, Routledge: London, 1989.

Randall, Margaret: *Sandino's Daughters*, Zed: London, 1981.

Randall, Vicky: *Women and Politics: An international perspective*, 2nd edn, Macmillan: Basingstoke, 1987.

Redclift, Nanneke: 'Rights in women: kinship, culture, and materialism', in Sayers, J., Evans, M. and Redclift, N. (eds): *Engels Revisited*, Tavistock: London, 1987, pp. 113–44.

Redclift, Nanneke and Mingione, Enzo: *Beyond Employment: Household, gender and subsistence*, Blackwell: Oxford, 1985.

Rees, Teresa: *Women and the Labour Market*, Routledge: London, 1992.

Rich, Adrienne: *Of Woman Born: Motherhood as experience and institution*, Virago: London, 1984.

Ríos, Palmira N.: 'Export-oriented industrialisation and the demand for female labor: Puerto Rican women in the manufacturing sector, 1952–1980', *Gender and Society*, vol. 4, no. 3, 1990, pp. 321–37.

Roberts, Helen (ed.): *Doing Feminist Research*, Routledge and Kegan Paul: London, 1981.

Roberts, Penelope A.: 'Rural women's access to labour in West Africa', in Stichter, S.B. and Parpart, J.L. (eds): *Patriarchy and Class: African women in the home and workforce*, Westview: Boulder, CO, 1988, pp. 97–114.

Robertson, Claire: 'Developing economic awareness: changing perspectives in studies of African women', *Feminist Studies*, 13 (1), 1987.

Robertson Elliot, Faith: *The Family: Change or continuity?*, Macmillan: Basingstoke, 1986.

Roesch, Otto: 'Rural Mozambique in the Baixo Limpopo', *Review of African Political Economy*, 41, 1988, pp. 73–91.

Rogers, Barbara: *The Domestication of Women: Discrimination in developing societies*, Tavistock: London, 1980.

Roldán, Martha: 'Renegotiating the marital contract: intra-household patterns of money allocation and women's subordination among domestic outworkers in Mexico City', in Dwyer, D. and Bruce, J.

(eds): *A Home Divided: Women and income in the Third World*, Stanford University Press: Stanford, CA, 1988, pp. 229–47.

Rosaldo, Michelle Z.: 'Woman, culture and society: a theoretical overview', in Rosaldo, M.Z. and Lamphere, L. (eds): *Woman, Culture and Society*, Stanford University Press: Stanford, CA, 1974, pp. 17–42.

Rosaldo, Michelle Z.: 'The use and abuse of anthropology: reflections on feminism and cross-cultural understanding', *Signs*, 5 (3), 1980, pp. 389–417.

Rosaldo, Michelle Z. and Lamphere, Louise (eds): *Woman, Culture and Society*, Stanford University Press: Stanford, CA, 1974.

Rose, Steven: *Molecules and Minds*, Open University: Milton Keynes, 1987.

Rowbotham, Sheila: *Women, Resistance and Revolution*, Allen Lane, Penguin: Harmondsworth, 1972.

Rowbotham, Sheila: *The Past Is Before Us: Feminism in action since the 1960s*, Pandora: London, 1989.

Rowbotham, Sheila and McCrindle, Jean: 'More than just a memory: some political implications of women's involvement in the miners' strike, 1984–5', *Feminist Review*, 23, 1986, pp. 109–24.

Rowbotham, Sheila, Segal, Lynne, Wainwright, Hilary: *Beyond the Fragments: Feminism and the making of socialism*, Merlin: London, 1980.

Rubin, Gayle: 'The traffic in women: notes on the "political economy" of sex', in Reiter, R.R. (ed.): *Toward an Anthropology of Women*, Monthly Review Press: New York, 1975, pp. 157–210.

Ruchwarger, Gary: *Struggling for Survival: Workers, women and class on a Nicaraguan state farm*, Westview: Boulder, CO, 1989.

Rudebeck, Lars: 'Kandjadja, Guinea-Bissau 1976–1986', *Review of African Political Economy*, 41, 1988, pp. 17–29.

Rueschemeyer, Marilyn and Szelényi, Szonja: 'Socialist transformation and gender inequality: women in the GDR and Hungary', in Childs, D., Baylis, T.A. and Rueschemeyer, M. (eds): *East Germany in Comparative Perspective*, Routledge: London, 1989, pp. 81–109.

Ruggie, Mary: 'Workers' movements and women's interests: the impact of labour-state relations in Britain and Sweden', in Katzenstein, M.F. and Mueller, C.C. (eds): *The Women's Movements of the United States and Western Europe*, Temple University Press: Philadelphia, PA, 1987, pp. 247–66.

Sacks, Karen: *Sisters and Wives: The past and future of sexual equality*, Greenwood: Westport, CT, 1979.

Sacks, Michael Paul: 'Women in the industrial labour force', in Atkinson,

D., Dallin, A. and Lapidus, G. (eds): *Women in Russia*, Harvester Wheatsheaf: Hemel Hempstead, 1978, 189–204.

Safa, Helen I.: 'Runaway shops and female employment: the search for cheap labour', *Signs*, 7(2) , 1981, pp. 418–33.

Safa, Helen I.: 'Female employment in the Puerto Rican working class', in Nash, J., Safa, H. *et al.*: *Women and Change in Latin America*, Bergin and Garvey: South Hadley, MA, 1986, pp. 84–105.

Safa, Helen I.: 'Women's social movements in Latin America' in *Gender and Society*, vol. 4, no. 3, 1990, pp. 354–69.

Saffioti, Heleieth B.: *Women in Class Society*, Monthly Review Press: New York, 1978.

Saffioti, Heleieth B.: 'Technological change in Brazil: its effect on men and women in two firms', in Nash, J., Safa, H. and contributors: *Women and Change in Latin America*, Bergin and Garvey: South Hadley, MA, 1986, pp. 109–35.

Salaff, Janet W.: 'Women, the family, and the state: Hong Kong, Taiwan, Singapore – Newly industrialised countries in Asia', in Stichter, S. and Parpart, J.L. (eds): *Women, Employment and the Family in the International Division of Labour*, Macmillan: Basingstoke, 1990, pp. 98–136.

Saliou, Monique: 'The processes of women's subordination in primitive and archaic Greece', in Coontz, S. and Henderson, P. (eds): *Women's Work, Men's Property*, Verso: London, 1986, pp. 169–206.

Sanday, Peggy: 'Rape and the silencing of the feminine', in Tomaselli, S. and Porter, R. (eds): *Rape*, Basil Blackwell: Oxford, 1986.

Sarti, Cynthia: 'The panorama of Brazilian feminism', *New Left Review*, 173, 1989, pp. 75–90.

Savané, Marie Angelique: 'The effects of social and economic changes on the role and status of women in sub-Saharan Africa', in Moock, J.L. (ed.): *Understanding Africa's Rural Households and Farming Systems*, Westview: Boulder, CO, 1986, pp. 124–32.

Sayers, Janet: *Biological Politics*, Tavistock: London, 1982.

Schirmer, Jennifer G.: ' "Those who die for life cannot be called dead": women and human rights protests in Latin America', in *Feminist Review*, 32, 1989, pp. 3–29.

Schminck, Marianne: 'Women and urban industrial development in Brazil', in Nash, J., Safa, H. *et al.*: *Women and change in Latin America*, Bergin and Garvey: South Hadley, MA, 1986, pp. 136–64.

Scott, Alison M.: 'Women and industrialisation: examining the "female marginalisation" thesis', *Journal of Development Studies*, 22(4), 1986, pp. 649–80.

Scott, Alison M.: 'Patterns of patriarchy in the Peruvian working class', in Stichter, S. and Parpart, J. (eds): *Women, Employment and the*

Bibliography

International Division of Labour, Macmillan: Basing-
pp. 198–220.

..: 'Informal sector or female sector?: gender bias in urban
market models', in Elson, D. (ed.): *Male Bias in the*
ment Process, Manchester University Press: Manchester,
, pp. 105–32.

ilda: *Working Your Way to the Bottom: The feminisation of*
overty, Pandora: London, 1985.

Scott, Joan and Tilly, Louise: 'Women's work and the family in nineteenth
century Europe', in Whitelegg, E. *et al.* (eds): *The Changing*
Experience of Women, Blackwell/Open University: Oxford, 1982,
pp. 45–70.

Secombe, Wally: 'The housewife and her labour under capitalism', *New*
Left Review, 83, 1974, pp. 3–24.

Secombe, Wally: 'Domestic labour: reply to critics', *New Left Review*, 94,
1975.

Segal, Lynne: *Is the Future Female? Troubled thoughts on contemporary*
feminism, Virago: London, 1987.

Select Committee: *Report of the Select Committee on Violence in*
Marriage, vol. 1, Report, HMSO: London, 1975.

Sen, Amartya K.: 'Gender and cooperative conflicts', in Tinker, I. (ed.):
Persistent Inequalities: Women and world development, Oxford
University Press: Oxford, 1990, pp. 123–49.

Sen, Gita: 'Women workers and the green revolution', in Benería, L. (ed.):
Women and Development: The sexual division of labour in rural
societies, Praeger: New York, 1982, pp. 29–64.

Sen, Gita and Grown, Caren: *Development, Crises and Alternative*
Visions: Third World women's perspectives, Earthscan: London, 1988.

Sharma, Ursula: 'Women, work and property in North-West India', in
Alavi, H. and Harriss, J. (eds): *Sociology of 'Developing' societies:*
South Asia, Macmillan: Basingstoke, 1989, pp. 160–9.

Sharma, Ursula: 'Public employment and private relations: women and
work in India', in Stichter, S. and Parpart, J. (eds): *Women,*
Employment and the Family in the International Division of Labour,
Macmillan: Basingstoke, 1990, pp. 229–46.

Shapiro, Judith: 'The industrial labour force', in Buckley, M. (ed.):
Perestroika and Soviet Women, Cambridge University Press: Cambridge, 1992, pp. 14–38.

Sharpe, Sue: *Double Identity*, Penguin: Harmondsworth, 1984.

Shostak, Marjorie: *Nisa: The life and words of a !Kung woman*, Penguin:
Basingstoke, 1983.

Showstack Sassoon, Anne (ed.): *Women and the State*, Hutchinson:
London, 1987.

Siddiqui, Hannah: 'Review essay on Letter to Christendom', in *Feminist Review*, 37, 1991, pp. 78–84.

Sidel, Ruth and Sidel, Victor: *The Health of China*, Zed: London, 1982.

Silverblatt, Irene: ' "The universe has turned inside out . . . there is no justice for us here": Andean women under Spanish rule', in Etienne, M. and Leacock, E. (eds): *Women and Colonisation: Anthropological perspectives*, Praeger: New York, 1980, pp. 149–85.

Simon, David: 'Agrarian policy in Zimbabwe', *Review of African Political Economy*, 34, 1985, pp. 82–9.

Slater, David: 'Socialism, democracy and the territorial imperative: a comparison of the Cuban and Nicaraguan experiences', in Forbes, D. and Thrift, N. (eds): *The Socialist Third World: Urban development and territorial planning*, Blackwell: Oxford, 1987, pp. 282–302.

Slocum, Sally: 'Woman the gatherer: male bias in Anthropology', in Reiter, R.R. (ed.): *Toward an Anthropology of Women*, Monthly Review Press, 1975: New York, pp. 36–50.

Smith, Joan: 'Feminist analysis of gender: a mystique', in Lowe, M. and Hubbard, R. (eds): *Woman's Nature: Rationalisations of inequality*, Pergamon: Oxford, 1983.

Snell, Mandy: 'Equal pay and sex discrimination', *Feminist Review* (ed.): *Waged Work: A reader*, Virago: London, 1986, pp. 12–39.

Spelman, Elizabeth V: *Inessential Women: Problems of exclusion in feminist thought*, The Women's Press: London, 1988.

Spender, Dale: *Man made language* (2nd edn), Routledge and Kegan Paul: London, 1985.

Spiro, Heather M.: 'Women farmers and traders in Oyo state, Nigeria: a case study of their changing roles', in Momsen, J.H. and Townsend, J.G. (eds): *Geography of Gender in the Third World*, State University of New York Press/Hutchinson: London, 1987.

Stacey, Judith: *Patriarchy and Socialist Revolution in China*, University of California Press: Berkeley, CA, 1983.

Stacey, Margaret: 'The division of labour revisited or overcoming the two Adams', in Abrams, P. *et al.* (eds): *Practice and Progress: British Sociology 1950–1980*, Allen and Unwin: London, 1981, pp. 172–90.

Stack, Carol: *All Our Kin: Strategies for survival in a black community*, Harper and Row: New York, 1975.

Stamiris, Eleni: 'The women's movement in Greece', *New Left Review*, 158, 1986, pp. 98–112.

Stamp, Patricia: 'Kikuyu women's self-help groups: towards an understanding of the relation between sex-gender system and mode of production in Africa', in Robertson, C. and Berger, I. (eds): *Women and Class in Africa*, Africana Publishing Company: New York, London, 1986, pp. 27–46.

Stamp, Paddy and Robarts, Sadie: *Positive Action: Changing the workplace for women*, National Council for Civil Liberties: London, 1986.

Stanworth, Michelle: 'Women and class analysis: a reply to John Goldthorpe', *Sociology*, 18 (2), 1984, pp. 159–70.

Staudt, Kathleen and Col, Jeanne-Marie: 'Diversity in East Africa: cultural pluralism, public policy and the state', in Gallin, R.S. and Ferguson, A. (eds): *The Women and International Development Annual*, vol. 2, Westview: Boulder, CO, 1991, pp. 241–64.

Stead, Jean: *Never The Same Again: Women and the miners' strike*, The Women's Press: London, 1987.

Stead, Mary: 'Women, war and underdevelopment in Nicaragua', in Afshar, H. (ed.): *Women, Development and Survival in the Third World*, Longman: Harlow, 1991, pp. 53–87.

Stichter, Sharon B.: 'Women, employment and the family: current debates', in Stichter, S. and Parpart, J. (eds): *Women, Employment and the Family in the International Divison of Labour*, Macmillan: Basingstoke, 1990, pp. 11–71.

Stichter, Sharon B. and Parpart, Jane: 'Introduction: towards a materialist perspective on African women', in Stichter, S.B. and Parpart, J.L. (eds): *Patriarchy and Class: African women in the home and workforce*, Westview: Boulder and London, 1988, pp. 1–26.

Stichter, Sharon B. and Parpart, Jane: *Women, employment and the Family in the International Division of Labour*, Macmillan: Basingstoke, 1990.

Stivens, Maila: 'Women, kinship and capitalist development', in Young, K., Wolkowitz, C. and McCullagh, R. (eds): *Of Marriage and the Market*, Routledge and Kegan Paul: London, 1984, pp. 178–92.

Stoler, Ann: 'Class structure and female autonomy in rural Java', *Signs*, 3 (1), 1977, pp. 74–89.

Stoler, Ann: 'Rice harvesting in Kali Loro: a study of class and labour relations in rural Java', in Tayor, J.G. and Turton, A. (eds): *Sociology of 'Developing' Societies: South East Asia*, Macmillan: Basingstoke, 1988, pp. 111–22.

Strathern, Marilyn: 'Self interest and the social good: some implications of Hagen gender imagery', in Ortner, S.B. and Whitehead, H. (eds): *Sexual Meanings*, Cambridge University Press: Cambridge, 1981, pp. 166–91.

Strathern, Marilyn (ed.): *Dealing with Inequality*, Cambridge University Press: Cambridge, 1987.

Strathern, Marilyn: 'Introduction' and 'Conclusion', in Strathern, M.

(ed.): *Dealing with Inequality*, Cambridge University Press: Cambridge, 1987a, pp. 1–32, 278–302.

Stubbs, Jean: *Cuba: The test of time*, Latin America Bureau: London, 1989.

Stubbs, Jean and Alvarez, Mavis: 'Women on the agenda: the cooperative movement in rural Cuba', in Deere, C.D. and León, M. (eds): *Rural Women and State Policy*, Westview: Boulder and London, 1987, pp. 142–61.

Sydie, Rosalind A.: *Natural Women, Cultured Men: A feminist perspective on sociological theory*, Open University Press: Milton Keynes, 1987.

Tadesse, Zenebeworke: 'The impact of land reform on women: the case of Ethiopia', in Benería, L. (ed.): *Women and Development: The sexual division of labour in rural societies*, Praeger: New York, 1982, pp. 201–22.

Terray, Emmanuel: *Marxism and 'Primitive' Societies: Two studies*, Monthly Review Press: New York and London, 1972.

Thomas, G.: *Women and Industry*, HMSO: London, 1948.

Thorogood, Nicki: 'Race, class and gender: the politics of housework', in Brannen, J., Wilson, G. (eds): *Give and Take in Families*, Allen and Unwin: London, 1987, pp. 18–41.

Threlfall, Monica: 'The women's movement in Spain', *New Left Review*, 151, 1985, pp. 44–73.

Tiger, Lionel and Fox, Robin: *The Imperial Animal*, Paladin: London, 1974.

Tilly, Louise and Scott, Joan: *Women, Work and Family*, Methuen: London, 1987.

Tinker, Irene (ed.): *Persistent Inequalities: Women and world development*, Oxford University Press: Oxford, 1990.

Tohidi, Nayereh: 'Gender and Islamic fundamentalism: feminist politics in Iran', in Mohanty, C.T., Russo, A. and Torres, L. (eds): *Third World Women and the Politics of Feminism*, Indiana University Press: Bloomington, IN, 1991, pp. 251–67.

Tomalin, Claire: *The Life and Death of Mary Wollstonecraft*, Weidenfeld and Nicolson: London, 1974.

Trenchard, Esther: 'Rural women's work in sub-Saharan Africa and the implications for nutrition', in Momsen, J.H. and Townsend, J.G. (eds): *Geography of Gender in the Third World*, State University of New York Press/Hutchinson: London, 1987, pp. 153–72.

Trivedi, Parita: 'To deny our fullness: Asian women in the making of history', *Feminist Review*, 17, 1984, pp. 37–50.

TUC (Trade Union Congress): *Equal Opportunities: Positive action programmes*, TUC, 1982.

TUC Report, 1966, 1984.

Turnbull, Colin: *Wayward Servants*, Eyre and Spottiswoode: London, 1965.

Turnbull, Colin: 'The ritualisation of potential conflict between the sexes among the Mbuti', in Leacock, E. and Lee, R. (eds): *Politics and History in Band Societies*, Cambridge University Press: Cambridge, 1982, pp. 133–56.

Turner, Mary: 'Women and development: the Caribbean and Latin America', in Parpart, J. (ed.): *Women and Development in Africa: Comparative perspectives*, Dalhousie African Studies Series, University Press of America: Lanham, MD, 1989, pp. 103–14.

Ungerson, Clare (ed.): *Women and Social Policy*, Macmillan: Basingstoke, 1985.

Urdang, Stephanie: 'The last transition?: Women and development in Mozambique', *Review of African Political Economy*, 27/28, 1984, pp. 8–32.

Urdang, Stephanie: *And Still They Dance: Women, war and the struggle for change in Mozambique*, Earthscan: London, 1989.

Vaughan, Megan: 'Household units and historical process in Southern Malawi', in *Review of African Political Economy*, 34, 1985, pp. 35–45.

Ventura-Dias, Vivianne: 'Modernisation, production organisation and rural women in Kenya', in Ahmed, I. (ed.): *Technology and Rural Women: Conceptual and empirical issues*, Allen and Unwin: London, 1985, pp. 157–210.

Vogel, Lise: *Marxism and the Oppression of Women*, Pluto: London, 1983.

Wainwright, Hilary: *Labour: A tale of two parties*, The Hogarth Press: London, 1987.

Walby, Sylvia: *Patriarchy at Work*, Polity: Oxford, 1986.

Walby, Sylvia: 'Gender politics and social theory', *Sociology*, 22 (2), 1988, pp. 215–32.

Walker, Alan (ed.): *Community Care*, Basil Blackwell and Martin Robertson: London, 1982.

Wallace, Ruth A. (ed.): *Feminism and Sociological Theory*, Sage: London, 1989.

Wallace, Tina with March, Candida (eds): *Changing Perceptions: Writings on gender and development*, Oxfam: Oxford, 1991.

Waters, Elizabeth: 'Restructuring the "woman question": perestroika and prostitution', *Feminist Review*, 33, 1989, pp. 3–19.

Webster, Paula: 'Matriarchy: a vision of power', in Reiter, R.R. (ed.): *Toward an Anthropology of Women*, Monthly Review Press: New York, 1975, pp. 141–56.

West, Jackie (ed.): *Work, Women and the Labour Market*, Routledge and Kegan Paul: London, 1982.

Werner, James F.: 'Diseases of the soul: sickness, agency and the men's cult among the Foi of New Guinea', in Strathern, M. (ed.): *Dealing with Inequality*, Cambridge University Press: Cambridge, 1987, pp. 255–76.

Wheelock, Jane: *Husbands at Home: The domestic economy in a post-industrial society*, Routledge: London, 1990.

White, Christine Pelzer: 'Socialist transformation of agriculture and gender relations: the Vietnamese case', in Taylor, J.G. and Turton, S. (eds): *Sociology of 'Developing' Societies: South East Asia*, Macmillan: Basingstoke, 1988, pp. 165–76.

White, G.: 'Revolutionary socialist development in the Third World: an overview', in White, G., Murray, G. and White, C. (eds): *Revolutionary Socialist Development in the Third World*, Harvester Wheatsheaf: Hemel Hempstead, 1983, pp. 1–34.

Whitehead, Ann: ' "I'm hungry, mum": the politics of domestic budgeting', in Young, K., Wolkowitz, C. and McCullagh, R. (eds): *Of Marriage and the Market*, Routledge and Kegan Paul: London, 1984, pp. 93–116.

Whitehead, Ann: 'Effects of technological change on rural women: a review of analysis and concepts', in Ahmed, I. (ed.): *Technology and Rural Women: Conceptual and empirical issues*, Allen and Unwin: London, 1985, pp. 27–64.

Whitehead, Ann: 'Food production and the food crisis in Africa', in Wallace, G. with March, C. (eds): *Changing Perceptions: Writings on gender and development*, Oxfam: Oxford, 1991, pp. 68–77.

Willis, Paul: *Learning to Labour*, Gower: Aldershot, 1977.

Wilson, Elizabeth: *Women and the Welfare State*, Tavistock: London, 1977.

Wilson, Elizabeth: *Only Halfway to Paradise*, Tavistock: London, 1980.

Wilson, Elizabeth with Weir, Angela: *Hidden Agendas*, Tavistock: London, 1986.

Wilson, E.O.: 'Human decency is animal', *New York Times Magazine*, 12 October 1975.

Wolf, Christa: *Cassandra*, Virago: London, 1984.

Wolf, Diane L.: 'Daughters, decisions and domination: an empirical and conceptual critique of household strategies', *Development and Change*, vol. 21, 1990, pp. 43–74.

Wolf, Diane, L.: 'Female autonomy, the family and industrialisation in Java', in Blumberg, R. (ed.): *Gender, Family and Economy: The triple overlap*, Sage: London, 1991, pp. 128–48.

Wolf, Margery: *Revolution Postponed: Women in contemporary China*, Methuen: London, 1987.

Wolpe, Harold: 'Capitalism and cheap labour power in South Africa: from segregation to apartheid', *Economy and Society*, vol. 4, no. 1, 1972, pp. 425–56.

Wong, Aline K.: 'Planned development, social stratification, and the sexual division of labour in Singapore', *Signs*, 7 (2), 1981, pp. 434–52.

Young, Kate: 'Modes of appropriation and the sexual division of labour: a case study from Oaxaca, Mexico', in Kuhn, A. and Wolpe, A.M. (eds): *Feminism and Materialism*, Routledge and Kegan Paul: London, 1978, pp. 124–54.

Young, Kate: 'The creation of a relative surplus population: a case study from Mexico', in Benería, L. (ed.): *Women and Development: The sexual division of labour in rural societies*, Praeger: New York, 1982, pp. 149–78.

Young, Marilyn G: 'Chicken Little in China: women after the Cultural Revolution', in Kruks, S., Rapp, R. and Young, M. (eds): *Promissory Notes: Women in the transition to socialism*, Monthly Review Press: New York, 1989, pp. 233–47.

Young, Michael and Wilmott, Peter: *The Symmetrical Family*, Routledge and Kegan Paul: London, 1973.

Youssef, Nadia Haggag: *Women and Work in Developing Societies*, Greenwood: Westport, CT, 1974.

Yuval-Davis, Nira and Anthias, Floya (eds): *Woman–Nation–State*, Macmillan: Basingstoke, 1989.

INDEX